Building Industrial Digital Twins

Design, develop, and deploy digital twin solutions
for real-world industries using Azure Digital Twins

Shyam Varan Nath

Pieter van Schalkwyk

Packt>

BIRMINGHAM—MUMBAI

Building Industrial Digital Twins

Publishing Product Manager: Pavan Ramchandani
Senior Editor: Sofi Rogers
Content Development Editor: Divya Vijayan
Technical Editor: Joseph Aloocaran
Copy Editor: Safis Editing
Project Coordinator: Manthan Patel
Proofreader: Safis Editing
Indexer: Manju Arasan
Production Designer: Aparna Bhagat

First published: September 2021

Production reference: 1290921

Published by Packt Publishing Ltd.
Livery Place
35 Livery Street
Birmingham
B3 2PB, UK.

ISBN 978-1-83921-907-8

www.packt.com

Foreword

Shyam and Pieter are both recognized professionals in the industrial internet, IoT, and Digital Twins community. They converted the OT/IT task group to the Digital Twins Interoperability task group at the Industry IoT Consortium (formerly known as the Industrial Internet Consortium). They also led the task group in the development of the "Digital Twins for Industrial Applications" whitepaper.

Shyam is the author of a book on industrial digital transformation, published by Packt. Pieter is currently the chair for the Natural Resources working group in the Digital Twin Consortium. He is actively developing a Digital Twin capability framework and a composable Digital Twin development methodology.

In this book, Shyam and Pieter walk you step-by-step through creating your first Digital Twin prototype. It explores the "what, why, and how" of Digital Twin through an example project, which covers the entire lifecycle of a Digital Twin prototype development on the Azure Digital Twins platform.

The authors' extensive knowledge and experience in developing and deploying real-world industrial Digital Twins project are evident in the practical guidance and rich repository of tools, like the Lean Digital Twin Canvas, that they provide in every chapter. Their easy-to-follow advice on setting up the Azure Digital Twins services and their step-by-step approach to creating Digital Twin models and instances on the service will get you started on your first Digital Twin prototype in a few hours.

This book is a valuable resource to anyone starting their first industrial Digital Twin project, not just for the technical content, but also for the clear guidance on using Digital Twins to solve real-world business problems.

Dan Isaacs

CTO – Digital Twin Consortium

Contributors

About the authors

Shyam Varan Nath is a Specialist Leader, Analytics and Cognitive, at Deloitte. Prior to this, he worked for Oracle, General Electric, IBM, and Halliburton. He is the primary author of two books, Industrial Digital Transformation, and Architecting the Industrial Internet. His expertise involves IIoT, cloud computing, databases, AI/ML, and business analytics. He has worked on driving digital transformation at several large companies. He is a Distinguished Toastmaster (DTM) and very active on Twitter; @Shyamvaran. He is the founder of the analytics user group called AnDOUC (formerly BIWA). He has an undergraduate degree from IIT Kanpur, India, as well as an MSc (in computer science) and an MBA from FAU, Boca Raton, Florida. Shyam is part of the Program Committee of IoTSWC and a regular speaker at large technology events. He can be contacted at ShyamVaran@gmail.com.

I wish to thank all my professional colleagues from the companies
I have worked at for the valuable experience I acquired during that time,
along with all those industry professionals in the fields of AI, IoT, Digital
Twins, and cloud computing, with whom I interact on a regular basis
and meet at technology events. I am grateful for the various activities and
publications from Industrial Internet Consortium (IIC) and Digital Twin
Consortium (DTC) that help me stay current. And finally, many thanks
to my co-author and friend, Pieter, and the editorial team at Packt,
who made this book possible.

Pieter van Schalkwyk, CEO at XMPro, is an experienced engineer and technologist who helps organizations use real-time, event-based Digital Twins to improve situational awareness, process efficiency, and decision making without disrupting operations. He is recognized as a thought leader in industrial digital transformation and has written and spoken extensively on topics including digital twins, IIoT, AI/ML, and industrial blockchain applications. Pieter holds a bachelor's degree in mechanical engineering and a master's degree in information technology. He chairs the Natural Resources Working Group in the Digital Twin Consortium (DTC). Prior to this, Pieter was the chair of the Digital Twin Interoperability Task Group within the Industrial Internet Consortium (IIC). In February 2019, Pieter received the IIC Technical Innovation Award. He describes himself as an entrepreneur at heart, technology enthusiast, team builder, and aspiring Ironman triathlete.

A big thank you to my colleagues at XMPro and the members of the Digital Twin Consortium who continue to challenge me to explore how to use digital twins to create safer, greener, and more responsible industrial operations faster. A special thank you to Gavin Green and Muhammad Ali for your technical help and support, Kirsten Schwarzer for brainstorming ideas, and Steve Howcroft for your continued encouragement with the book. Shyam, thank you for inviting me to co-author the book with you and thank you to the Packt editorial team, who made it a reality. Finally, I'd like to thank my wife, Andri, for letting me indulge my passion. I admire your amazing patience, and I'm so grateful to go through life with you.

About the reviewers

Joseph Philip is the director of PSOTS Ltd., based in London, UK, offering consultancy services since 2013 to the digital twins industry in the energy sector. Joseph has been delivering operator training simulators and digital twins in the oil and gas, chemicals, energy, and petrochemical sectors for more than 30 years.

These systems have been delivered all over the world to major companies including BP, Shell, Total, and many others, and he has also been responsible for delivering power plant simulators to Australia and Asia while working for Yokogawa Australia. He moved to the UK in 2001 and started working for AspenTech. In 2004, he began working for Honeywell, before moving to Invensys (Schneider Electric) in 2007, delivering OTS and DT systems in Europe, the US, China, and the Middle East.

Jayendra Ganguli has over two decades of experience in the design (CAD/CAE/PLM), manufacturing, and operational feedback domains of the aerospace and automotive sectors. He has led company-wide initiatives in the architecture and implementation of PLM, MES, MRO, and digital thread/twin solutions in two of the world's top three aerospace companies.

Jayendra also heads up the interoperability and standards architecture, both internally and at external standards bodies such as the ISO. He is currently focused on developing digital thread and digital twin modeling, traceability, interoperability, and data-driven architectures for the aerospace domain. He collaborates with major PLM and data vendors on the topic of the digital thread and twin interface.

Dan Isaacs is Chief Technology Officer of **Digital Twin Consortium** (**DTC**), responsible for technical direction, liaison partnerships, and business development support for new memberships. Dan was Director of Strategic Marketing and Business Development at Xilinx, responsible for Automotive Business Development - Automated Driving and ADAS systems and responsible for emerging technologies: AI/ML, and the ecosystem strategy for the IIoT.

Dan has 25 years' experience in working at Automotive, Mil/Aero and Consumer-based companies including Ford, NEC, LSI Logic and Hughes Aircraft. Dan has delivered keynotes, seminars, served as panelist and moderator at World Forums and Global conferences. Dan is a member of international advisory boards with degrees in Computer Engineering: EE from Cal State University and B.S. Geophysics from ASU.

Dr. Zoya Alexeeva is an experienced digital transformation and strategy executive who has worked in the manufacturing, process automation, automotive, and smart grid domains. Her expertise includes IIoT business cases, strategy definition, IT and OT systems and their integration, complex solution delivery, and market and technology analysis. She has held numerous roles, including digital and IT strategy director, digital solutions portfolio manager, and solutions architect.

Table of Contents

Section 2: Building the Digital Twin

3

Identifying the First Digital Twin

4

Getting Started with Our First Digital Twin

Section 3: Enhancing the Digital Twin

8

Enhancing the Digital Twin

Interview on Digital Twins with William (Bill) Ruh, CEO of Lendlease Digital

Interview on Digital Twins with Anwar Ahmed, CTO at GE Renewable Energy

Other Books You May Enjoy

Index

Preface

Digital twins are increasingly being used to improve the life cycle of complex products. This applies to improving both the product's manufacturing process as well as its operations throughout its lifetime. As a result, both **information technology** (**IT**) and operations professionals are becoming interested in learning about Digital Twins. This book will apply the concept of Digital Twins by building a prototype for a wind turbine as an industrial asset for the field of renewable energy.

You will understand how the technology selection is done for a Digital Twin. Then, you will learn how to evaluate the possible business outcomes from a Digital Twin, leading to analysis of the return on investment. The tutorial approach to building a Digital Twin using Azure Digital Twins will provide hands-on experience. Finally, you will see how this first industrial Digital Twin fits into the entire renewable energy generation ecosystem.

Who this book is for

The audience for this book will be a mix of IT leaders, operational **line of business** (**LOB**) leaders, and **subject-matter experts** (**SMEs**) looking for guidance on the use of Digital Twins to drive digital transformation that delivers quantifiable value for industrial operations. This book is aimed at mid-career subject experts or business technologists such as engineers and operations managers, building the first prototype of a Digital Twin of a wind turbine as part of this book. It will enable these business technologists to assess the resource requirements and capabilities of Digital Twins across the complete design, development, and deployment life cycle of real-world Digital Twins.

What this book covers

Chapter 1, Introduction to Digital Twin, describes the concept of Digital Twins and provides a brief history of its origins, and a definition for a common understanding of the Digital Twin concept. It provides an understanding of the use and application of Digital Twins with some industry examples.

Chapter 2, Planning Your Digital Twin, identifies the key criteria to assess the use of a Digital Twin for your specific industrial challenge or opportunity. The chapter addresses prerequisites for Digital Twins and organizational factors to consider.

Chapter 3, Identifying the First Digital Twin, covers the selection of Digital Twin candidates for a prototype, each from the perspective of the type of organization that is evaluating Digital Twins for their use cases.

Chapter 4, Getting Started with Our First Digital Twin, explains the planning framework, how to validate the problem statement and expected outcomes, and the proposed business process for developing your Digital Twin. It identifies the different types of technology platforms that can be used to create the first Digital Twin prototype of a wind turbine.

Chapter 5, Setting Up a Digital Twin Prototype, provides practical step-by-step guidance for selecting and setting up the infrastructure on a cloud platform in preparation for building the Digital Twin prototype in the next chapter.

Chapter 6, Building the Digital Twin Prototype, describes the end-to-end process of building a real-world Digital Twin prototype on the Microsoft Azure Digital Twins platform. The chapter covers the complete development process, including testing, technical evaluation, and business validation steps.

Chapter 7, Deployment and Value Tracking, guides you through the functional testing of the Digital Twin prototype and evaluates different deployment models for scaling the prototype to an operational production solution. The chapter further suggests value tracking approaches that demonstrate the value of the Digital Twin solution to the different stakeholders in an industrial enterprise.

Chapter 8, Enhancing the Digital Twin, describes the possibilities beyond the first Digital Twin prototype. The chapter looks at the "art of possible" with Digital Twins and some of the emerging opportunities for Digital Twins to provide safer, greener, more responsible industrial operations with positive returns on the value at stake for all stakeholders. This chapter goes in depth into the application of Digital Twins for renewable energy generation.

To get the most out of this book

You will get the most out of this book if you have basic technical proficiency in programming concepts such as JSON and Azure Functions. These skills are not prerequisites.

The examples in the book provide guidance on the potential application of Digital Twins in your organization, but you will get additional value from the book if potential applications are identified as you read the book and create your first prototype.

Software/hardware covered in the book	Operating system requirements
Azure Digital Twins on the Azure cloud platform – free trial subscription available	None – solutions are browser-based
JSON	

If you are using the digital version of this book, we advise you to type the code yourself or access the code from the book's GitHub repository (a link is available in the next section). Doing so will help you avoid any potential errors related to the copying and pasting of code.

The readers can stay in touch with the authors and post their questions and discussion topics in the Slack Group for this book:

`industrialdigitaltwin.slack.com`

Download the example code files

You can download the example code files for this book from GitHub at `https://github.com/PacktPublishing/Building-Industrial-Digital-Twin`. If there's an update to the code, it will be updated in the GitHub repository.

We also have other code bundles from our rich catalog of books and videos available at `https://github.com/PacktPublishing/`. Check them out!

Download the color images

We also provide a PDF file that has color images of the screenshots and diagrams used in this book. You can download it here: `https://static.packt-cdn.com/downloads/9781839219078_ColorImages.pdf`.

Conventions used

There are a number of text conventions used throughout this book.

`Code in text`: Indicates code words in text, database table names, folder names, filenames, file extensions, pathnames, dummy URLs, user input, and Twitter handles. Here is an example: "Mount the downloaded `WebStorm-10*.dmg` disk image file as another disk in your system."

A block of code is set as follows:

```
html, body, #map {
  height: 100%;
  margin: 0;
  padding: 0
}
```

When we wish to draw your attention to a particular part of a code block, the relevant lines or items are set in bold:

```
[default]
exten => s,1,Dial(Zap/1|30)
exten => s,2,Voicemail(u100)
exten => s,102,Voicemail(b100)
exten => i,1,Voicemail(s0)
```

Any command-line input or output is written as follows:

```
$ mkdir css
$ cd css
```

Bold: Indicates a new term, an important word, or words that you see onscreen. For instance, words in menus or dialog boxes appear in **bold**. Here is an example: "Select **System info** from the **Administration** panel."

> **Tips or Important Notes**
> Appear like this.

Get in touch

Feedback from our readers is always welcome.

General feedback: If you have questions about any aspect of this book, email us at customercare@packtpub.com and mention the book title in the subject of your message.

Errata: Although we have taken every care to ensure the accuracy of our content, mistakes do happen. If you have found a mistake in this book, we would be grateful if you would report this to us. Please visit www.packtpub.com/support/errata and fill in the form.

Piracy: If you come across any illegal copies of our works in any form on the internet, we would be grateful if you would provide us with the location address or website name. Please contact us at copyright@packt.com with a link to the material.

If you are interested in becoming an author: If there is a topic that you have expertise in and you are interested in either writing or contributing to a book, please visit authors.packtpub.com.

Share Your Thoughts

Once you've read *Building Industrial Digital Twins*, we'd love to hear your thoughts! Scan the QR code below to go straight to the Amazon review page for this book and share your feedback.

https://packt.link/r/<1839219076>

Your review is important to us and the tech community and will help us make sure we're delivering excellent quality content.

Section 1: Defining Digital Twins

This part of the book will introduce the concept of Digital Twins to a novice and why Digital Twins are needed. You will also understand the purpose and benefits of Digital Twins.

This section comprises the following chapters:

- *Chapter 1, Introduction to Digital Twin*
- *Chapter 2, Planning Your Digital Twin*

1
Introduction to Digital Twin

The Digital Twin is a concept that has gained a lot of popularity recently. Many analysts, vendors, and customers agree that it is poised for proliferation as its value is realized and recognized, specifically in industrial environments.

This book aims to enable you to build your first Digital Twin prototype or minimum viable Digital Twin. Before we start looking at the Digital Twin's technical aspects, it is essential to understand what a Digital Twin is, how it came to be, and the business value of Digital Twins. Also, what are the ideal prospects for Digital Twins, especially if you are just starting out?

The generic concepts, characteristics, and principles around Digital Twins will be described in this chapter without us focusing on any specific technology for Digital Twins. In later chapters, we will focus on the technical development of a sample Digital Twin to demonstrate how to create your first Digital Twin prototype. This chapter aims to provide you with a shared understanding of Digital Twins, their characteristics, and how they can be applied. This understanding will be used later in this book when you configure your first Digital Twin.

We will start by providing a brief history of the development of the Digital Twin concept, focusing specifically on the industrial application of Digital Twins. This historical overview will provide some insight into the intent of Digital Twins, as well as what the original thought leaders and creators had in mind when describing the first Digital Twins.

Following this, we will define the term Digital Twin, which we will be using throughout this book as the guiding reference for the twin you are about to create. There are various definitions out in the market, but we must have a shared understanding of what we refer to as a Digital Twin for this book. We will expand the definition so that it includes some of the characteristics that we see as required or optional.

We will also provide some examples of industry use cases and how these apply across the overall life cycle of the Digital Twin entity. These use cases will provide you with some ideas on applying Digital Twins to your specific environment or business. This will offer further insight into the value proposition of Digital Twins for different requirements. Finally, we will provide some initial guidance on identifying potential applications of Digital Twins in an industrial setting.

The rest of this book will focus on helping you build your first Digital Twin and will start with planning your Digital Twin, identifying the right candidate for your first Digital Twin, and then guidance on setting up, building, deploying, and validating the outcomes of your Digital Twin prototype. Let's start by establishing a common understanding of the concepts, definitions, and value, and how this all came about.

This chapter will cover the following main topics:

- History of the Digital Twin
- Industry use of Digital Twins
- The value proposition of Digital Twins
- Identifying opportunities

History of the Digital Twin

In this section, we will explore the Digital Twin concept's origins and intent by the original creators as we define the Digital Twin for this book and identify its key characteristics. The initial goal of a Digital Twin is to provide the same or better information than could be obtained by being in physical possession of the physical twin, in contrast to simulation and modeling to predict behavior based on "what-if scenarios."

Origin of the Digital Twin concept

The concept of a Digital Twin was first described by Dr Michael Grieves of the University of Michigan in a presentation to the Society of Manufacturing Engineering in October 2002. Grieves originally named it the **Mirrored Spaces Model** (**MSM**), but the name evolved, and he ascribed the term "Digital Twin" to John Vickers of NASA, who worked with Grieves on product life cycle management for complex systems.

Grieves and Vickers observed that technological advances in physical products and assets made systems more complex. New technologies also brought new capabilities, such as communication and computing, that could not be represented in the physical (mechanical and electronic) space. These capabilities increased the complexity of systems and required a mechanism to mitigate system complexity by providing improved information about the physical product or entity:

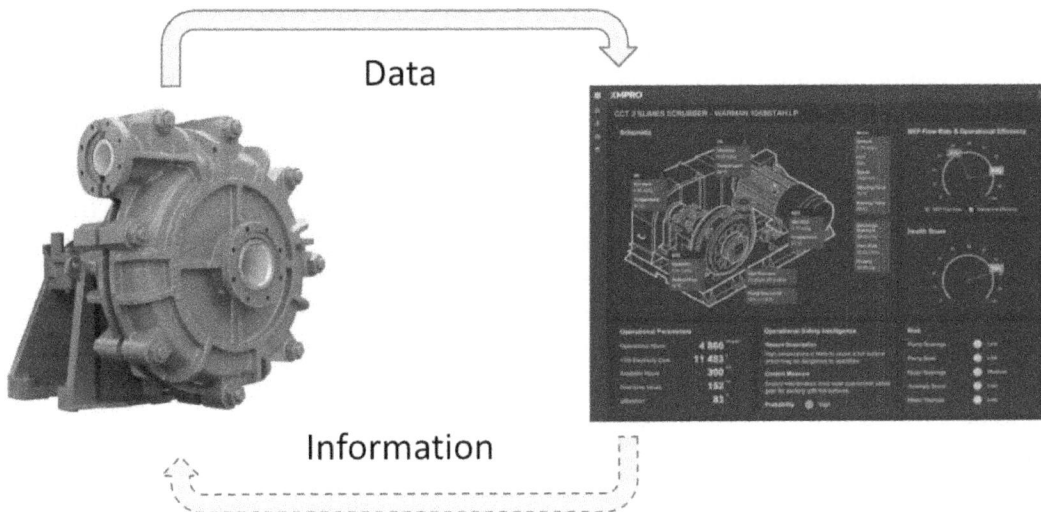

Figure 1.1 – Physical and virtual products combined to create a Digital Twin

MSM provides some insight into Grieves' approach to having a Digital Twin "mirror" a Physical Twin through the flow of data, from the physical product to the digital instance, and then how this information was exchanged and sent back to the physical one:

"The Digital Twin is the information construct of the Physical Twin. The intent of the Digital Twin is that it can provide the same or better information than could be obtained by being in physical possession of the Physical Twin. The key assumption is that the type, granularity, and amount of information contained in the Digital Twin is driven by use cases."

Grieves, Michael. (2019). Virtually Intelligent Product Systems: Digital and Physical Twins. 10.2514/5.9781624105654.0175.0200.

Three key concepts characterized these early Digital Twins. **Digital Twin Prototype (DTP)** is the "type" or model representation of the physical twin. It was also described as the "design version with all its variants." The DTP of a centrifugal pump, for example, is a single description and information model for the specific model of a pump. There is only one DTP or model, but multiple pumps may use that same model description. This brings us to the instance of a Digital Twin.

The **Digital Twin Instance (DTI)** is each instance of every physical entity, based on the DTP. We may have 150 pumps in the centrifugal pump example, and each pump may represent a unique instance, all of which is based on the common DTP for that specific model of the pump. It is possible to have only one instance based on a single model. A building is a typical example of such a configuration. There is only one building (DTI) and only one model of DTP. It is worth noting that any changes to the DTP will require the DTI to be updated to maintain the fidelity of the instance to the prototype.

Physical entities such as buildings and other complex products can often not be described by a single DTI. It is generally more of a collection or composition of different instances to make up the overall building definition. Grieves and Vickers addressed this challenge by introducing aggregation of instances. The following diagram illustrates the progression from a DTP model based on a physical entity, and how this is instantiated as a DTIs for individual physical entities that conform to the same Digital Twin Prototype:

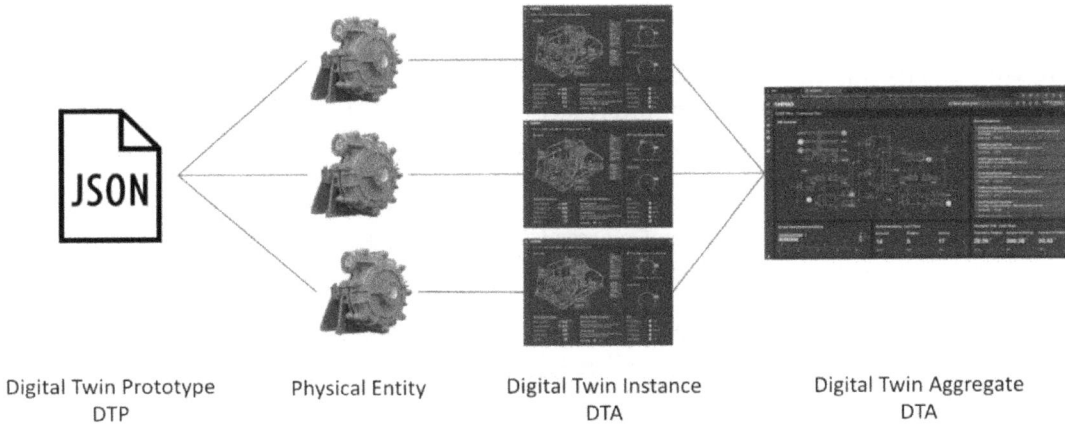

Figure 1.2 – Relationships between Digital Twin concepts

It also shows how multiple DTIs can be combined to create a Digital Twin Aggregate, which we will introduce next.

A **Digital Twin Aggregate (DTA)** is an aggregate collection of DTIs and other DTAs, and the mechanisms to query them. DTIs can exist independently of other instances, but DTAs cannot. The DPI of a single centrifugal pump can exist in isolation, whereas the aggregate of a grouping of pumps are dependent on a collection of instances. A DTA can provide additional insight into the behavior of the aggregate, which cannot be achieved at the instance level. For example, we could monitor the pressure difference across the slurry pumps for a specific processing area, which will give us a different insight into the overall operation of this part of the mining process plant versus the information that we can gather from the DTI of a single pump.

It is important to note that DTPs and their corresponding DTIs are different from **Computer-Aided Drawing (CAD)** files. A CAD file can describe the physical dimensions of a component, but it lacks the file structure to capture, store, and maintain the properties of all the components based on the CAD file. DTPs and DTIs are typically based on file structures such as **JavaScript Object Notation (JSON)** or **Extensible Markup Language (XML)** to manage the extended metadata of a Digital Twin.

Many descriptions and definitions emerged from vendors, analysts, and research organizations over the years based on this initial work by Grieves and Vickers, but they are outside the scope of this book.

In 2012, NASA described a Digital Twin as a multiphysics, multiscale, probabilistic, ultra-high fidelity simulation that reflects the state of a corresponding twin based on historical data, real-time sensor data, and a physical model.

What is a Digital Twin?

There are numerous vendor and analyst definitions of Digital Twins, each describing features that reflect the capabilities or interests of the authors. The Digital Twin Consortium's definition provides a vendor- and technology-agnostic definition that describes the what, when, why, and how of Digital Twins at a high level:

"A Digital Twin is a virtual representation of real-world entities and processes, synchronized at a specified frequency and fidelity.

Digital Twins can represent the past and present and simulate predicted futures.

Digital Twin Systems transform business by accelerating holistic understanding, optimal decision-making, and effective action.

Digital Twins are motivated by outcomes, tailored to use cases, powered by integration, built on data, and implemented in IT/OT systems."

We propose a more focused definition of a Digital Twin for this book that relates to the process that we will describe to help you build your first Digital Twin. It contains the necessary elements and common understanding for your initial Digital Twin:

"A Digital Twin is a synchronized instance of a digital template or model representing an entity in its life cycle and is sufficient to meet the requirements of a set of use cases."

Our definition addresses the critical elements of a Digital Twin that we will require in the remaining chapters as we demonstrate how to create our first Digital Twin. It highlights the requirement for a prototype or template model of a physical entity. It recognizes that there may be multiple instances that represent multiple assets of the same type. It also highlights the requirement that the Digital Twin should address specific business challenges or use cases and that they could be at any stage of the entity's life cycle.

> **Important Note**
> We differentiate between the life cycle of the entity and the life cycle of the Digital Twin. This distinction will be described later in this chapter.

Entities are not limited to physical assets, and we prefer the description of an entity from the ISO organization:

> *"entity is an item that has recognizably distinct existence, e.g., a person, an organization, a device, a subsystem, or a group of such items."*

International Organization for Standardization (ISO) 24760-1:2011

In addition to the conventional physical asset view of a Digital Twin, this description of an entity allows us to include Digital Twins of processes, supply chains, organizations, and governments, among others. It can also be used in extreme examples, such as a hurricane or bushfire, in an emergency response use case. We will cover more examples in the *Industry use of Digital Twins* section.

A vital element of the Grieves and Vickers approach was that Digital Twins synchronized with a physical entity. This means that a digital model that only provides a simulation with no input from a physical asset does not qualify as a Digital Twin. It can be used to start the process of creating a Digital Twin as it may represent the DTP or DTA, but it requires the instance and the data to be synchronized to qualify as a Digital Twin. Examples of these digital models include 2D and 3D CAD design drawings, **Building Information Management** (BIM) models, planning simulation models, and AR visualizations based on design parameters.

Entity life cycle and Digital Twin development life cycle

Physical entities, products, and assets have life cycles, from planning and design through manufacturing or construction, operations, maintenance, and, finally, retirement or disposal. The asset life cycle represents the phases of physical twin development and use. The twin's digital version is a software-based digitalization that includes models, data, connectivity, analytics, and actions. The twin's digital version requires a software engineering approach, whereas the physical twin is based on engineering management practices such as **product life cycle management** (PLM).

It is important to note that we distinguish between the asset life cycle/Physical Twin and the Digital Twin development life cycle, as shown in the following diagram. We will be referring to both life cycles throughout this book, so this differentiation is important to keep in mind:

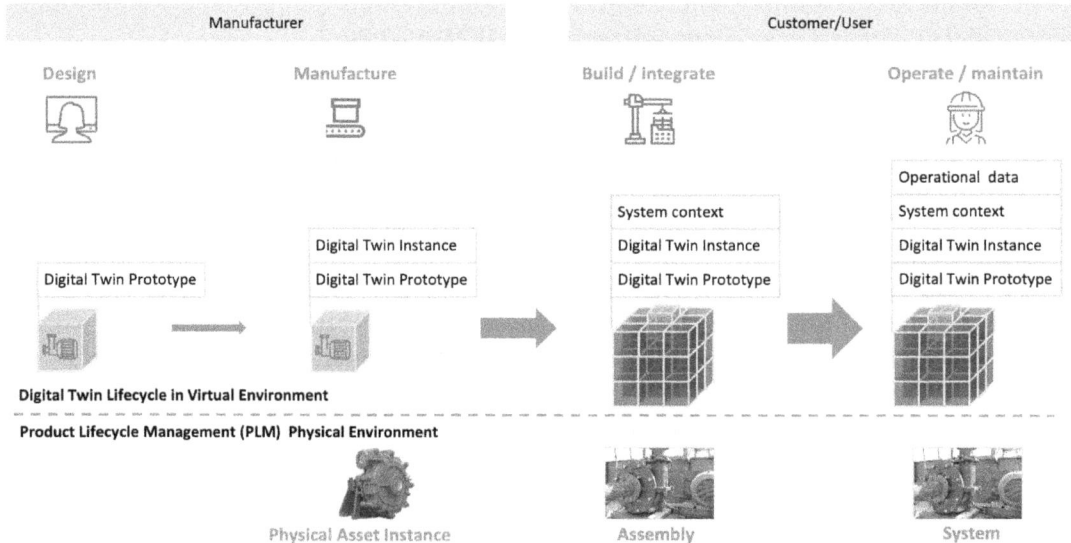

Figure 1.3 – Digital Twin and product life cycle relationship

Developing Digital Twins requires both traditional engineering as well as software development practices so that they work in harmony. This convergence of **Operational Technology (OT)** and **Information Technology (IT)** is a positive development for Digital Twins as it creates a shared understanding of both the physical and the digital requirements.

It is not the aim of this book to provide guidance on PLM for the physical twin. The digital development life cycle will be addressed in the remaining chapters as we build our first DTP. Also, it is not this book's aim to provide guidance on the digital development methodology that an organization should follow.

Our preference is an agile-based approach for our initial minimum viable Digital Twin in this book, but other software engineering approaches, such as the V-Model and Waterfall, can be used if you are more familiar with these methodologies. The V-Model approach is popular for designing and manufacturing complex systems in aviation and the military, but that is beyond the scope of this book.

Types of Digital Twins

The types of Digital Twins that we'll describe here are not a full taxonomy of a Digital Twin or a formal classification system. Still, this will highlight that different use cases have different types of Digital Twins.

Discrete versus composite

The scope and scale of a Digital Twin will vary based on the use case or problem that it is addressing. A key consideration when choosing your first Digital Twin is the level of complexity that your use case will require. More complex Digital Twins are typically composed by assembling different discrete or standalone Digital Twins:

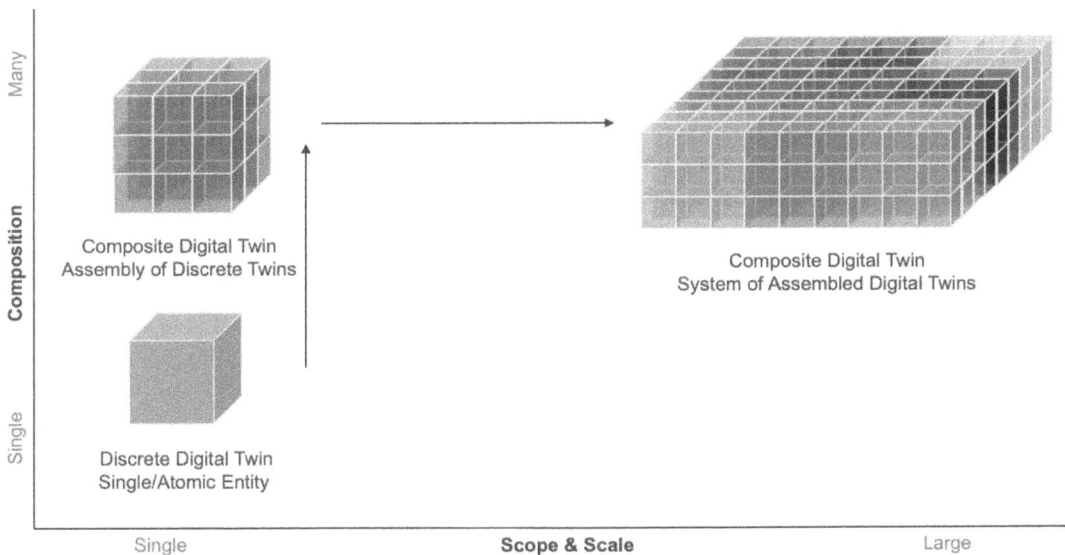

Figure 1.4 – Discrete and composite Digital Twin relationship

The preceding diagram shows the relationship between a discrete Digital Twin and a composite Digital Twin.

A discrete Digital Twin is the lowest level of abstraction that is sufficient to meet the requirements of a specific use case. It is often a single or atomic entity where no value would be added by breaking it down into components or parts, such as the gearbox or motor for a ball mill in mining. It doesn't need to be broken down into its component parts as its status and monitoring processes are reported at this entity level.

A composite Digital Twin is a combination of discrete Digital Twins that represent an entity comprising multiple individual components or parts. A composite Digital Twin can be an Assembly Twin, such as a ball mill in mining, or a System Twin that comprises multiple Assembly Twins, such as processing and refinement plants. A Composite Digital Twin is a system of systems with a more complex life cycle management challenge.

A discrete Digital Twin is typically a standalone component or asset that can function on its own to address a specific use case. An electrically driven centrifugal pump and its electric drive is a typical example of a discrete Digital Twin as monitoring and reporting is done at this level. An example of the discrete pump Digital Twin use case would be to predict pump failures based on a predictive analytics model.

A composite Digital Twin is an assembly of several discrete Digital Twins to create a new functional, composite asset. Combining several discrete pump Digital Twins with discrete autoclave Digital Twins creates a composite Digital Twin of a gold processing plant, which is used for production optimization.

A predictive maintenance use case example for a composite plant Digital Twin is more extensive than the predictive maintenance use case of the discrete pump Digital Twin, even though the pump is used in the plant use case.

The DTP that we will design and develop in this book will follow the Discrete Digital Twin pattern. The difference between the pump and the gold recovery plant leads to the second type of classification we need for Digital Twins.

Product versus facility

Industrial Digital Twins based on physical entities can broadly be applied to two prominent use cases. The first is a Digital Twin representing a manufactured product such as a pump, electric motor, hand drill, X-ray machine, automobile, or any other asset-based entity. The primary objective of the Digital Twin is to monitor the use of this specific entity, which may include indications of failures or sub-optimal operation.

The second type of industrial Digital Twin use case is around manufacturing or production facilities, which generally consist of a composition of individual assets. The Digital Twin is used to provide insight into the operations of the facility. The facility Digital Twin will consist of an assembly of unique product twins.

The discrete product Digital Twin can be used in two different ways in the composite facility Digital Twin; for example, where the product is part of the facility, such as a robotic arm on an assembly line.

The second use case is where the Digital Twin is part of the manufactured product, for example, an electric motor, a jet engine, or wind turbine, in the manufacturing facility.

A smart manufacturing use case, for example, uses a combination of product and facility Digital Twins. The product Digital Twin is used on the manufacturing line to determine the machine setup, tooling, and parts requirements.

Product Digital Twins are currently predominantly used in manufacturing scenarios, and manufacturers have no visibility of the use of the product once it has been shipped. As the adoption of Digital Twins increases, this scenario will likely change.

Product manufacturers are keen to extend access to the Digital Twin of the product beyond the point of the manufacture. Manufacturers provide Digital Twin solutions that allow them to collect operations and usage data that will be used for product improvements and new service-based products.

The Digital Twin can provide insights into how products are used, and this can be fed back into the product's design for improvements. These insights will enable manufacturers to develop and manufacture products that are more fit for purpose and at higher quality levels.

The real opportunity for many manufacturers is to provide not only the product but also the maintenance services around the product. Access to the operating product's Digital Twin will provide the necessary insight to predict when failures are likely to happen, or when the product is due for servicing or replacement. This opens up a new business model for many manufacturers with new revenue streams, which wasn't possible without the Digital Twin technology.

Simulation versus operational

During the early stages of the product or asset life cycle, the Digital Twin use cases focus more on simulation scenarios. In contrast, use cases in the later stages of the product tend to focus more on operational and maintenance challenges.

We can broadly classify Digital Twins into simulation and operations twins. This does not mean to say that simulation cannot be used in operations, but the predominant application is to manage operations. During the design phase, the principal use cases simulate different scenarios to determine the product or facility's ideal design:

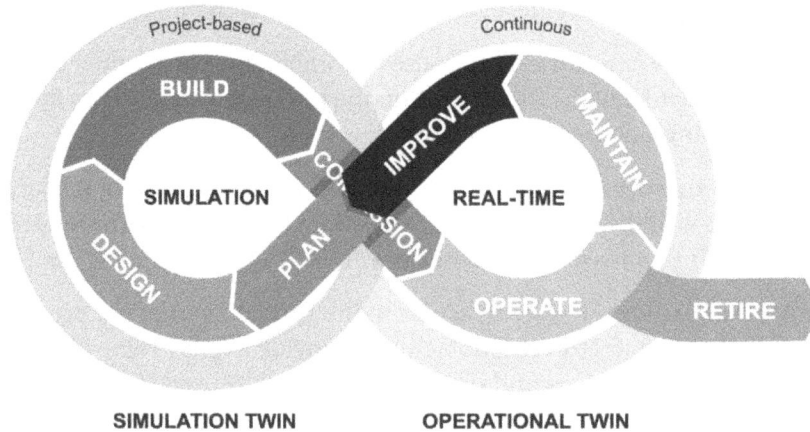

Figure 1.5 – Simulation and operational Digital Twin types

Simulations also tend to be more project-based, whereas operational use cases are continuous over the operations and maintenance life cycle of the entity. The infinity loop model best describes this, as shown in the preceding diagram. The plan, design, build, and commissioning phases are typically project-based simulations for Digital Twins with very slow synchronization or twinning rates.

The operate, maintain, and improve phases are continuous and often real-time applications of Digital Twins. Recommendations from the improve phase may require us to make modifications to the product that would lead back into the planning and project-based designing manufacturing cycle. It is important to note that this is not a qualifying criterion for classification but rather a typical pattern when using industrial Digital Twins.

Analytics versus physics-based

The digital models that represent the entity can be based on analytics and physics-based algorithms. These algorithms can use historical and real-time data to enable simulation and predictions of the current and future state or behavior:

- **Analytics-based** algorithms are statistical or mathematical techniques that are used to predict entity behavior based on historical data. These models are most often based on AI or machine learning techniques. Predicting the remaining useful life of equipment such as a centrifugal pump using a regression model is an example of an analytics-based application.

- **Physics-based** algorithms are based on the physical laws of using engineering equations of state and material properties to provide insight into the current or predicted state of a product. A **Computational Fluid Dynamic (CFD)** could use design parameters or real-time data to provide insights into a centrifugal pump's behavior under specific conditions. Finite element analysis is another example of a physics-based algorithm that's used to provide insights into a product's structural integrity under simulated or real-time conditions.

Simulation and operational twins can use both analytics and physics-based models for simulation or operational analysis and predictions.

Characteristics of a Digital Twin

The characteristics described in this book are focused on the key elements that will be required when you develop your first DTP. There may be additional characteristics in other more complex use cases, but these provide a great starting point for Digital Twin evaluation:

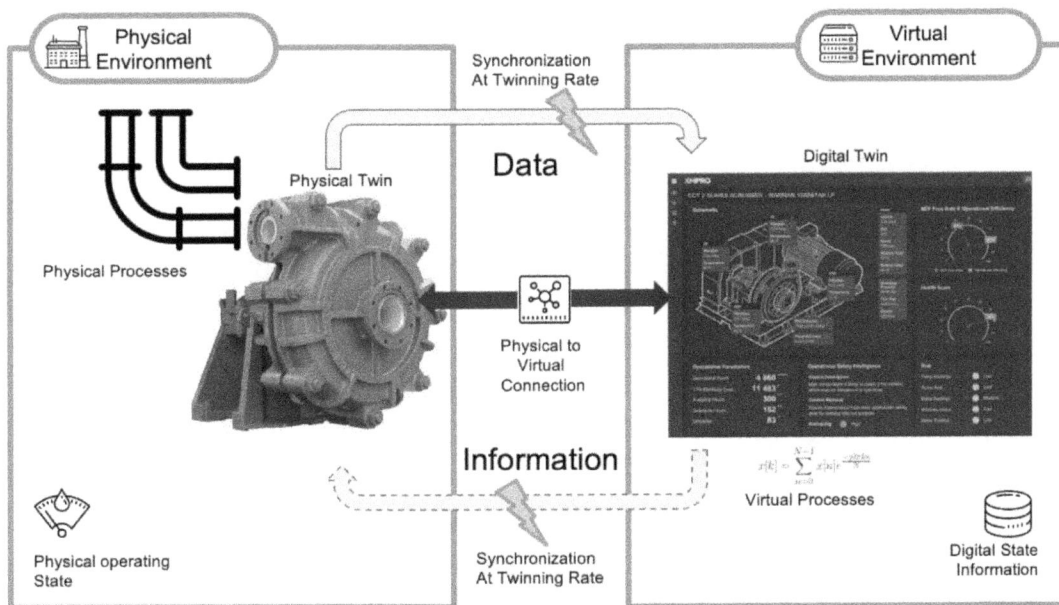

Figure 1.6 – Digital Twin characteristics

The preceding diagram provides a visual representation of the characteristics of a Digital Twin that are based on the Digital Twin definition:

Characteristic	Description
Physical Entity (Physical Twin)	"An entity is an item that has recognizably distinct existence, e.g., a person, an organization, a device, a subsystem or a group of such items" ISO/IEC 24760-1:2011
Physical Environment	The real-world environment that the Physical Twin exist in (factory, oil platform, hospital, nature reserve, etc.)
Virtual Entity (Virtual Twin)	The virtual Digital Twin prototype (DTP) and instance(s) synchronized with the physical entity at a twinning rate
Virtual Environment	The technology-based environment that the virtual Twin exists in
Synchronization (twinning)	Synchronization or updating the state of the physical twin and virtual twin
Twinning Rate	The rate or frequency at which synchronization happens
State	The values of all the parameters of both the physical and virtual Twins in its environments
Physical to Virtual Connection (bi-directional)	The communications and data connections or processes used to establish this synchronization of the state at the prescribed twinning rate
Physical Processes	The processes in the real-world environment that will change or impact the state of the physical twin
Virtual Processes	The processes in the virtual environment (such as analytics or physics-based calculations) That will change or impact the state of the virtual twin

Figure 1.7 – Key characteristics

Digital Twin fidelity is not necessarily a characteristic and more of a result of the model's sophistication and twinning rate. We are seeing an increase in Digital Twin fidelity as the computing capabilities in the virtual environment continue to expand exponentially according to Moore's law.

Metrology is also an essential requirement for twinning as it involves accurately measuring the state parameters. It is not a characteristic, but it is essential to ensure accurate representations of the physical state.

As we start building the first DTP in this book, we will continue to refer to these characteristics. It is useful to document the specific aspects of your Digital Twin in this table format when you choose your ideal candidate. It will provide an initial test to help determine if a particular use case or scenario would qualify as a Digital Twin.

Models and data

Virtual twins exist in virtual environments in a digitized format and rely on different data sources and models to turn data into information. There is a wide variety of data sources and models that provide virtual twin data capabilities. For this book, we have simplified them into six main categories:

1. **Temporal or Time Series Data**: This data provides time-stamped, real-time synchronization of physical state data through sensors, automation, and control and IoT systems. It is stored and accessed from time series databases, historians, and IoT platforms.

2. **Master Data**: Master data is generally slow-changing contextual data that's stored in systems. It is used to describe assets or entities such as **enterprise asset management systems (EAM)** and **enterprise resource management systems (ERP)**, as well as in Digital Twin services such as Azure Digital Twins.

3. **Transactional Data**: Operational, transactional data such as production records, maintenance records, supply chain information, and other business records related to the Digital Twin are generally stored in ERP, **Computerized Maintenance Management Systems (CMMS)**, **Manufacturing Execution Systems (MES)**, **Business Process Management (BPM)**, and production systems.

4. **Physics-Based Models**: Physics-based and engineering calculations use real-time, transactional, and master data to describe or predict the physical entity's state. Examples include **finite element methods (FEM)** and **computational fluid dynamics (CFD)**, as well as other laws of nature, such as the laws of thermodynamics.

5. **Analytical Models**: These are mathematical and statistical models in the virtual environment that use the same data sources described previously to predict the current and future state of the physical twin and its environment. This includes AI and machine learning for predictive maintenance and operations use cases.

6. **Visual Models**: These are digitalized visualization modeling capabilities such as **Computer Aided Design (CAD)**, **Augmented Reality (AR)**, **Virtual Reality (VR)**, **Building Information Modeling (BIM)**, **Geographic Information System (GIS)**, and geophysics models. These models are often used to reduce system complexity and provide a visual analysis of the different data sources.

The heterogeneous nature of all these different data sources contributes to the fact that integration remains a significant challenge when creating Digital Twins. We will refer to this point when we start building the DTP in the technical chapters of this book. Integration and interoperability can consume a large part of the resources in a Digital Twin project. It is essential to understand the data requirements, as well as what physics and analytical models will be required to address the specific business problem that the Digital Twin set out to solve.

Digital Thread

Digital Thread is a term that gained popularity at the same time as Digital Twins. It is sometimes confused or associated with Digital Twins. The Digital Thread can exist without formal Digital Twins, but Digital Twins are built on Digital Thread information.

The Digital Thread evolved from PLM, which captured the process from design to manufacture for physical products. The Digital Thread creates a traceable, unique birth record with the actual data for each composite entity or product assembly and all its components. It captures all its interactions and transactions throughout its life cycle through to retirement. It extends the life cycle record beyond the PLM's focus into operations, maintenance, and disposal.

The Digital Twin's focus on the life cycle phase is to address specific use cases, whereas the Digital Thread is the data aggregator across all life cycle phases. The Digital Thread provides component traceability regarding its design iterations, manufacturing processes, testing, and quality measures. It often includes environmental metadata such as manufacturer information, storage temperature, and humidity for specific components. The Digital Thread may also include information on the relationship between components, including **Bill of Material** (**BOM**) structures and maintenance records.

Some Digital Twins may extend beyond a single phase or blend phases, such as operate and maintain, but it is unlikely to extend across the full life cycle. Digital Twin components such as models, analytics, and real-time sensor data may be reused, but there is generally not a single Digital Twin that spans all of the asset life cycle phases.

Digital Threads integrate data from multiple design, manufacturing, and operational data sources. They may not replicate the information from CAD, MES, EAM, and ERP systems, but they maintain references to the source data for the "birth record to death certificate" for products and components.

The Digital Twin of an aircraft fleet, for example, may be used to prioritize maintenance for individual aircraft, where the Digital Thread for the aircraft will assist in **Failure Mode and Effect Analysis** (**FMEA**) and **Root Cause Analysis** (**RCA**) in the event of a component failure. It can provide insight into the design, manufacture, and maintenance of the component. A Digital Twin can also assist in identifying aircraft that may have the same faulty component:

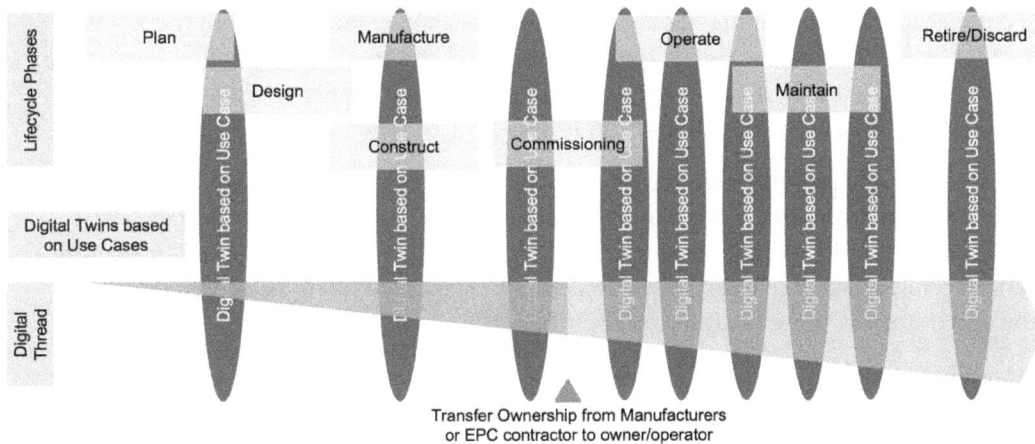

Figure 1.8 – Digital Twin versus Digital Thread

The preceding diagram shows the development of the Digital Thread across the overall life cycle of the entity, where the Digital Twin use cases address specific challenges within one or possibly two life cycle phases. How this is used in practice will be explained in the next section.

Industry use of Digital Twins

Throughout this book, you will learn how to create your first industrial Digital Twin. Before we get started, though, it is essential to understand who the key stakeholders are that have an interest in the value of Digital Twins, as well as some of the high-level applications in different industries.

Digital Twin stakeholders

Let's distinguish two different high-level scenarios when using Digital Twins in industrial applications. The first scenario is where the asset that is twinned is a standalone product that's used by an end user. The specific model of an **electric vehicle (EV)**, such as a Tesla Model 3, might be the product, while the consumer is the end user. The vehicle manufacturer will be the **Original Equipment Manufacturer (OEM)**.

The second scenario is a manufacturing asset such as a smart factory, where the EV is produced. The Digital Twin is the factory itself and has different use cases and applications during the smart factory's life cycle phases. This production facility could also be a gold mine, an oil platform, a power distribution micro-grid, or a nuclear power plant.

For this scenario, the stakeholders include the owner/operator that commissions **Engineering, Procurement, Construction, and Manufacture (EPCM)** contractors to design and build these production facilities. OEMs provide equipment for facilities, and Operations and Maintenance service providers are often used by owners/operators to operate and maintain these facilities on their behalf.

Traditionally, OEMs did not have access to their products and their usage data after they left their factories, but OEMs are increasingly supplying their product Digital Twins with physical assets and, in process, aim to get access to real-time usage data. We are starting to see the reach of OEM Digital Twins extend beyond their own factories' boundaries.

Service providers for Digital Twins aim to extend their capabilities across the full life cycle of the product and facility's Digital Twins. This includes connectivity, compute, storage, integration, modeling, analytics, visualization, and workflows.

The following diagram shows the typical roles of stakeholders during the asset life cycle phases:

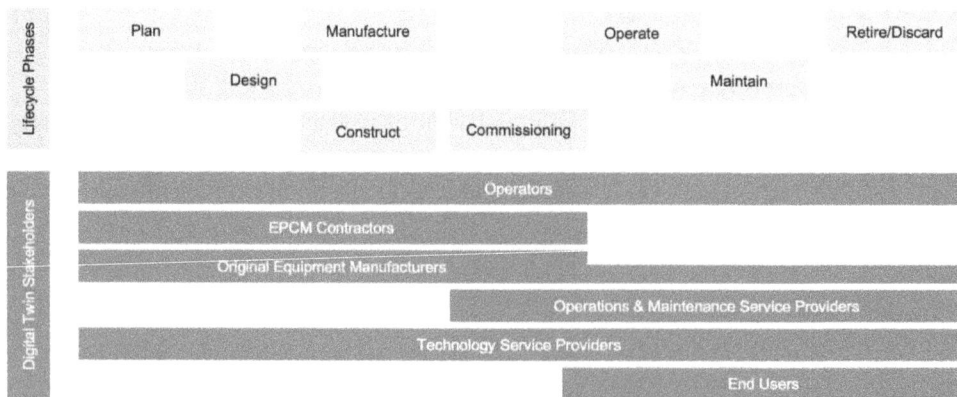

Figure 1.9 – Key stakeholders during the life cycle of an entity

All of these stakeholders have had a vested interest in Digital Twins at some stage during the product or facility's life cycle. Information or Digital Twin sharing between stakeholders increases as Digital Twin use cases start to span multiple stakeholders across multiple phases. It significantly increases the Digital Twins' business value, but it also increases complexity and leads to interoperability challenges. Some of these challenges will be addressed later in the book.

Industrial Digital Twin applications

Digital Twins exist across the whole life cycle of assets and products, as we saw earlier in this chapter. Let's look at a few examples of industrial Digital Twin use cases in different industries. This is not an exhaustive list, but it does provide examples that highlight some of the challenges that can be addressed by Digital Twins. This can help you decide on the type of Digital Twin you would like to build as your prototype.

Discrete manufacturing

- Optimize **Overall Equipment Effectiveness** (**OEE**) in real time during operations.

- Predictive quality improvement during operations to reduce the scrap rate and rework.

- Enhance product designs with insights from operations and maintenance data.

Process manufacturing

- Manage batch-based processes to "golden batch" in real time to improve product quality and process optimization.

- Predict equipment failure with machine learning models based on real-time operational data and models built on historical failure data.

- Monitor real-time compliance with safety and regulatory requirements for classified equipment during operations.

Energy (power)

- Predict the energy demand per consumer through dynamic machine learning models in an operations-planning Digital Twin.

- Improve grid distribution and management by utilizing simulation models based on real-time data input for **Distributed Energy Resources** (**DERs**).

- Improve solar array maintenance by detecting anomalous behavior that indicates dirty panels, for example.

- Predictive maintenance for wind farms to improve the "first-time fix rate" and reduce truck rolls and the spares inventory that's carried by the field service teams.

Oil and gas

- Perform real-time **Finite Element Method** (**FEM**) analytics to determine offshore oil platforms' structural integrity based on weather and oceanic data.

- Update subsurface reservoir models with drilling and exploration data to support investment decisions.

- Monitor rotating equipment (such as pumps and compressors) in real time to improve equipment availability and asset performance. This includes condition-based and predictive maintenance.

Mining and metals

- Improved recovery yields on mineral processing plants during operations such as gold recovery or coal washing.

- Monitor mine tailings and other environmental waste in real time and provide recommendations based on expert business rules.

- Provide real-time casting guidance to blast furnace operators based on real-time process parameters and metallurgical (physics) models.

Automotive

- The Digital Twins of vehicles provide feedback to manufacturers with usage data that is incorporated in design improvements.

- Real-time telemetry in the Digital Twin of a car enables manufacturers and their service agents to offer maintenance services based on condition monitoring and predictive analytics.

- The Digital Twins of autonomous vehicles opens up new business models for service providers, such as ride-share operators.

Life sciences and medical

- Reduce the risk of critical stock and logistics challenges with a real-time Digital Twin of the end-to-end supply chain.

- Reduce downtime on expensive **High-Performance Liquid Chromatography (HPLC)** systems with real-time conditioning monitoring and failure prediction.

- The Digital Twin of a patient providing a holistic view to improve the quality and efficacy of medical treatment (though this is currently challenged by privacy and security concerns).

Infrastructure

- Enable off-site and on-site pre-fabrication by updating the dimensional and structural data in design Digital Twins, through to additive manufacturing during the construction and delivery phases.

- Provide real-time insights and situational awareness during natural disasters and severe weather events.

- Provide real-time insights into foot traffic in retail infrastructures such as malls and shopping centers.

Aerospace

- Track and Trace Digital Twins provide insights into real-time material and supply chain management in aviation manufacturing.

- The predictive Digital Twin of aircraft landing gear extends the life of components and reduces maintenance costs.

- Airport Digital Twins with real-time aircraft movement improve bay utilization and cycle times, thereby increasing revenue.

Defense

- Improved equipment reliability and maintainability of complex military equipment with condition monitoring and predictive maintenance Digital Twins.

- Strategic warfare Digital Twins based on real-time situational data provide planning scenarios to tactical command and leadership.

- A Spatial Digital Twin with a single, dynamic dataset that represents the physical world with sufficient resolution to act as the reference point for all systems requiring mission data.

Other

The Digital Twin concept is increasingly used to model and manage less tangible entities. Some of these include the following:

- Digital Twin of the Earth
- Digital Twin of organizations
- Digital Twin of bushfires

These different examples show a diverse range of Digital Twin applications. There are many more that have not been included in this list. The range of potential applications is only limited by the imagination of those who are actively building these Digital Twins.

A key element of all these examples is that they have clear and measurable value to the stakeholders of the Physical Twin or entity.

The value proposition of Digital Twins

Digital Twin systems transform businesses by accelerating holistic understanding, optimal decision-making, and effective action.

Reduce complexity to improve understanding

Grieves and Vickers' initial objective was to manage assets and systems that were becoming increasingly complex with simpler, but representative, virtual instances. Digital Twins that are synchronized with physical entities provide situational awareness and other operational insights tailored to specific problems you are trying to address.

Better insights into real-time and simulated behavior support making better decisions faster. Insights from Digital Twins are often more reliable than traditional approaches of searching for data in multiple enterprise systems. The consolidated data integration approach of a Digital Twin provides more reliable, comprehensive insights that improve the quality of the decisions that are made on that data. The structured information approach of a Digital Twin also lends itself to decision automation rather than just decision support.

Having this improved understanding and better insights provides value in two key operational perspectives. We will look at these in the following subsections.

Improved situational awareness

Businesses are increasingly forced to work in real time or near real time. Every day, companies are exposed to more and more internal and external events that need to be responded to in real time. These events can come from a multitude of sources:

- The actions of people in a business

- The actions of competitors, customers, legislators, or suppliers and supply chains.

- Equipment breakdowns, process failures, and weather events

- Real-time intelligence from business applications, and near real-time data from web services

- More recently, the influx of information from IoT with sensor-based or smart device machine-borne data in IoT platforms

Real-time situational awareness is a concept that came from the US Air Force when training fighter pilots to anticipate the actions of an enemy fighter. It is based on gathering information on the current state and environment of the situation, determining what the information means, and projecting the future state to create a corresponding action. It was described in military terms as the **Observe – Orient – Decide – Act (OODA)** loop.

Digital Twins might not require the same millisecond response times as a military jet fighter, but the real-time synchronization of a Digital Twin representing a physical asset provides critical situational awareness that drives critical decisions. The supporting information for decisions can be augmented with predictive models, physics, and/or analytics-based data to provide operators with comprehensive decision support. Combining rules with decision information creates an opportunity for Digital Twins to become prescriptive and take autonomous action through decision automation.

Both decision support and decision automation focus on delivering better business outcomes based on the situational awareness that's gained through the Digital Twin.

Improved business outcomes

Digital Twins improve business outcomes in various ways, but we will focus on the impact of an industrial Digital Twin that represents a physical asset or entity such as a motor drive, a production plant, or a factory.

The business impact of Digital Twins can be measured based on four major impact categories, as shown in the following table:

Increase Revenue	• Improved Productivity
	• Increased machine uptime
	• Monetizing digital information and services (business model innovation)
Reduce Cost	• Reduced machine or equipment failures
	• Optimized inventory and better supply chain management
	• Reduce rework and improved quality
Improve Customer and Employee Experience	• Provide real-time situational awareness to customers and business users
	• Provide decision support through simulation, analytics augmented and virtual reality, and business rules embedded in the Digital Twin
	• Provide holistic or 360-degree visualization of an asset and its operating environment
Improve Compliance and Reduce Risk	• Monitor real-time compliance on Health, Safety, and Environment
	• Improve transparency on operational use and maintenance of assets, specifically for classified equipment such as pressure vessels and pressure relief valves. (Insurance and asset integrity inspection services)
	• Automate compliance with Operational Excellence for business KPIs and balanced scorecards.

Figure 1.10 – The business impact of Digital Twins

Each category represents a business value driver where a Digital Twin can act as a lever to influence overall business outcomes.

Transformational value

The transformational value of Digital Twins in industrial applications focuses primarily on the impact on digital business transformation, as well as the development of new or improved products based on the transformation of Digital Twins.

Business transformation through digital transformation

A Digital Twin is a change agent for formal digital transformation. A Digital Twin typically represents a specific initiative or use case around a business goal. Due to the digital nature of a Digital Twin, the particular use case or initiative is generally the project that drives specific digital transformation toward the business goal or outcome:

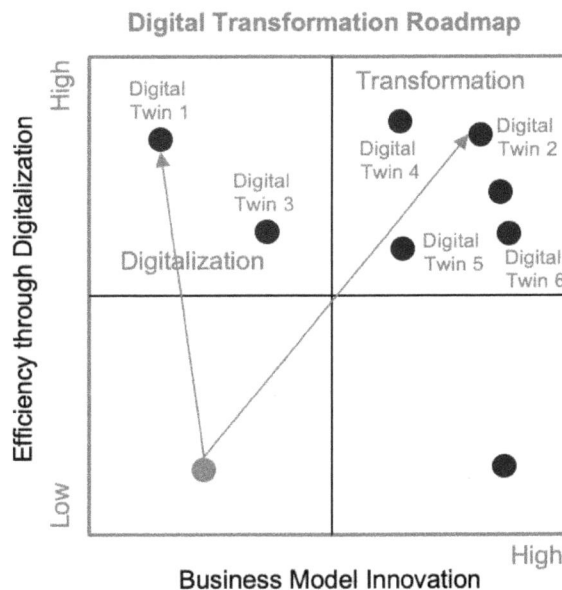

Figure 1.11 – Digital transformation versus digitalization

Digital Twins can affect business transformation by either improving efficiency through digitalization or providing added value by enabling new business models. The four quadrants in the preceding diagram show the impact of different Digital Twin initiatives that improve business process efficiency with digitalization and real-time data. Alternatively, it can monetize and leverage real-time data to change an organization's operating business model. The top right-hand quadrant represents opportunities where businesses can, for example, sell new services based on their equipment, such as support contracts and consumable replenishment, based on the real-time data from their products and customers.

Many organizations start with digitalization projects that improve efficiency. As they gain maturity when using Digital Twins, they move to the top right quadrant and look for ways to monetize these new digital assets.

New or improved products

There are different ways to monetize these new digital assets, including selling operational and maintenance intelligence to operators and users. Equipment manufacturers can also use this information to provide ongoing services based on conditions or predictions gathered from real-time data.

Original Equipment Manufacturers (**OEMs**) can also use information about the use and performance of their equipment in the field to provide feedback to help improve the design of their products and services. The actual use of assets in an industrial environment provides a wealth of information for Design Digital Twins, which can now use this information for better simulation, specifically in physics-based models.

Value at stake

The World Economic Forum value at stake framework provides an alternative perspective on assessing the impact of digital transformation with technology-based approaches such as Digital Twins.

The "value at stake" framework assesses the value in terms of the economics for the industry or the business and the impact on society. It has a simple representation, especially when communicating value to business executives and other stakeholders, who have a limited interest in the technical aspects of the Digital Twin but need to make the decisions to invest in Digital Twin technology.

The digital value to the industry is based on two elements:

*   Value migration, which represents how revenue can shift between stakeholders such as competitors, customers, and other industry players. This aligns with the business model innovation opportunity described earlier in this chapter.

*   Value addition, which represents the regular business operational opportunities, such as increased revenue and reduced cost.

The digital value to society focuses on three impact points:

- The traditional economic measures for customers and employees in terms of cost, time saving, and efficiency improvements.

- The societal impact in terms of job creation, new skills development, reduced traffic congestion, and safer working environments.

- The environmental impact can be described by reducing CO_2 emissions or improving the management of tailings in mining:

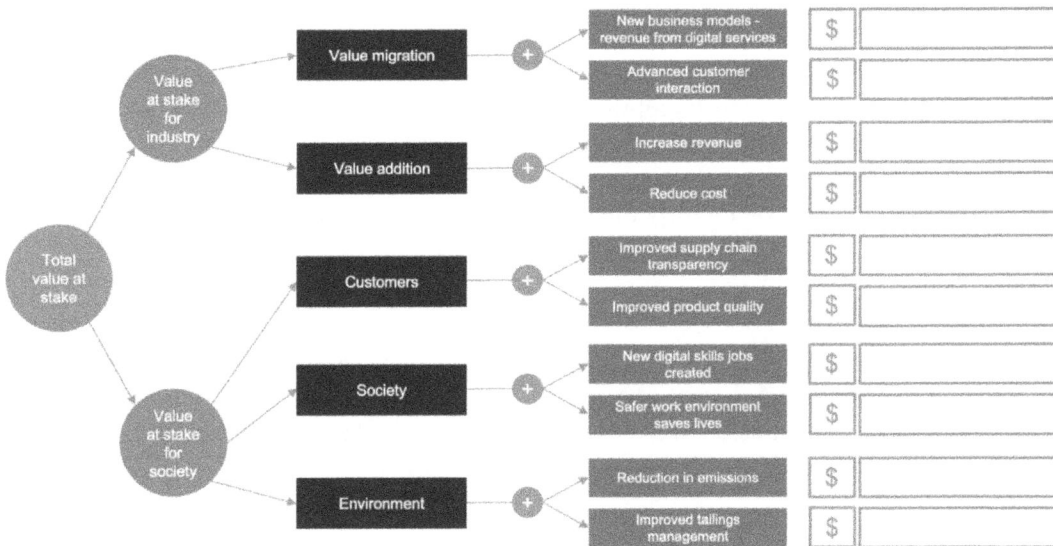

Figure 1.12 – Example of a value at stake analysis for a Digital Twin

> **Note**
> The preceding diagram has been adapted from `https://reports.weforum.org/digital-transformation/introducing-value-at-stake-a-new-analytical-tool-for-understanding-digitalization/`.

The single-page view of the value at stake for a Digital Twin, shown in the preceding diagram, provides a simple yet powerful way to describe a Digital Twin's value proposition.

Now that we can describe the value of a Digital Twin, the next key step is identifying ideal candidates for Digital Twins in your business.

Identifying opportunities

Digital Twins focus on addressing specific business challenges or exploiting new opportunities, as we saw in the value at stake description of Digital Twin applications. These challenges and opportunities provide guidance for identifying opportunities for Digital Twins in industrial applications. This will be covered in more detail in *Chapter 4, Getting Started with Our First Digital Twin.*

The remainder of this book will focus on selecting and building your first Digital Twin, but let's provide a summary of the high-level guiding principles that can be used to identify a potential pilot from a pool of candidates.

For Digital Twins that focus on improving asset performance, reducing downtime, and increasing production or throughput, the ideal starting point is to identify current "bad actors." This approach is based on using current failure data, production loss information, or failure mode analysis on previous downtime incidents. Applying the 80/20 Pareto principle will help you identify the initial shortlist of entities that cause the bulk of the downtime.

> **Important Note**
>
> The Pareto principle states that for many outcomes, roughly 80% of consequences come from 20% of the causes (the "vital few"). Other names for this principle are the 80/20 rule, the law of the vital few, and the principle of factor sparsity: `https://bit.ly/DTPareto8020`.

Digital Twins that focus on exploiting new revenue opportunities are generally more strategic and have well-described business cases. The technical feasibility of these opportunities is typically also a factor when designing the new service. Real-time data access, sensor information, and other functions of the Digital Twin are built from the start.

The next step for both scenarios is to rank the business impact against the Digital Twin's technical feasibility. Technical feasibility is generally a factor of infrastructure, connectivity, data access, appetite for change, and organizational maturity.

It is a high-level ranking that can easily be done in Excel, and a template is available at `https://bit.ly/DTPriority`:

XMPRO Business Value Assessment

#	Use Case/Scenario	Business Impact					Economic	Technical Feasibility				
		Safety	Downtime	Throughput	Quality	Cost	Value/year	Automation	IT Systems	Analytics	Environment	Project
1	Use Case 1	Medium	High	High	High	High	> $10m	High	High	Medium	High	High
2	Use Case 2	Low	Low	Medium	customer satisf	High	> $10m	High	High	Low	High	High
3	Use Case 3	Low	Low	Low	Low	Low	> $1m	High	High	Low	High	High
4	Use Case 4	Low	Low	Low	Low	Low	> $1m	High	High	Low	High	High
5	Use Case 5	Low	Medium	High	Low	Medium	> $10m	Medium	High	Low	High	High
6	Use Case 6	Medium	Medium	Medium	Medium	Medium	> $1m	High	High	High	High	High
7	Use Case 7	Low	Medium	Medium	Medium	Low	> $1m	High	High	High	High	High
8	Use Case 8	Medium	Medium	Medium	Medium	Medium	> $10m	High	High	High	High	High
9	Use Case 9	Medium	High	High	High	High	> $1m	High	High	High	High	High
10	Use Case 10	High	Medium	Low	High	Low	> $1m	Medium	Medium	Medium	High	High

Figure 1.13 – Business impact and technical feasibility assessment

In this example, the following technical assessment criteria are being used:

- OT complexity
- IT complexity
- Analytics
- System complexity
- Project readiness

The technical assessment criteria can be adjusted to fit the business's requirements, but for this example, the criteria are for a typical industrial installation:

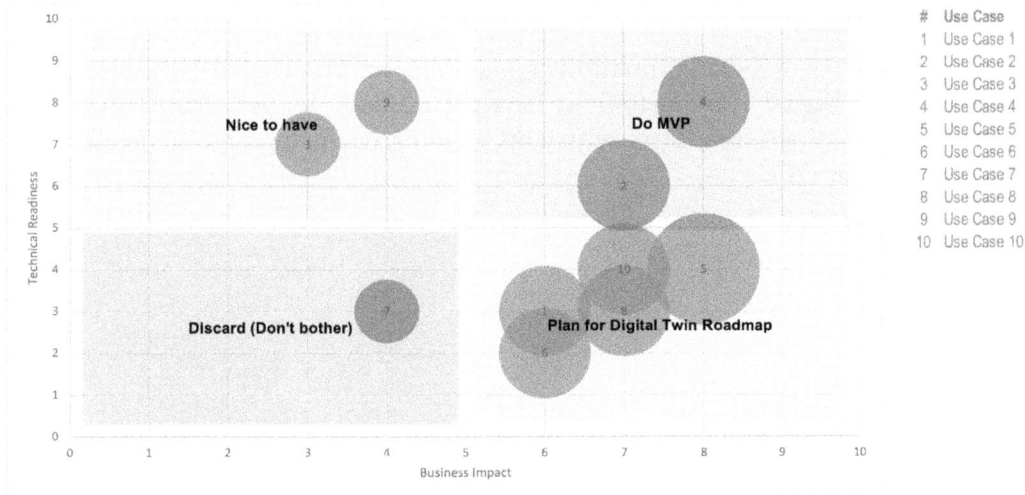

Figure 1.14 – Digital Twin prioritization matrix

This order of magnitude is visually represented in a bubble chart, with the business impact and technical readiness scores as the two significant measures. The weighted average values of each of these measures are placed on the graph, which is divided into four quadrants. The value of the economic impact determines the size of the bubble. The four quadrants represent the business readiness for each of the Digital Twin scenarios. The **Do Minimum Viable Product** (**MVP**) quadrant represents a high business impact and a high level of technical readiness.

The opportunities on the quadrant's far right-hand side, with the biggest bubble size, often represent Digital Twin projects with the highest likelihood of success for all stakeholders.

This is a very simple approach to ranking possible candidates for your first Digital Twin; the next chapter will provide more guidance on planning your Digital Twin project.

Summary

In this chapter, we started by taking a brief look at the history of Digital Twins and the original intent behind the concept. We discussed the difference between discrete and composite Digital Twins, and then we identified the elements required for something to qualify as a Digital Twin. We introduced several typical use cases across the life cycle of a Digital Twin, discussed the difference between a Digital Twin and a Digital Thread, and provided guidance on describing the value proposition of a Digital Twin. Our Digital Twin prioritization matrix provides a framework to perform a high-level assessment of the use cases for your first DTP.

You now have an understanding of what a Digital Twin is, its key characteristics, the value of a Digital Twin, and assessing where a Digital Twin may apply in your business.

The remaining chapters will guide you through building your first Digital Twin, beginning with planning your Digital Twin, identifying the right candidate for your first Digital Twin, and then providing guidance on setting up, building, deploying, and validating the outcomes of your DTP.

2
Planning Your Digital Twin

In the previous chapter, we learned why we need Digital Twins and how to use them to drive specific business outcomes. We explored the history of the Digital Twin and the various industries in which it presents opportunities.

Now, let's examine how to plan for an industrial Digital Twin in an enterprise setting. We will identify the key criteria that can be used to determine whether the industrial Digital Twin is applicable to the business scenarios. Additionally, we will explore how to develop the business case for investments in the Digital Twin. Following this, we will explore the prerequisites for the Digital Twin in an enterprise, including the functional and non-functional requirements. This will allow us to identify the underlying digital technologies required for the Digital Twin. Note that we will not lose sight of the organizational factors that are in play for the success of the industrial Digital Twin initiatives.

In this chapter, we will learn about the following topics:

- Key criteria
- Expected business outcomes
- Prerequisites for the Digital Twin
- Organizational factors
- Technological needs

Key criteria

Here, we will identify the key criteria to help an enterprise decide when the introduction of an industrial Digital Twin makes sense. The Digital Twin can be for a physical asset system or a process such as a manufacturing process in a plant. Depending on the target of the Digital Twin, objective criteria have to be established to ensure that the Digital Twin will add business value. Here, business values and outcomes are used in a broader sense, and they could include the following:

- Improved life of the asset
- Process efficiency gains
- Operational optimization or lower operating costs
- New digital revenues
- Competitive advantage
- Improved end customer satisfaction
- Improved safety
- A social good such as the reduction of the carbon footprint

As a result, once the key criteria have been established, it is easier to evaluate the direct and indirect investments and opportunity costs versus the broader business value generated. *Figure 2.1* shows this visually:

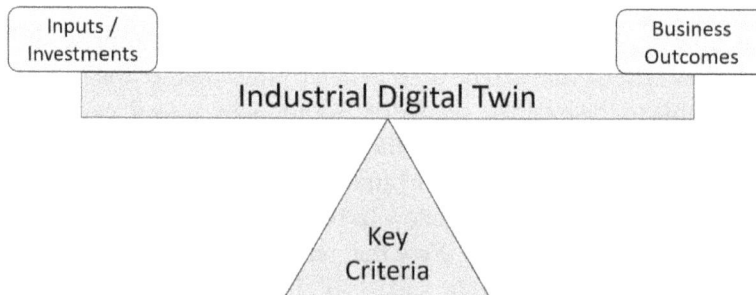

Figure 2.1 – Evaluation of the business benefits of the Industrial Digital Twin

In *Chapter 1, Introduction to Digital Twin*, we discussed the business value and transformational value as a result of the deployment of Digital Twins in the industry. The transformation value that is added can, often, be in form of new digital revenues. The monetization of Digital Twins can be based on a single Digital Twin or an ecosystem of twins, such as the concept of the **Twin2Twin (T2T)** ecosystem. (Please refer to `https://www.hcltech.com/blogs/twin2twin-new-paradigm-enterprise-digital-transformation`). The concept of T2T is similar to **Digital Twin Aggregate (DTA)**. However, T2T can also include disparate twins, such as twins of buildings and spaces along with twins of **heating, ventilation, and air conditioning** (HVAC) and security systems to efficiently operate a commercial building. These T2T twins are not hierarchical in nature.

A single Digital Twin can be monetized by the **original equipment manufacturer (OEMs)**, that is, by charging the customer for the use of the Digital Twin of the physical product. Such a Digital Twin can be sold as an add-on to the physical product and have a specific purpose, such as the predictive maintenance of the asset. The article on T2T, as referenced earlier, states that Digital Twins from different stakeholders in a value chain can help "to create a vibrant TWIN2TWIN economy." This will provide monetization opportunities to the different providers in the industry value chain. Today, marketplaces are common in the cloud computing world. One such example is Oracle's Cloud marketplace, which allows various stakeholders to create a vibrant ecosystem of cloud computing services that they can monetize jointly. (Please refer to `https://cloudmarketplace.oracle.com/marketplace/oci`.)

We believe similar ecosystems of the Digital Twin will arise in which the different participants of the ecosystem will contribute to the interdependent parts of the Digital Twin of the system or Digital Twin aggregate.

The commercial sector is often driven by profitability, so the Digital Twins should drive business value in general. However, in the public sector, the driver might be a social good, offering sustainability or an improved citizen experience. Singapore is experimenting with its own Digital Twin of a city. The government agency National Research Foundation has created Virtual Singapore, which is useful for simulating traffic or emergencies. (Please refer to `https://www.youtube.com/watch?v=QnLyy0owGL0&feature=youtu.be`.) Therefore, it is clear that the key criteria for a Digital Twin would vary based on the stakeholders.

In the next section, we will take a deeper look at the expected business outcomes for a specific industry in the commercial sector along with public sector scenarios.

Expected business outcomes

In the *Industry use of Digital Twins* section of *Chapter 1, Introduction to Digital Twin*, we discussed the applicable industry segments for the industrial Digital Twin. Now, let's take a look at the more specific business outcomes that are expected, or are possible, in some of these scenarios.

The manufacturing industry

When dealing with physical products, the manufacturer is responsible for the following:

- Product design and development
- Manufacturing/assembly
- Supply chain and distribution
- Product warranty and reputation
- Optional service contracts

Let's take a further look at discrete and process manufacturing within this context.

Discrete manufacturing

Let's take the example of aircraft manufacturing. A commercial aircraft is a fairly complex product and consists of assemblies such as the body or the fuselage, wings, two or four engines, landing gears, and the stabilizer. To build the Digital Twin of the aircraft as a composite asset, the prerequisite would be the Digital Twins of the major parts of the aircraft. These parts can be manufactured with different OEMs; for instance, the aircraft could be manufactured by Boeing but the engine could come from **General Electric** (**GE**). The Boeing-designed landing gear might be manufactured by United Technologies, which is now called Raytheon Technologies Corporation. *Figure 2.2* depicts an aircraft and its major parts:

Vertical Stabiliser

Rudder

Wing Upper Surface

APU Exhaust

Upper Fuselage

Spoilers

Elevator

Leading Edge Slats

APU Inlet

Horizontal Stabiliser

Trailing edge Flaps

Aileron

Angle of Airflow Sensor
(2 locations)

Wing Tip

Static Ports
(both sides)

Radome

Engine Intake

Static Ports
(both sides)

Pitot Tubes
(both sides)

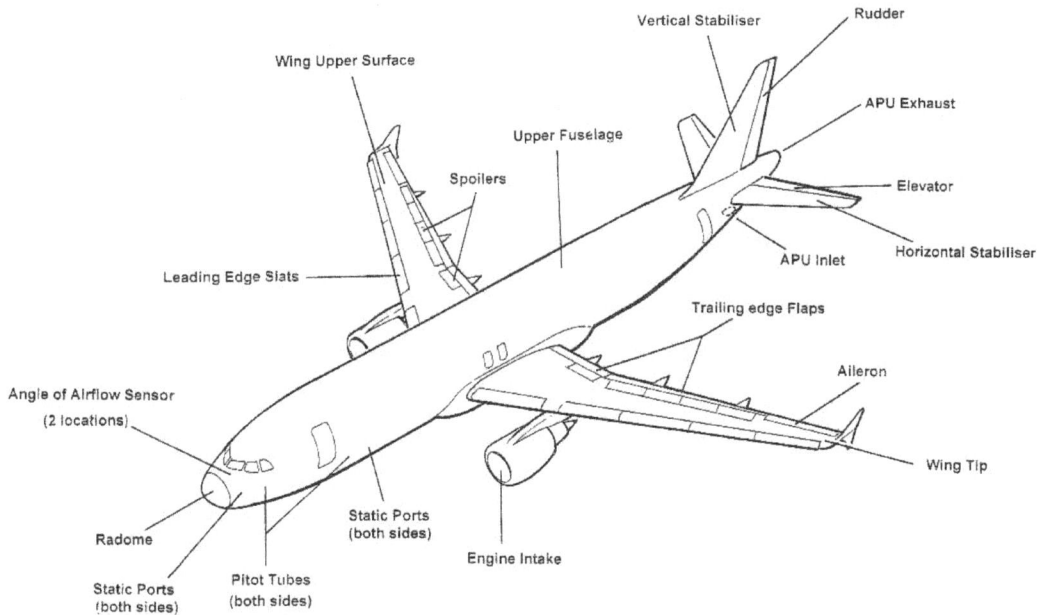

Figure 2.2 – The major parts of an aircraft

When the composite asset, such as an aircraft, is an assembly of supplier-provided assemblies, the composite Digital Twin would depend on the collaboration of the entire supply chain. In turn, each of the major OEMs, such as GE and United Technologies (now Raytheon), depends on several supplies for the smaller components.

Since we are looking at a commercial aircraft, which is used by airlines to fly passengers and cargo, we can list the high-level business outcomes as follows:

- **Aircraft manufacturer**: They provide reliable aircraft to the airlines.

- **Aircraft services provider**: The manufacturer might also be the provider of the maintenance services, and responsible for ensuring reliability, uptime, and safety in operations.

- **Aircraft owner or operator**: The airline that operates the aircraft is responsible for the safe and on-time operations of flights offered to its passengers.

- **The airline's passenger**: The end customer expects timely and safe flights at air travel costs that are on par or better than other airlines.

The preceding list consists of easy-to-understand business outcomes in the context of a discrete manufacturing industry where the product is the aircraft. This is a good example of a **business-to-business-to-consumer (B2B2C)** business model where a business such as Boeing or Airbus is selling to another business such as American Airlines or British Airways and, in turn, offering services to an individual end consumer who is an airline passenger.

Now that we understand the simplified value chain of the commercial airline industry, we can evaluate how an industrial Digital Twin of an aircraft would fit here. If the Digital Twin of the aircraft helps the manufacturer to build better aircraft or provide better service offerings to the airlines, then it delivers in terms of the business outcomes. Likewise, if the Digital Twin helps to reduce downtime – especially any unscheduled downtime for the aircraft – and improve the safety and efficiency of flights, then it delivers the business value.

While the airline passenger is not directly making a decision about the adoption or use of the Digital Twin of the aircraft, their customer satisfaction will provide direct inputs to the business outcomes of the airlines. Likewise, if the Digital Twin of the aircraft, and the jet engine as part of it, helps to improve fuel efficiency or carbon emissions, then it improves regulatory compliance and promotes social good. In our over-simplified model of the aircraft value chain, we have not looked at several other non-aeronautical stakeholders such as the airports and the ground services providers. However, every stakeholder benefits from efficiency in the basic aeronautical value chain. If the use of a Digital Twin of an aircraft leads to less unscheduled disruption of flights, airport operations run smoothly.

In order to provide the required business outcomes that were discussed in the preceding section, let's summarize the key business outcomes that are expected from the industrial Digital Twin of a commercial aircraft:

- It will help improve the current and future models of the aircraft.
- It will reduce the unscheduled downtime of the aircraft – this is often measured as **Aircraft on Ground (AOG)**. (Please refer to `https://www.proponent.com/causes-costs-behind-grounded-aircraft/`.)
- It will improve fuel efficiency and the carbon footprint.
- It will improve safety and reliability and reduce the variability within operations.

In the next section, we will take a look at an example from process manufacturing.

Process manufacturing

In the *Discrete manufacturing* section, we looked at the example of commercial aircraft. The aviation industry is heavily dependent on fuel, which is one of its largest operating costs. Hence, a natural segue would be the oil and gas industry where process manufacturing is critical.

Process manufacturing is often used in the oil and gas, chemical, semiconductor, plastics, metal, pharmaceutical, and biotechnology industries along with consumer packaged goods, including the food and beverage industry. Process manufacturing uses liquid and other forms of ingredients that are often mixed according to established recipes. Propane gas is an outcome of process manufacturing, although the final packaged product sold might be measured in discrete number of cylinders.

The petroleum industry consists of three major segments. They include the following:

1. **Upstream industry**: This is involved in the exploration, drilling, and production of crude oil or natural gas via oil wells.

2. **Midstream industry**: This is involved in the storage and transportation of petroleum products.

3. **Downstream industry**: This is involved in the refining and distribution of petroleum products so that they reach end consumers via gas stations.

Figure 2.3 shows these three segments of the industry:

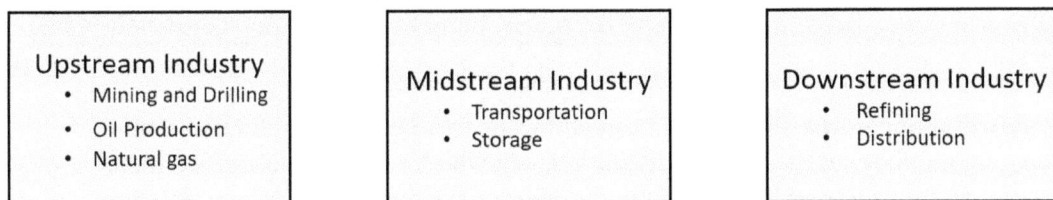

Upstream Industry	Midstream Industry	Downstream Industry
• Mining and Drilling • Oil Production • Natural gas	• Transportation • Storage	• Refining • Distribution

Figure 2.3 – The three segments of the oil and gas industry

Now, let's take a look at the applicability of the Digital Twins in the different parts of the oil and gas industry. Oil wells use a critical piece of equipment, called a **blowout preventer (BOP)**. BOP is used to monitor, seal and control the oil and gas wells, to prevent a blowout. However, a BOP is manufactured via discrete manufacturing. In the downstream industry, the refinery is a part of process manufacturing. A petrochemical refinery, as shown in *Figure 2.4*, is an important part of the production of fuel for the transportation industry, including aircraft:

Figure 2.4 – A petroleum refinery

Now, let's examine how a Digital Twin can add value to a petroleum refinery. In this context, a commonly used term is a digital refinery, which refers to the digitization of refinery operations to provide an end-to-end view of the operations. A few initiatives will be listed here, such as the Digital Twin of the **crude distillation unit (CDU)**. In 2018, TANECO and ChemTech partnered to create a Digital Twin of the CDU, where the business objective was to optimize the oil fractionation process. This Digital Twin used the thermodynamic model of the production process. (Please refer to https://www.hydrocarbonprocessing.com/news/2018/06/taneco-and-chemtech-create-digital-twin-of-refinery.) AspenTech has also focused on the Digital Twin of the CDU to reduce the operational risk within a plant.

Often, the petrochemical industry is challenged to control its environmental impact due to emissions. Bharat Petroleum Corporation Ltd, in India, is working with AspenTech on a Digital Twin for the Refinery-Wide Emission Model, to help control the impact on the environment and stay within the regulatory guidelines when operating a refinery. (Please refer to `https://www.worldofchemicals.com/media/digital-twin-for-refinery-wide-emission-and-efficiency-monitoring/4697.html`.)

In the preceding section, we looked at two major industries, namely, the aviation industry and the oil and gas industry. We studied examples of discrete manufacturing and process manufacturing and how both provide opportunities for the use of a Digital Twin to help drive business outcomes.

Next, we will take a look at the role of industrial Digital Twins in smart manufacturing.

Smart manufacturing

Smart manufacturing, or a smart factory, is a broad term that is used for improving the manufacturing industry by applying digital technologies such as Digital Twins, the **Internet of Things** (**IoT**), and additive manufacturing (also called 3D printing). The providers of factory automation equipment such as industrial automation providers, namely, Siemens, Rockwell, and GE, have focused on providing connected equipment, to facilitate smart manufacturing. However, here, we will focus on robotics providers such as Kuka and ABB (formerly Asea Brown Boveri). A Digital Twin provides opportunities for the providers of such manufacturing robots to deliver digital services to its customers. *Figure 2.5* shows this concept at a high level:

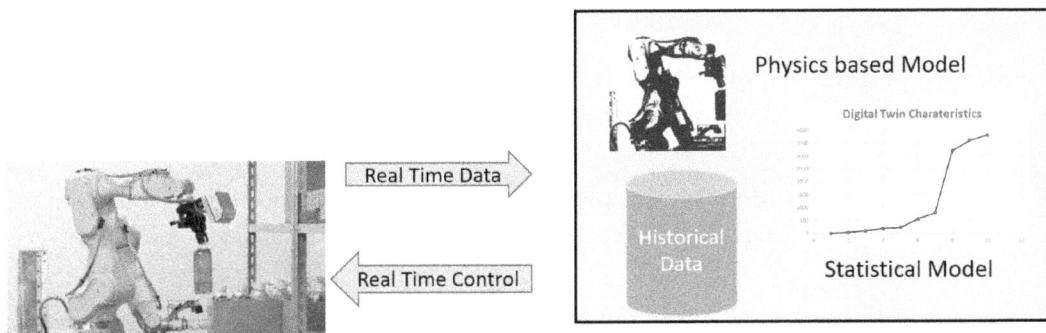

Robot in Manufacturing Shop   Digital Twin

Figure 2.5 – The Digital Twin of a manufacturing robot

When a robot is used in the assembly line process of discrete manufacturing, such as a car in an automobile factory, a specific stage of the process can be digitized to optimize that stage. In this case, a Digital Twin of the robot, provided by its manufacturer (such as Kuka in *Figure 2.6*), can be used to map out the assembly process digitally, leading to simulation models to optimize the performance, including throughput and quality. This scenario allows Kuka to sell digital services powered by the Digital Twin of the robot to the factory operator. In turn, the factory operator can operationalize it for smart manufacturing and improve its throughput and the quality of the physical assets it is manufacturing. Finally, this digital data helps us to capture the birth record of the manufacturing process, contributing to the digital thread of the asset. Such service leads to the possibility of **Robots as a Service** (**RaaS**) for providers such as ABB or Kuka.

A Digital Twin of the human heart and the smart pacemaker is a similar application if you think of the human body as a biological factory. Just like a smart robot can augment and improve factory operations, a pacemaker can improve the human body when the heart weakens. The pacemaker tries to replicate the human heart both mechanically and electrically. A Digital Twin of the pacemaker helps to personalize the physical asset – in this case, the pacemaker – to the human's heart, who is using this specific pacemaker. The signals from the pacemaker, which have been digitally captured and modeled, help improve the delivery of care to the patient. (Please refer to `https://www.reuters.com/article/us-healthcare-medical-technology-ai-insi/medtech-firms-get-personal-with-digital-twins-idUSKCN1LG0S0`.)

In this scenario, the Digital Twin provides the following possible outcomes:

- The manufacturer of the pacemaker can gain insights into their product to improve its design over time.

- The manufacturer can provide additional data and analytics services around the product to the physicians or the patient, as the understanding of the data and its patterns increase over time.

- This allows care providers, such as physicians, to improve the monitoring and care of the patient including when to replace the battery in the pacemaker, which is an invasive process.

- This allows the patient to self-monitor their own heart-related activities with the help of a smartphone- or tablet-based application.

In the previous sections, we explored various scenarios, such as optimizing the assets in discrete manufacturing, the optimization of process manufacturing, and the smart factory. All of these areas can drive additional business outcomes by embracing the industrial Digital Twin. *Figure 2.6* summarizes, in a simple visualization, how the Digital Twin adds value by providing insights into the intervention of the physical asset.

This invention of the real-world object does not need to be automatic and can include a human in the loop in the early generations of the solution:

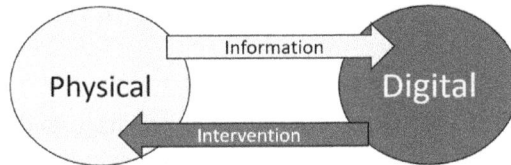

Figure 2.6 – A feedback loop of the physical asset and Digital Twin

The information regarding the physical object is a combination of the real-time sensor data and the historical knowledge of the asset. In a more advanced scenario, other sources of information might include third-party data, such as weather data or macroeconomics data, along with enterprise data from the IT systems at the enterprise.

Next, let's take a look at the industrial Digital Twin of systems, that is, **Supply Chain Management (SCM)**.

Supply chain management

SCM connects raw material providers to manufacturers. Then, on the distribution side, it connects the manufacturers to the business (B2B) or end user consumers (B2C). *Figure 2.7* shows the relationships between these different entities in a supply chain process:

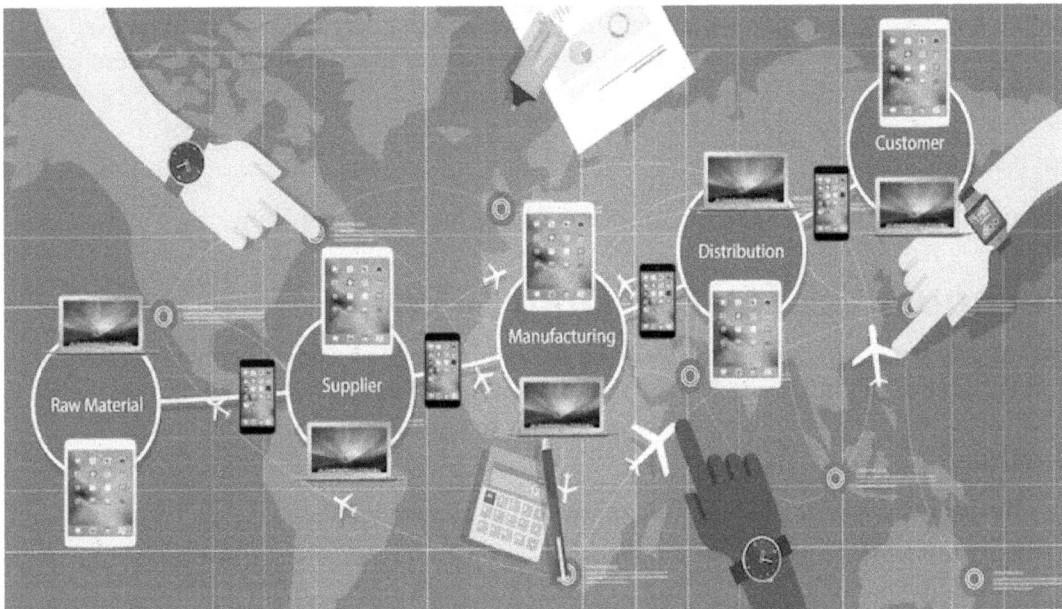

Figure 2.7 – The supply chain process

> **Note**
>
> Image source: `https://geobrava.wordpress.com/2019/04/16/how-ai-innovation-transforms-supply-chain-planning/`

In *Figure 1.5* of *Chapter 1, Introduction to Digital Twin*, we discussed the relationship between the Digital Twin and the digital thread from the perspective of a physical asset. The Digital Twin of the supply chain focuses on efficiency from the system perspective and is independent of a specific physical asset being produced. In Gartner's *Hype Cycle for Supply Chain Strategy*, published in August 2020, you can see the digital supply chain twin is in the innovation trigger phase. (Please refer to `https://www.supplychainquarterly.com/articles/3877-gartner-says-iot-technology-is-two-to-five-years-from-transformational-impact`.) This positioning of a Digital Twin for a supply chain suggests that it will reach its "plateau of productivity" within 5+ years; however, we believe that in certain segments of the industry, it will provide substantial business value much earlier.

In the previous sections, we looked at different scenarios in which quantifiable business outcomes can be delivered via industrial Digital Twins. We looked at the potential beneficiaries of the outcomes, which is key for decision-makers who are either investing in the Digital Twin initiatives or are paying for the services and benefits as consumers. The business outcome expected from the industrial Digital Twin is well supported by prominent analyst firms such as Gartner. They projected that Digital Twins will be used by approximately half of the large industrial enterprises by 2021. This will make these organizations 10% more effective in their business endeavors. (Please refer to `https://www.gartner.com/smarterwithgartner/prepare-for-the-impact-of-digital-twins/`.)

In the next section, we will examine the prerequisites for the Digital Twin.

Prerequisites for the Digital Twin

To justify investment in the Digital Twin, we should frame the business problem in such a way that the applicability of the Digital Twin is clearly understood. Let's take the example of fuel costs in the trucking industry. Now, let's try to figure out the prerequisites in this context:

- **Business problem**: The high cost of fuel for the trucking fleet
- **Business objective**: To reduce the cost of fuel without any adverse impact on trucking operations
- **Proposed solution**: To build a Digital Twin of the truck(s) or trucking operations and optimize the fuel cost

Based on the simplified statement of the business problem and proposed solution involving the Digital Twin, let's take a look at the prerequisites:

- **Model**: As per *Chapter 1, Introduction to Digital Twin*, a physics-based or analytics-based model would be needed to create the Digital Twin of the truck. Either such a model should exist or should be easy to create based on the data and knowledge of the physical asset and the operations.

- **Framework**: The framework refers to the software or the system that can be used to instantiate this model and apply it to the asset, which, in our case, is the truck. This framework should be able to ingest the sensor data and other contextual data to create the Digital Twin or keep it current.

- **Application**: In order to achieve the business objective, such as reducing the fuel cost for the trucking fleet, an application on top of the framework is required to provide the actionable steps to the business user. In this case, this application can guide the truck driver periodically or in near real time.

In a nutshell, the model, framework, and application are the key prerequisites for the successful adoption of a Digital Twin within the organization. There are various viewpoints from which to observe the building blocks of the Digital Twin. Notably, Futurithmic defined it as the three critical components of the Digital Twin. (Please refer to https://www.futurithmic.com/2020/04/14/how-digital-twins-driving-future-of-engineering/.) The three components are as follows:

1. The data model
2. Algorithms or analytics
3. Executive controls

In this view, the data model will also correspond to the asset model of the physical entity. Simply put, if an asset has sensors for temperature, pressure, and vibration, the data model or the asset model will provide information about the metadata of the sensor data. This will help us to decide which stream of time-series data is the value of the temperature and the corresponding engineering units (in Celsius or Fahrenheit). The algorithm will tell us about the importance of the sensor data and its correlation to the health of the asset. A simple example would be if the asset temperature increases by 5 degrees in 10 minutes, along with an increase in vibration levels, then it creates an alarm. The executive controls would refer to the orchestration of the actions such as triggering a human action due to rapid increase in temperature and vibration, in this case. The interventions in response, could be to shutdown the asset thus responding to change in its behavior measured via the sensor data namely temperature and pressure and rate of changes in these attributes.

A paper, titled *Digital twin requirements in the context of Industry 4.0*, by Durao, Haag, Schutzer, and Zancul has a more exhaustive list of the prerequisites or requirements for Digital Twins based on the survey of related literature. The list is in descending order of the number of occurrences of these prerequisites for Digital Twins, within the surveyed literature:

- Real-time data from the asset
- Integration
- Fidelity
- Interaction
- Communication
- Convergence
- Automatically updated
- Autonomy
- Connectivity
- Data acquisition
- Data capture
- Data quality
- Data security
- Data warehousing
- Efficiency
- Expansibility
- Globally available in real time
- Independently expanded
- Interoperability
- Modularity
- Process planning
- Real-time location
- Scalability/scalable
- Stable data acquisition
- Stable operation

Based on this viewpoint, the most important requirement for the Digital Twin is its ability to handle real-time data followed by integration and fidelity. Let's analyze these further. To generate data, the asset has to be instrumented with appropriate sensors. These sensors can be part of the asset or retrofitted onto the surface or within the surroundings of the asset. The real-time data requirement refers to the ability to collect this information at a rate that makes sense for the application served by the Digital Twin. The real-time data ensures the current view of the asset's behavior and allows us to devise a timely intervention. For instance, an aircraft sends snapshot or summary information during a flight of its critical systems, such as the jet engine. This real-time information is processed in a timely manner so that a critical decision can be made about the health of the aircraft for the next flight. Hence, here, the term "real time" is relative. In this case, the time horizon of the decision based on applying the aircraft data to its Digital Twin is from minutes to the order of one hour. However, in the case of a pacemaker augmenting a human heart, the time grain could be much finer.

The second requirement of data integration refers to the stitching of data from different subsystems of the twin or, in the case of a fleet of assets, from different assets. A commercial aircraft can have two or four engines. In most cases, an aircraft is designed to operate safely when one engine fails mid-flight. By design, the in-flight shutdown of one engine is supposed to be harmless to the aircraft and not even noticeable by the passengers. In such scenarios, the data integration between the different components of the composite asset, that is, the aircraft and its engines, is critical. Not only do we need data integration but near real-time data. This is so that the sister engine(s) on the aircraft can be corrected to increase the level of thrust generated to maintain the aircraft posture with one less engine.

A rapid decline in engine oil pressure might be the leading indicator of engine failure mid-flight. To fly safely with one engine or one less engine, the pilot might adjust the airspeed or the altitude.

As discussed in *Chapter 1, Introduction to Digital Twin*, Digital Twin fidelity is often the result of a model's sophistication. The degree of fidelity makes the industrial Digital Twin resemble the physical asset. While a higher fidelity Digital Twin can be used for more complex applications of the Digital Twin, it also increases the computational complexity and, hence, the costs of managing the whole process.

Now we have a better understanding of the prerequisites and requirements of Digital Twins. In the next two sections, we will take a look at the organizational and technological requirements of the Digital Twin initiatives.

Next, we will take a look at the organizational and cultural factors.

Organizational factors

The adoption of Digital Twins by industrial giants will drive a key digital transformation in these companies. They will become software companies of some sort. This phenomenon can already be seen in many large industrial giants in the last 5–7 years. Let's take a look at the examples of companies such as Honeywell, GE, Siemens, ABB, Hitachi, Bosch, Schneider Electric, and more:

- Honeywell: In July 2019, Darius Adamczyk, the CEO of Honeywell, said that the company is moving toward "a premier software-industrial company, with connected software sales continuing to grow at a double-digit rate organically." It created the **Honeywell Connected Enterprise** (HCE) unit to focus on such digital technologies as **Industrial IoT** (**IIoT**) software solutions.

- GE: GE decided to become a digital industrial company in the mid-2010s. GE's vision of a digital industrial company can be viewed in an infographic, which can be downloaded at `https://www.ge.com/digital/sites/default/files/download_assets/What-is-a-digital-industrial-company-infographic.pdf`. GE created GE Digital under the **Chief Digital Officer** (**CDO**) to act on this vision. GE Digital was a software company-like business unit. The goal was to create an industrial internet platform that can be used to create and maintain the Digital Twins of industrial assets manufactured by GE. The same platform could be used to apply generic twins to similar assets of other manufacturers or allow the building of custom Digital Twins for third-party assets used by GE's customers. An example of a third-party asset could be a de-icing machine used by an airline that uses an aircraft powered by GE's jet engine. GE Digital also created an extensive ecosystem of partners around this and has played a key role in the emergence of the **Industrial Internet Consortium** (**IIC**) in 2014.

- Siemens: Along similar lines, Siemens expressed its vision for a comprehensive Digital Twin, saying "We blur the boundaries between industry domains by integrating the virtual and physical, hardware and software, design and manufacturing worlds." (Please refer to `https://www.sw.siemens.com/`.)

Emerging technologies such as IoT and Digital Twins require a number of changes in the organization to take full advantage of them. We discussed some examples of large industrial companies such as Honeywell, GE, and Siemens going through some similar changes. We will group these into factors, as follows:

- **Digital technologies and talent**: This can include technical skills in areas such as IoT, simulation, cloud computing, and more.

- **Ecosystems and alliances**: To take full advantage of the benefits of the industrial Digital Twin, enterprises need to collaborate across the ecosystem they operate in and create partnerships and alliances as needed.

- **Organizational structure and culture**: Companies that are agile and can change their culture and organizational structure to align with the new initiatives are more likely to succeed in benefitting from an industrial Digital Twin.

Digital technologies and talent

A Digital Twin could involve a combination of emerging technologies such as IoT platforms to manage the sensor data from connected devices or operations. Additionally, the building of a Digital Twin might involve additional software capabilities for the modeling and visualization of the twin. Often, the IoT platform might consist of an IoT Core within the cloud and edge computing environment located close to the assets or the operations. Likewise, conceptually, the Digital Twin of the asset could reside in the cloud or on the edge, depending on the use case. The organization will need the corresponding digital talent to identify, build, and maintain the technology requirements.

Ecosystems and alliances

Often, organizations have to work with both the internal resources and the players in the ecosystem. For example, earlier, we looked at an aircraft, which includes a complex assembly of components from suppliers. For instance, Boeing might buy the necessary jet engines from GE or Rolls-Royce. In such cases, the Digital Twin of the entire aircraft would heavily depend on the participation of the entire ecosystem. Historically, different players in the supply chain often competed with each other and did not have many incentives to cooperate. This made it harder for the industry segments to foster collaboration across their value chain.

In recent years, we have witnessed the growth of industry consortiums such as the IIC and **Digital Twin Consortium** (**DTC**). Such organizations as IIC and DTC have been able to bring stakeholders from the industry together to work on common frameworks and guiding principles, to accelerate the adoption of emerging technologies such as IoT and industrial Digital Twins.

Organizational structure and culture

In our opinion, an industrial Digital Twin requires close coordination between the **subject matter experts** (**SMEs**) and the technologists. Hence, the Digital Twin might not be wholly owned by the IT organization under the **Chief Information Officer** (**CIO**). Likewise, it cannot be fully owned by a **Line-of-Business** (**LoB**) leader such as the VP of Manufacturing. Instead, we have seen the emergence of new organizations and roles in large enterprises that own such techno-functional responsibilities. One such role is the CDO. Often, divisions such as the CDO's division are tasked with the success of initiatives, such as an industrial Digital Twin. In such settings, the CDO's group is then responsible for identifying the associated technology and the development of the digital talent pool around it. They might also foster the participation of the company in relevant consortiums and create alliances and partnerships to accelerate the development and value creation from Digital Twins. This process may lead to rapid adoption of emerging technologies. In this book we explain how Digital Twin and innovation in renewable energy come together.

The culture of innovation and experimentation is key when adopting emerging technologies. This also requires technologists and functional SMEs to be able to interact and work together across departmental barriers. Sometimes, this is achieved by collocating such cross-functional professionals under one roof such as in a **Center of Excellence** (**CoE**). In other cases, such groups might be visual but with a higher degree of communication and collaboration.

The outcomes of organizational agility

Indeed, to validate that such organizational and cultural changes help drive value, let's take a look at some of the quick success stories of some of the companies discussed earlier. The Honeywell asset Digital Twins capability has been used by Lundin in Oslo, Norway. This oil and gas company operating in the North Sea uses Honeywell Forge's Enterprise Performance Management software to monitor its offshore oil platform's processes and equipment with the goal of maximizing the productivity of people, processes, and assets.

Lundin is using the Honeywell asset Digital Twins to create "energy loss" reports, which help it to calculate CO_2 emissions. The Digital Twin of the energy generation process, helps Ludwin to do a full energy accounting, at the energy generation asset level.

Now, let's take a look at the technology needs of the industrial Digital Twin.

Technological needs

In the preceding sections, we comprehensively discussed the prerequisites and requirements around the industrial Digital Twin. Now, let's take a look at the technological needs arising out of those requirements. Some of the recent emerging and digital technologies will come in handy here. We will examine areas such as the following:

1. The framework and the model: IIoT systems and cloud versus on-premises
2. Connectivity: From the asset to the edge, the edge to the cloud, and the cloud to the cloud
3. Data capture and storage
4. Edge computing
5. Algorithms and analytics: The **Central Processing Unit (CPU)** and the **Graphics Processing Unit (GPU)**
6. Platforms and applications
7. Visualization: The dashboard, alerts, and **Augmented Reality (AR)** or **Virtual Reality (VR)**
8. Insights and actions: A human in the loop and field services
9. Feedback: Product feedback, processes/operations, and training
10. Software development paradigms and low code

The preceding list is not meant to be exhaustive. Additional considerations include the sensors required to collect the data, the placement of the sensors in the asset, the power source, and the battery life.

The framework and the model

Here, we will take a look at the software system that is used to manage the different aspects that are needed to understand the context of the Digital Twin and manage the metadata of the assets, processes, or systems involved in the Digital Twin. In general, we will find that there is a significant overlap between IIoT platforms and systems for Digital Twins. Often, Digital Twin systems are part of the IIoT platform. Some examples of commonly discussed Digital Twin systems include the following:

- The Oracle IoT Digital Twin Framework (`https://docs.oracle.com/en/cloud/paas/iot-cloud/iotgs/iot-digital-twin-framework.html`)
- The Azure Digital Twin (`https://azure.microsoft.com/en-us/services/digital-twins/`)

- IBM Digital Twin Exchange (`https://www.ibm.com/internet-of-things/trending/digital-twin/` or `https://digitaltwinexchange.ibm.com/`)

- Ansys Twin Builder (`https://www.ansys.com/products/systems/ansys-twin-builder`)

- GE's Predix Platform (`https://www.ge.com/digital/applications/digital-twin`)

Of the preceding list, GE, Microsoft, Oracle, and IBM are also well known for their offerings around the IIoT platforms. Here, we will not go into further details about these technical systems; however, we will do a deep dive in later chapters.

Connectivity

Connectivity can be broadly classified into the following categories:

- Connectivity between the sensors and the asset: Sensors can be built into the physical asset, retrofitted during servicing, or retrofitted aftermarket, such as on the surface of the asset. In all of these cases, the sensor needs to communicate with one central system either per asset or per location. Not all sensors can have wired connectivity. Additionally, some might have their own batteries as not all physical assets have their own power source. Remember, an aircraft on the ground without its engines on uses the ground power unit. Additional capabilities such as protocol conversions might be needed here.

- From assets or sensors to the gateway/edge device: The asset might be wired to the aggregator or the gateway device at the location. In such cases, it will need wireless communication such as **Bluetooth Low Energy** (**BLE**) or Wi-Fi. This setup allows one gateway device (or a minimal number of devices) to manage the connectivity for all the assets from one location to the IoT Core/Digital Twin system, which might be in the cloud or on a remote data center. These devices might also aggregate or process the data.

- From the edge/gateway to the cloud: Assuming that the IoT or the digital system is in a public cloud or on a remote data center, the edge devices need to connect to the core and send the data in a secure manner. In some cases, the edge device might process or store the data to some extent. The emergence of 5G technologies could help to centrally view or maintain the Digital Twin of the remote field assets in one central location. Nokia and Bosch are working toward such initiatives. The actuation of systems in the asset, as a result of the insights from such a connected Digital Twin system, is a possibility in the near future. Often, assets in factories or power plants are connected via a wired network to cloud-based systems.

- From cloud to cloud: In some cases, the data collection and data processing systems could be different and might be on different clouds. In such scenarios, we might need communication between the clouds. Cybersecurity becomes important when data is stored off-premises.

In the previous section, we looked at the different scenarios of data connectivity requirements. These connectivity scenarios are required to facilitate different architecture paradigms of the Digital Twin framework.

Data capture and storage

The asset data needs to be ingested, stored, and organized in the Digital Twin system. The most common format of data from sensors is time-series data, and often, these are stored in Historians or time-series databases. Other forms of unstructured data, such as video or sound files, which are often referred to as big data, might also have to be stored in such systems. Often, Hadoop systems might fit in here. The metadata or asset data along with the enterprise data could be stored in relational databases. In summary, the data store requirements could be met by a combination of technologies such as SQL, NoSQL, and Hadoop technologies.

Edge computing

Often, data originates in the sensors and assets and traverses to the core via the edge. However, in many cases, the edge might have an important role in data shaping or in preprocessing, analyzing, storing, and communicating the data. Depending on the requirement, the Digital Twin system components might be distributed between the edge system and the core system. The Digital Twins of an entire fleet of geographically dispersed assets can only exist in the core or the central location. The edge can be used to deploy the twin of a single asset on the fleet.

Algorithms and analytics

The edge might be able to run a limited form of algorithms and analytics in near real time for a given asset. Hence, in a generic Digital Twin system, the algorithms and analytics models at the asset level should, ideally, be written once and be allowed to be deployed either at the edge or within the core. Depending on the volume, nature, and speed of computation required in the edge, it might use a CPU and a GPU. A typical example of the necessity of a GPU is when dealing with video data and the need for processing it on the edge. Even in the core, the system running the IoT or Digital Twin platform might use a combination of virtual machines, bare-metal servers, or **high-performance computing** (**HPC**), which is often equipped with GPUs.

Additionally, GPUs are deployed when learning with complex **Artificial Intelligence (AI)** algorithms, including deep learning. More details regarding this will be covered in later chapters of this book.

Platforms and applications

The generic capabilities of the building blocks of the Digital Twin system are often referred to as the platform. The platform prevents the rebuilding of the same collection of generic capabilities over and over again. GE's Predix Platform or the Microsoft Azure platform could fall into that category for IoT platforms. These serve a wide variety of use cases across multiple industries. However, the applications built on top of these platforms could serve a very specific purpose. The same platform might be able to manage the Digital Twin of a pacemaker, aircraft, or automobile. However, the application and objectives of these applications could be very different. Sometimes, a layered approach is taken where, on top of the IoT platform, an industry-specific or functionality-specific (asset monitoring versus manufacturing) application family might be developed, such as for the aviation or healthcare industry. This layer might try to generalize the common application needs that are often seen in that industry along with the industry-specific security and compliance requirements. Then, another layer of the application might be for a specific set of assets such as the jet engine in the aviation industry or a pacemaker in the healthcare/medical devices segment.

Visualization

The platform might provide basic visualization capabilities such as the visualization of the Digital Twin, an asset monitoring dashboard with alerting capabilities, or a fleet view of the asset twins. The application users can reuse or customize these capabilities or build their own Digital Twin visualizations with specific outcomes in mind. In more sophisticated solutions, AR or VR might be used for enhanced interaction with the asset Digital Twins.

Insights and actions – a human in the loop and field services

The broad set of capabilities that allow human operators to gain insights into the assets via the Digital Twin, and take appropriate actions, would fall in this category. A field service professional might use AR/VR to augment their interaction with the asset in the field setting, such as when dealing with unscheduled maintenance.

Feedback – product feedback, processes/operations, and training

The overall solution for Digital Twins must provide a feedback loop. This is so that insights gained from the twins can be captured via knowledge management systems. The product designer and engineers should be able to mine that information to improve future products or, in the case of software-defined products (such as a Tesla car), provide the future revisions of the product in the field. Tesla uses **over-the-air** (**OTA**) updates to its software in the car to improve the current product over its lifetime; please refer to *Figure 2.8*:

Figure 2.8 – OTA updates to the car

Software development paradigms and low code

Finally, the software development framework should be robust and functionally rich to allow agile and rapid development. A few commonly used terms include the following:

- A cloud-native or microservices framework

- A low-code development framework

- A **Software Development Kit** (**SDK**) and **Application Programming Interface** (**API**) to allow the collaboration between different teams and companies in the entire ecosystem.

In the preceding section, we looked at the technological requirements for industrial Digital Twin systems. In future chapters, we will dive deeper into some of these aspects, as we begin to decide how to select these technological components for a specific problem that can be solved with the Digital Twin.

Summary

In this chapter, we looked at the planning process for the industrial Digital Twin. Additionally, we looked at the key criteria based on the nature of the Digital Twin application and the desired expected outcomes. We examined the technical and non-technical prerequisites for the success of the Digital Twin in an enterprise. We looked at examples from different industries in order to apply this decision process, such as in the aviation industry, the oil and gas industry, and the medical devices industry. Hence, the general framework of the Digital Twin, developed in this chapter is agnostic of the industry domain, it is applied to. We want to consider and look at the business justification for the industrial Digital Twin.

Chapter 1, Introduction to Digital Twin and *Chapter 2, Planning Your Digital Twin* wrap up the part of the book where we focused on the "what" and "why" of the industrial Digital Twin. *Chapter 1* covered the background and definition of the Digital Twin. Then, this chapter built on that information and set the stage for the evaluation and assessment of the prerequisites of the Digital Twin.

In *Section 2* of this book, we will focus on identifying, planning, and building the Digital Twin. In *Chapter 3, Identifying the First Digital Twin*, we will discuss how to go about evaluating the right candidates for the Digital Twin. We will explore the different roles and responsibilities in this context. This evaluation process will help to narrow down the finalist for building a prototype of an industrial Digital Twin in this book.

Questions

Here is a list of questions to test your understanding of this chapter:

1. What are some of the expected business outcomes of an industrial Digital Twin?

2. Are Digital Twins applicable to the process manufacturing industry?

3. What organizational factors can contribute to the success of the digital twin initiative?

4. What is the role of cloud computing in a Digital Twin?

Section 2:
Building the
Digital Twin

In part two of the book, we will look at how to go about building the first Digital Twin and then test and validate it, relative to the intended purpose of the twin, as well as how to stabilize the operations of the Digital Twin and eventually scale this process.

This section comprises the following chapters:

3
Identifying the First Digital Twin

In *Chapter 2*, *Planning Your Digital Twin*, we discussed the key criteria for Digital Twins in enterprises and their expected business outcomes. We looked at this from the perspective of different industry sectors and their ecosystems. We analyzed the prerequisites for Digital Twins, including the organizational and cultural factors. Finally, we went over the technology requirements for Digital Twins.

In this chapter, we will discuss the evaluation process for a Digital Twin in the context of a wide range of companies. This will provide you with wide exposure to the relevance of Digital Twins both for internal and external opportunities. We will tie this to the actual roles and responsibilities being created and advertised by companies today. We will cover these topics:

- Evaluating Digital Twin candidates
- Roles and responsibilities
- Experimentation and interactions
- The finalist

In a nutshell, this chapter will cover the process of arriving at the first Digital Twin to build, in alignment with the nature of the business and achievable outcomes. This makes the identification and evaluation of the first Digital Twin crucial. This process will be covered comprehensively here.

Evaluating Digital Twin candidates

In this section, we will identify the prospects for industrial Digital Twins and then evaluate the one we want to move forward with. This evaluation has to be done in the context of your company or initiative, to be relevant to you. We will do the evaluation for multiple scenarios here and that should help for a wide range of cases.

Here are a few settings where a Digital Twin may be evaluated:

- An industrial conglomerate
- A large enterprise in a single industry sector
- A public sector entity
- A large software company or public cloud provider
- An **Independent Software Vendor** (**ISV**)
- A large **System Integrator** (**SI**) or management consulting firm
- A small/niche service company

Let's now look at each of these scenarios.

Industrial conglomerates

Companies that would fit in this category are **General Electric** (**GE**), Siemens, ABB, Hitachi, Honeywell, Johnson Controls, Schneider Electric, Bosch, and Emerson Electric. Such industrial global companies have in recent years created a digital competency center within their company, with the goal of accelerating the industrial digital transformation. Some examples are GE Digital and Honeywell Connected Enterprise. We will look at both scenarios where the digital organization is evaluating the Digital Twin candidate or the **Line of Business** (**LOB**). Let's look at the digital organization first.

Digital twin at digital competency

The digital competency is usually a horizontal LOB with the goal of servicing different LOBs as well as, in some cases, external customers directly, with the goal of developing new markets or new digital revenue streams. When the digital group evaluates the candidates for a Digital Twin, it will look at considerations such as the following:

- Which LOB has identified one or more business use cases for the Digital Twin?
- Is the Digital Twin going to drive internal efficiency in the LOB or is it going to be adopted by its customers?

- Is the LOB willing to commit its **Subject Matter Experts (SMEs)** to work with the digital group?

- Will the Digital Twin framework be reusable for another LOB?

- What is the current status of the data from the physical asset, such as availability and ownership of the data?

- What is the current status of the physics- or math-based models and do these need to be developed from scratch for the Digital Twin of the physical asset or the process?

Now that we have listed the key considerations for the Digital Twin, we are ready to identify the candidates. Let's take a scenario where the digital group is working with an aviation and power generation business. The aviation business builds jet engines for aircraft and provides services to airline customers. The power business builds generators that are used by electric utility companies. The utility company also buys long-term service contracts from the manufacturer. Based on these, the digital group is evaluating three candidates for its first Digital Twin. These are the following:

- Work with the aviation LOB to build the Digital Twin of the engine, E, that it manufactures.

- Work with the power LOB to build the Digital Twin of the gas generator, G, that it manufactures.

- Build a generic Digital Twin of a generator that is agnostic of the manufacturer. Since there are only a few engine providers for commercial aircraft, a generic jet engine model will not be very useful.

Now, let's compare each of the three scenarios in the following table:

Criteria	Twin of Engine, E	Twin of Gas Generator, G	Twin of Generic Gas Generator
First customer/user	Yes	Yes	Not yet
Reusability of twin	Low	Possible for other generators	High
Productivity/ efficiency use case	Yes	Yes	No – external only
New digital revenues	Possible	Possible	Yes
Investment	Moderate	Moderate	High

The preceding table shows how the digital group may list the objective criteria to help decide the pecking order for the Digital Twin identification for the starting point. The table shows that the twin of the engine, E, and gas generator, G, would primarily be internal use cases driven by the LOB. The investments can be justified by productivity gains obtained by the business by the use of the twins. However, when the use case for the twin involves only external customers, it may require a higher initial investment.

In the next section, let's look at similar scenarios from the viewpoint of the LOB.

Digital twin at the LOB

The LOB of an industrial conglomerate may look at the same scenario through their own lens before deciding to invest in the Digital Twin initiative. In this case, the LOB may look at three different criteria:

- The LOB's own readiness for the Digital Twin initiative, whether is it complementary to its own business strategy or could be a possible distraction
- The ability to quantify productivity or efficiency delivered by the twin
- Technology direction

The LOB would look at its current business strategy and then see where the Digital Twin would be a good fit. For instance, aviation and power generation businesses would normally sell the physical asset once and then sell long-term services to their customers. In such cases, the LOB would invest in the Digital Twin, to help improve the predictive maintenance services. Since these contracts are long-term, the top-line revenue is not likely to change due to the introduction of the use of a Digital Twin for predictive maintenance. However, the delivery of the services and margin on them could be substantially improved by the use of a Digital Twin. Hence, it will go well with the business strategy for the LOB. A similar case study of the Digital Twin of an aircraft's landing gear is available here: `https://www.ge.com/digital/customers/predictive-insights-aid-aircraft-landing-gear-performance`. This prototype of the Digital Twin was built by GE and Infosys and one of the authors of this book (Nath) was involved in it.

While we see that qualitatively speaking, the investment in the Digital Twin makes sense for the aviation LOB, it may further have to build the business case quantitatively. In order to do so, the LOB would have to estimate with sufficient confidence the improvement in the service contract margins due to proper use of the Digital Twin versus additional investments. This business case has to make sense in the long term, but should be measurable in the short to mid-term as well, to ensure they are moving in the right direction.

Finally, the LOB has to look at the technology considerations. This may include the software platform as well as the infrastructure for data and connectivity of the physical asset. The LOB would have to work with the asset owner or operator to obtain the data for the purposes of the Digital Twin. If the LOB decides to work with the digital group, or its conglomerate, then they need to make sure the digital platform can handle the data and modeling needs of their asset. For instance, while the gas generators, as shown in *Figure 3.1*, work in a fixed location, such as in a power plant, it is easy to connect them to a high-speed network for data collection, as long as the utility customer is on board with that:

Figure 3.1 – Gas generator

Note
Image source: http://commons.wikimedia.org/wiki/ File:Turboprop_T-53.jpg

Power plants such as the one shown in *Figure 3.2* house the gas generators. Often, the utility company buys a long-term service contract from the manufacturer, to transfer the risk of maintenance and downtime to them. In turn, the utility company would often agree to allow the collection and sharing of the data from the generator and its operation with the manufacturer, for the perceived value of better services and lower downtime:

Figure 3.2 – Electric power plant

> **Note**
>
> Image source: `https://commons.wikimedia.org/wiki/`
> `File:Turboprop_T-53.jpg`

Aircraft are typically only connected with very low-bandwidth satellite connections that are used for critical data transmission only. As a result, the collection of detailed data from jet engines would need an offline mechanism to collect massive amounts of data from the prior flight(s). The LOB would have to make sure that the digital group can provide the digital platform to facilitate such data collection for the Digital Twin of the engine, E, such as the one shown in *Figure 3.3*:

Figure 3.3 – Rolls-Royce aircraft engine and landing gear

> **Note**
>
> Image source: `https://www.aeronef.net/2011/12/boeing-777-300-with-rolls-royces-jet.html`

Here, we looked at the key considerations in industrial conglomerate companies about the adoption and investment of a Digital Twin. We looked at the decision process for the central digital group as well as from the viewpoint of the LOBs.

Large enterprises in a single industry sector

Continuing the theme of aviation and power, let's look at some large enterprises that primarily operate in a single industry. Some examples of such companies are Boeing and Airbus, which are the two largest aircraft manufacturers, as well as Exelon, which is a large energy company. Such companies would be comparable to our LOB assessment in a conglomerate.

Let's take the example of Boeing or Airbus. They manufacture aircraft that are primarily sold to airlines or, in some cases, to the defense sector. However, the definition of "airlines" has changed over time and companies such as FedEx, UPS, DHL, and Amazon operate like an "airline" as well. FedEx, UPS, and DHL each have over 250 aircraft. According to an article from September 2018 (see `https://www.aviationtoday.com/2018/09/14/boeing-ceo-talks-digital-twin-era-aviation/`), the CEO of Boeing claimed that they were able to improve their first-time quality of the sub-systems and parts of aircraft by 40% by leveraging Digital Twin asset development models.

The aircraft manufacturers will have to evaluate how they will monetize the Digital Twin before making investment decisions. They would likely consider the following:

- Improvement of the product quality during manufacturing by using a Digital Twin for simulations and as part of the digital thread

- Improvement in the **Maintenance, Repair, and Overhaul** (**MRO**) services provided to the commercial airlines and cargo handlers while considering the relationships with large parts providers such as GE, Rolls-Royce, and Honeywell

- Digital twin-based offerings sold as new revenues including to defense customers (see `https://www.machinedesign.com/automation-iiot/article/21139448/full-throttle-digital-twins-boost-airworthiness-in-legacy-airplanes`)

Such considerations will help decide which type of Digital Twin to prioritize in the aviation industry. Dassault Systèmes, which is a company with about 20,000 employees, has built Digital Twin capabilities as well (see `https://www.3ds.com/3dexperience/cloud/digital-transformation/digital-twin-technology`). It had a big presence in the aviation industry but is not limited to that industry.

Energy sector companies such as Exelon operate in power generation, transmission, and distribution. Power generation would be from renewable and non-renewable sources. A company such as Exelon would typically purchase the majority of its equipment (including generators) from other manufacturers. As a result, they would have to decide whether to go to the manufacturer to obtain the Digital Twin of their equipment such as GE's power generator or to build a generic model that can be used across different manufacturers' generation equipment. Likewise, Exelon would have to look at internally prioritizing whether generation efficiency is more important than reducing any outages caused by the transmission and distribution capabilities. Exelon could focus on working with Siemens and Bentley Systems for their digital services for brownfield transmission and distribution (see `https://www.bentley.com/en/about-us/news/2019/october/22/bentley-systems-introduces-assetwise-digital-twin-services`). In this case, Exelon would adopt and build upon the OpenUtilities Digital Twin services for asset and network performance for its own use.

If renewable power generation is a priority for Exelon, they may start with the Digital Twin of a wind turbine or the wind farm as a whole. Often, wind farms are in the middle of a desert or on top of a mountain and connectivity is a key consideration. The alternative can be the deployment of the Digital Twin of the asset and the fleet at the wind farm level.

Finally, let's look at a large medical device manufacturing company for the use of a Digital Twin. In 2020, due to the pandemic (Covid-19), there has been a renewed focus on medical devices and life sciences companies. Some large medical device companies include Medtronic, Thermofisher, **Johnson & Johnson (J&J)**, and Abbott. Medtronic makes medical devices such as pacemakers, and while the Digital Twin for a complex device such as a pacemaker would seem like a good starting point, Medtronic has talked about the Digital Twin of its supply chain in 2020 (see `https://www.forbes.com/sites/stevebanker/2020/06/19/medtronics-digital-twin-supports-their-ability-to-respond-in-the-pandemic/?sh=d4819b6857ee`). The Digital Twin of the supply chain helps to make the operations and decision processes more agile, which is definitely needed in 2020, as part of industrial digital transformation.

Public sector

The public sector is usually not driven by profitability or competitive advantage, but rather by the focus on citizen experience. As a result, leaders in the public sector may look at the use of Digital Twins to improve the public health, safety, and convenience of their constituencies. In the context of public health, the concept of a human Digital Twin is gaining popularity. *"Over time, my medical record could be a Digital Twin of me"* (see `https://www.challenge.org/insights/the-next-era-of-public-sector-digital-transformation/`). This is a concept different from the Digital Twin of an industrial physical asset, but here the human being is the "asset."

Digital twins of cities have been considered in Europe (see `https://www.digitalurbantwins.com/post/why-the-public-sector-should-look-to-digital-twins-for-better-policy-making`). Such twins of cities can be used for the analysis of public policy changes, traffic analysis, and air quality analysis. The **China Academy of Information and Communications Technology (CAICT)** has also done some work on the architecture for Digital Twins of cities.

The public sector may have to prioritize its Digital Twin-related initiatives based on funding and grants from higher levels of governmental bodies, as well as other non-technical considerations. However, it does not limit cities and counties from seeking public-private partnerships and being creative in the initial stages to pilot the Digital Twin.

Federal and defense agencies such as the US Navy are also exploring the use of Digital Twins, such as for naval ships (see `https://federalnewsnetwork.com/federal-insights/2020/05/navy-using-digital-twins-to-speed-innovation-to-the-fleet/`):

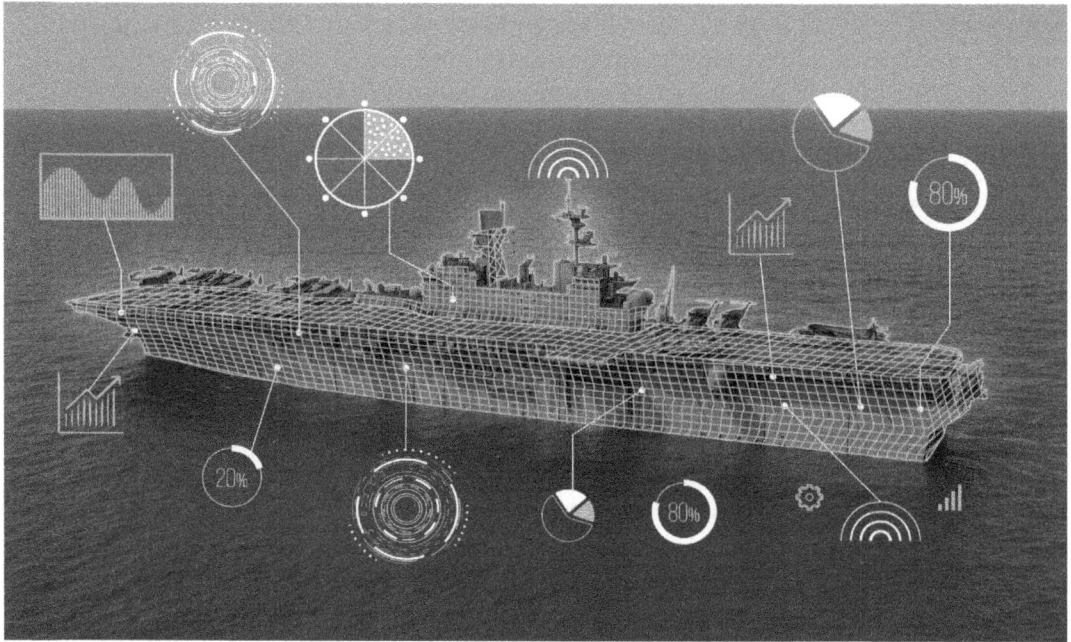

Figure 3.4 – Digital twin of a navy ship

We looked at a few examples of the use of Digital Twins in the public sector. Next, let's look at software and public cloud providers and their adoption of Digital Twins and related capabilities.

Software and public cloud providers

We will cover two main categories of software providers here. These are the following:

- Business application software providers such as Oracle, SAP, and Saleforce.com
- Public cloud providers such as Amazon – AWS, Microsoft – Azure, Google – GCP, Oracle – OCI, IBM, and Alibaba

Business applications providers such as Oracle and SAP have a large customer base of enterprises who use **Enterprise Resource Planning (ERP)**, **Human Capital Management (HCM)**, **Customer Relationship Management (CRM)**, and related software. These enterprises often look to their business application providers for emerging technology solutions as well. So, when they are considering a Digital Twin, they may often look at these providers to see whether they have Digital Twin offerings and how well these are integrated into their current business application offerings. As a result, companies such as Oracle and SAP have invested in the **Internet of Things (IoT)** platforms and built capabilities for a Digital Twin around that. Companies such as Oracle and SAP are less likely to use a Digital Twin for their internal use; they are mainly concerned about providing a framework to allow their customers to build an industrial Digital Twin. They may provide a sample of Digital Twins, to help accelerate the customer's own journey. Such business software companies may provide use cases for integration of the Digital Twin with enterprise software such as ERP with a focus on manufacturing and **Supply Chain Management (SCM)** modules.

> **Note**
>
> SAP has talked about its customers Kaeser Kompressoren and Netzsch using a Digital Twin here: `https://www.sap.com/products/supply-chain-management/digital-twin.html`.

Now, let's look at public cloud providers. You would have noticed that Oracle appears in both categories – namely business applications and public cloud providers. Public cloud providers have focused on cloud infrastructure, namely **Infrastructure as a Service (IaaS)**, **Platform as a Service (PaaS)**, and in some cases **Software as a Service (SaaS)**. Most large enterprises run their software systems on the public cloud, to a varying degree. As a result, these enterprises often look at the available IoT and digital capabilities in the public cloud of their choice. They try to minimize the number of cloud providers for their IT and **Operation Technology (OT)** solutions. As a result, public cloud providers have started to add IoT and Digital Twin capabilities to their public cloud platforms. Microsoft Azure Digital Twins and the Oracle Digital Twin framework are such examples. The public cloud providers are again focused on providing the tools and capabilities to their customers for building Digital Twins and are not the primary consumers of Digital Twins for their own operations. The public cloud providers may, however, provide a security framework as data flows from the edge to the cloud.

ISVs

ISVs include companies such as AspenTech, AVEVA, and Bentley. However, Schneider Electric acquired AVEVA in 2018. Companies in this category would work with other larger software providers, whether it is a public cloud provider or a similar company, to provide a Digital Twin solution to the end user or operating companies. Earlier in this chapter, we read that Bentley was working with SAP to provide a Digital Twin solution for Exelon. Likewise, AspenTech is working with their partner Equinox, helping to implement a Digital Twin for **Abu Dhabi National Oil Company** (**ADNOC**), for the Shah gas plant (see `https://www.aspentech.com/en/blog/blog/GLOBal_Threads_of_ Sustainability_From_Digital_Transformation`).

We can see that ISVs maintain a symbiotic relationship with other software and service providers to bring Digital Twin offerings to operating enterprises. ISVs tend to build reusable software offerings around the Digital Twin and usually try to stay focused on a narrow range of industries. They often rely on the first few pilot customers to help enrich their offering.

SIs

SIs and management consulting companies such as Accenture, Deloitte, **Tata Consultancy Services** (**TCS**), Infosys, and Capgemini focus on consulting services around strategy and implementation, for industry 4.0-related solutions. Typically, their customer bases are large enterprises. Generally, SIs do not build any reusable software products and instead partner with the technology provider of the IoT platform and Digital Twin systems. They may, however, decide to invest in the education and training of their consulting workforce, as well as building prototypes of the Digital Twin, to help evangelize their services. The Digital Twin of an aircraft's landing gear was built by Infosys with the help of GE. In this case, Infosys was the SI partner to GE, who provided the domain knowledge and the **Industrial IoT** (**IIoT**) platform.

Niche companies

As Digital Twins are still an emerging technology, many specialized and niche providers are in this space. To name a few companies, we have C3.ai, Uptake, and XMPro (see `https://xmpro.com/digital-twins-the-ultimate-guide/`). We will increasingly see specialized offerings from such niche providers, often via the marketplace of public cloud providers, such as the following:

- iGeneration – Digital Twin on Azure (see `https://azuremarketplace.microsoft.com/en-us/marketplace/apps/adfolks.igenerations-implement?tab=Overview`)

- Asset Performance Management – L&T Technology Services (see `https://azuremarketplace.microsoft.com/en-us/marketplace/apps/ltts.rapm_asset_performance_management?tab=overview`)

These are primarily offerings for use by operating companies in their Digital Twin journey. We will increasingly see start-ups entering this space, to build a new business around Digital Twin technology. Different kinds of Digital Twins have a prominent place in Gartner's Hype Curve of Emerging Technology, 2020.

In this section, we looked at different ways to evaluate the value of Digital Twins in different business settings. Now, let's look at the people and roles that are often responsible for the Digital Twin in different organizations.

Roles and responsibilities

In this section, we will identify the different personas and roles that would be part of the Digital Twin initiatives. One of the standard ways to represent roles and responsibilities is with a **RACI matrix**. The origin of the acronym RACI is from the four major responsibilities:

- Responsible
- Accountable
- Consulted
- Informed

The level of ownership decreases down the list, as shown in *Figure 3.5*:

RACI Matrix Definitions

R	Who is Responsible	Team or person assigned to do the work
A	Who is Accountable	Team or person who makes the final decision and has the ultimate ownership
C	Who is Consulted	Team or person who must be consulted before a decision or action
I	Who is Informed	Team or person who must be informed about a decision or action

Figure 3.5 – Description of the RACI matrix

Let's construct a sample RACI matrix for the industrial conglomerate example:

	CDO/CTO	LOB Leader	Architect	Developer
Digital Twin Ideas	RA	C	I	
Validating the Idea	A	RA	C	
Prototype	R		RA	C
Test/Validate	I		A	R
Production/Market Readiness	R	A	C	I

This sample RACI matrix provides pointers to roles that will be part of the Digital Twin initiative according to the specific situation in the company. Often, once the business leaders decide to transition from selling products to bundles of products and services, they will start focusing on the Digital Twin as an enabler. This stage is often called the servitization of the product. The CEO and board of the company may set the direction of the company for servitization or may delegate it to a role such as the **Chief Digital Officer (CDO)**. In some organizations, instead of the CDO, a **Chief Technology Officer (CTO)** role may take the lead to work with the LOB leaders on ideation of the Digital Twin. According to a recent *Wall Street Journal* article, the Digital Twin market was worth $3.8 billion in 2019, and is expected to reach $35.8 billion by the year 2025 (see `https://deloitte.wsj.com/cio/2020/06/23/digital-twins-bridging-the-physical-and-digital`).

Usually, technology initiatives are driven by CIOs; however, in our experience, Digital Twin initiatives are primarily led by other technologist roles in large enterprises, who work closely with the LOB leaders. The CIO's team would typically get involved when the technology, platform, and infrastructure decisions are being made. In an interesting article about the possible role of CIOs in the Digital Twin landscape, the concept of **Engineering Technology** (**ET**) has been introduced (see `https://thansyn.com/why-cios-must-better-engage-with-engineering-technologists-to-leverage-digital-twins/`). The following table summarizes the information from the article:

	Nature of Digital Twin	Owner/Users	Use Case	CIO's Role
1	Physical properties model	Plant engineers, product designers	Plant maintenance Accelerated prototyping of new products	Provide High-Performance Computing (HPC) and Product Life Cycle Management (PLM) capabilities
2	Electrical properties model	Facilities in charge, electrical engineer	Reduce power consumption	Data center strategy
3	Chemical or thermodynamic properties model	Plant engineer, process engineer	Alternative product and process	Integration of simulation and production systems
4	Process operations model	Process operations engineer	Faster problem resolution in operations and improved efficiency	Tie disparate systems together, such as ERP, MES, and plant operations
5	Reliability model	Maintenance engineers	Reduced maintenance costs and higher uptime	Tie together maintenance systems and time series data
6	Economic model	CFO/finance team	Better economic performance	Integrate the financial planning and profitability systems

While the concept of the Digital Twin has now been around for almost two decades, mainstream adoption is still an emerging area. It is an important question as to whether innovation and reinvention can be done by professionals who have been working for a long time in that area or by those who have come from different fields. Professionals working for decades in the same field understand the area very well and have built products and solutions that work a certain way today. Sometimes asking them to reinvent and think in different ways is a very difficult proposition. Let's take an example of an aircraft on the runway during landing. A commercial aircraft with two or four jet engines only needs one engine for the purpose of taxiing, whereas most pilots in different airlines do not switch off the other engines right after landing, as that is how it has been done for years. The **Federal Aviation Administration** (**FAA**) handbook does not address that (see `https://www.faa.gov/regulations_policies/handbooks_manuals/aviation/airplane_handbook/media/10_afh_ch8.pdf`). However, the airline Air Asia was able to save about 9 liters of fuel per flight by adopting this process (see `https://climatechange-theneweconomy.com/aviation-airasia`). This reduced the CO_2 footprint by 28 kilograms per flight. In this case, GE had provided this innovative, fuel-saving tip to Air Asia.

The preceding example shows that when we look at the roles and responsibilities for any Digital Twin initiative, it is important to form a team that consists of insiders and outsiders. Outsider could simply mean individuals who are not from the same domain and does not necessarily mean those who are from outside the company.

We did a brief survey of job descriptions where Digital Twin-related skills were explicitly mentioned. In the table below are a few examples as of December 2020:

Company	Size	Role	Job Description
Tesla	4,800	Senior virtual commissioning engineer	Tesla is seeking a highly motivated engineer for a Senior Virtual Commissioning Engineer position that focuses on developing code as well as testing and simulation for digital manufacturing equipment and its sub-assemblies. This position concentrates specifically on industrial Virtual Commissioning, Digital Twin integration, Industrial PC/PLC software simulation/emulation, code development using Structured Text/object-oriented programming and automatic testing.

Company	Size	Role	Job Description
Nokia	98,000	Mirror X Bells Labs summer intern	Robots, mixed reality devices, infrastructure and other sensors will provide the proximal sensing necessary to create a Mirror World/Digital Twin of the Physical world - in real time. Such a Digital Twin will be a key element in the digitalization of enterprises.
Idaho National Lab	2,200	Digital twin research scientist	Idaho National Laboratory's (INL) Digital and Software Engineering group within the Energy, Environment, Science and Technology Directorate is seeking forward-thinking, professionals interested in exploring a technical career at INL as a Digital Twin Research Scientist.
Johnson & Johnson	1,30,000	Post-doctoral scientist	The Postdoctoral Scientist will be responsible for leading a collaborative project to build a Digital Twin model of Janssen's upstream platform process. The goal of the project is to create an accurate, genome-based model that will serve as a digital representation of large scale-production reactors, and to use the model to guide upstream process development from cell line selection through the production bioreactor.
PTC	6,000	IoT and AR sales regional director	PTC technology helps companies to quickly unlock the value now being created at the convergence of the physical and digital worlds through the IoT, AR, 3D Printing, Digital Twin, and Industrie 4.0.
Autodesk	10,000	Support program manager	Come join the Autodesk Tandem™ team at Autodesk! Our mission is to create Digital Twin technology and solutions that will transform how buildings are designed, built, and operated.

Company	Size	Role	Job Description
Principal Power	2,600	Senior Naval architect	Global Performance engineering and analysis work relating to Digital Twins such as: scaled model test design and planning, verification, and validation of Digital Twin software versus numerical models and asset performance.
Rivian	100	Senior virtual engineer	Define a road map to enable delivery of a full Digital Twin and automation to keep the digital model up to date.
Bright Machines	330	Senior software engineer – 3D graphics	You will be joining a team of software engineers who are currently building a Digital Twin for Bright Machines' microfactories. At Bright Machines we're building Digital Twin software that serves as a virtual 3D environment where our users design, program, debug and test microfactories – an environment where mistakes are cheap and iterations are fast.
IBM	3,46,000	Digital Twin Architect	Leading the design and delivery of Digital Twin solutions for our clients, Providing technical leadership to clients on how Digital Twin, AR and IoT solutions can transform their business and operations, Presenting IBM's Digital Twin Point of View to C-level client executives, Providing technical leadership to presales and proposal teams, Developing IBM intellectual property and technical eminence in Digital Twin and IoT.

The preceding jobs span large and medium companies from the public to the private sector as well as consulting services companies such as IBM. Thus, different companies are addressing their roles and responsibilities related to Digital Twins, by both hiring for such skills as well as internally grooming them. This is good news for those of you who may want to explore new directions in your career. It is important to know that sometimes Digital Twin-related offerings may cannibalize existing business and services and it is important to be cognizant of this and plan for disruption around it.

In the next section, let's look at the methodologies that can be used to ideate, develop, and validate the ideas around the Digital Twin, with the goal to accelerate the decision cycle and the time to market.

Experimentation and interactions

Emerging technologies often require a lot of experimentation and the ability to learn from previous iterations. *Figure 3.6* shows the process of rapid experimentation and iterations, leading to a smaller set of success stories:

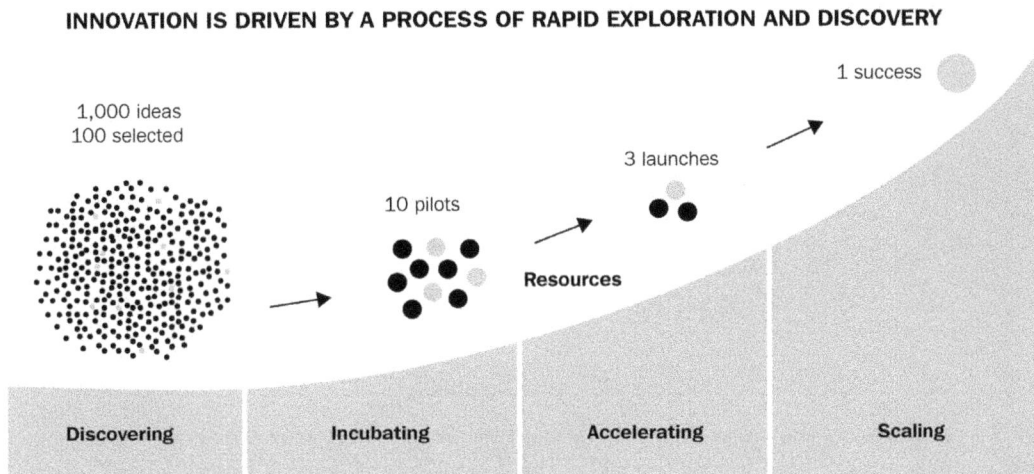

INNOVATION IS DRIVEN BY A PROCESS OF RAPID EXPLORATION AND DISCOVERY

1 success

1,000 ideas
100 selected

3 launches

10 pilots

Resources

Discovering   **Incubating**   **Accelerating**   **Scaling**

Figure 3.6 – Rapid exploration and discovery of the Digital Twin candidate

Agile Manifesto

The Agile Manifesto refers to a document that explains the values and principles of Agile software development. It is visually shown in *Figure 3.7* and was first published in 2001. These values and principles are described here: `https://www.visual-paradigm.com/scrum/agile-manifesto-and-agile-principles/`. The Agile methodology provides an alternative to the traditional heavy-weight waterfall method of developing software. The Agile methodology fits the rapid experimentation that Digital Twin initiatives often need. The use of the Agile methodology in the context of Digital Twins, by Siemens and Accenture, is described here: `https://blogs.sw.siemens.com/thought-leadership/2018/01/26/using-agile-processes-and-digital-twin-technology`. We suggest you view the video shared on this Siemens blog page, from the Digital Twin Summit (see `https://youtu.be/ETT1Tq88oHU`).

Figure 3.7 – Agile Manifesto

Figure 3.7 summarizes the spirit of the Agile methodology where smaller iterations lead to bigger outcomes while reducing the risks. The development work is often divided into the following:

- Releases
- Epics
- Stories
- Sprints

- Daily standups
- Test cases
- Demo and user acceptances
- Iterations (pivot or persevere)

Another way to look at the Agile methodology at work is visually shown in *Figure 3.8*, in their natural order:

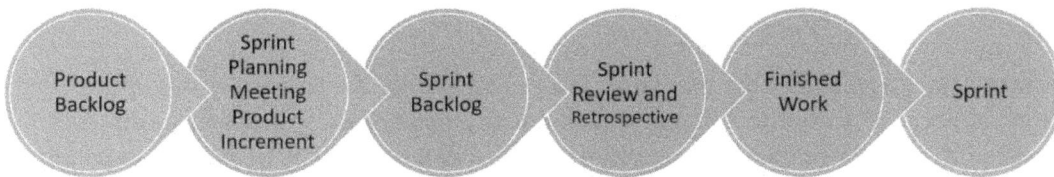

Figure 3.8 – Scrum methodology

The product backlog is defined in terms of releases, epics, and stories. The stories and epics are worked on during the Sprints, which can often be as short as 1-2 weeks. The Sprints involve their own planning so that stories are mapped to the Sprint Backlog. Once the developer completes the assigned tasks measured in story points, their work is reviewed or may be demoed to the business users. This leads to the wrapup of the Sprint and iteratively working on the product backlog.

As we further explain this terminology, let's use a realistic example. **Western Digital Corporation** (**WDC**) described their 12-week-long Digital Twin experimentation here: `https://blog.westerndigital.com/digital-twins-optimize-robot-manufacturing-ops/`. They called it a rapid learning cycle with the goal to create an **Autonomous Robot Vehicle** (**ARV**). Let's attempt to create the high-level Scrum artifacts for this initiative.

Release

A release is defined as an application that can be distributed to business users or a control group. This can be beta software or a pilot product or can be a generally available version of the software product. In the WDC case, the release would consist of some version of the ARV application, developed with the help of the Digital Twin process. A release is usually defined in terms of features that are on the product roadmap. These features may be described as epics.

Epic

An epic is a unit of work for development that logically groups related requests or needs of the user community of the application. Epics help the team to estimate the time and effort required for a logical grouping of work. Epics should be written in a manner that the business users can easily understand and validate at the end of the cycle. In the case of WDC, the epic can be stated as "the ARV pilot using the Digital Twin." Epics are broken down into stories, which can then be estimated more precisely and allocated to the members of the development team.

Story

The story, also referred to as the user story, is a description of the characteristics of the software application from the different stakeholders' perspectives. Stories are meant to be small units of work but tangible in nature. These stakeholders may be the end users or IT folks who maintain the final solution or the business sponsor of the project. A story should have these characteristics:

- Articulate how the characteristics of the application are valuable to the stakeholders.

- Describe how these can be demonstrated, tested, and verified for acceptance.

- Focus on the "what" and not particularly on the "how." This allows the technical team to figure out the best way to build the application.

- Be easy to estimate the work effort required by the Scrum team, while reducing the risk.

The best practice is to vertically slice the story. To take a simple analogy, a pizza consists of layers of dough, pizza sauce, cheese, and toppings. If a story only contains the dough, the user or the tester will only get to taste the dough by itself and will not be able to provide good feedback on the "acceptance" of the final pizza. On the other hand, by the principle of "vertical slice," if the story is to make a small slice of pizza, then the user can provide a lot more meaningful feedback and the risk to the acceptance of the final pizza will be much lower. While this "vertically sliced story" is highly desired, it may not always be feasible.

To look at the possible stories for the WDC epic, here are some possible stories:

- Twin of ARV movement in the second floor of the semiconductor fabrication plant (fab) of Shanghai, China
- History of the wait time and service time distribution for the **Device Under Test (DUT)** at the fab

This can be the starting point with two stories for the WDC epic. The stories can be finished in one or more Sprints. However, the goal is to be able to demo the progress at the end of each Sprint to the stakeholders.

Sprints

A Sprint is a short interval of time, often 1-2 weeks. Sprints are used to complete work such as the user stories. A release is often broken down into multiple Sprints. In the WDC example, for instance, the 12-week exercise could be broken down into 6 sprints of 2 weeks each. As these sprints progress, the measurable units of work are completed and tested according to the often-documented test cases.

Daily standups

A daily stand-up meeting is an Agile ritual used for tracking daily progress. It can be held once or twice a day. When twice, it is at the beginning and then end of the working day. Good communication is key to the success of Agile methodology and the daily standups are the key part of synchronizing the whole team. Often, each member may discuss these three items:

- What work did you do yesterday or today (when the standup is at the end of the day)?
- What work will you do today or tomorrow?
- Are there any blockers to your work?

When the whole or the majority of the team is working from a single office, the team gathers around the information radiator or the Scrum board during the daily standups. *Figure 3.9* shows such an information radiator:

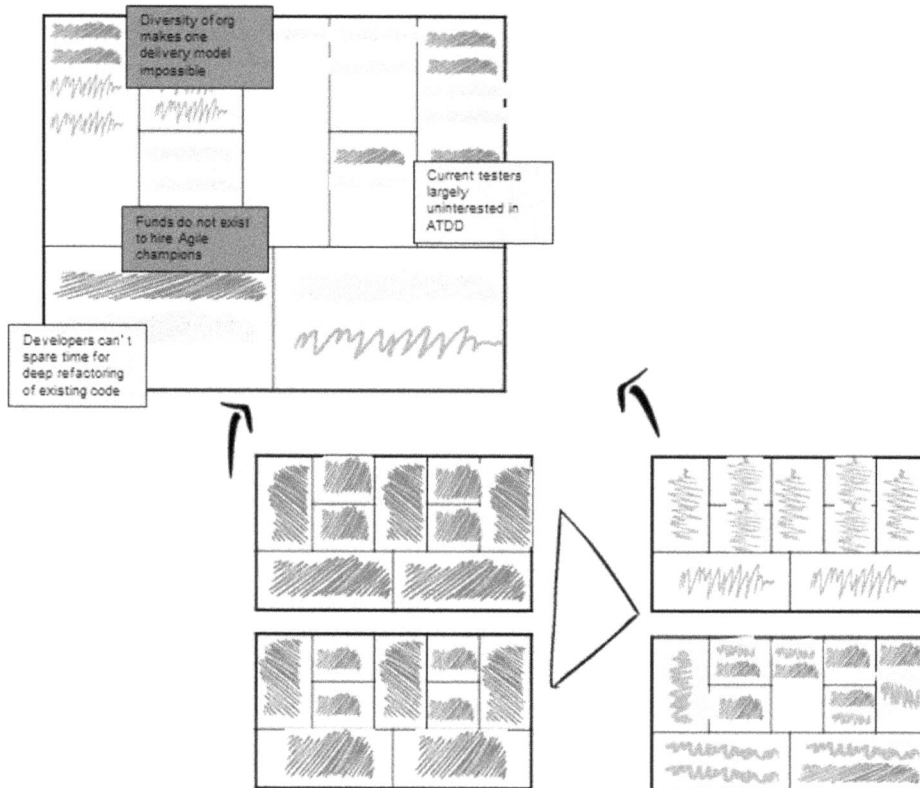

Figure 3.9 – Scrum information radiator

> **Note**
>
> Image source: http://agileconsulting.blogspot.com/2013/09/agile-transformation-cadence-model_495.html.

The use of the information radiator during the daily standups and in the area where the Scrum teams work provides a high level of visibility to the overall progress of the Sprints and the releases. In scenarios where the majority of the team is not working under a single roof, electronic versions of such information radiators and Scrum boards are used and the daily standup may take place via video conferencing systems. *Figure 3.10* shows one such electronic Scrum board:

Digital Twin Sprint Burndown

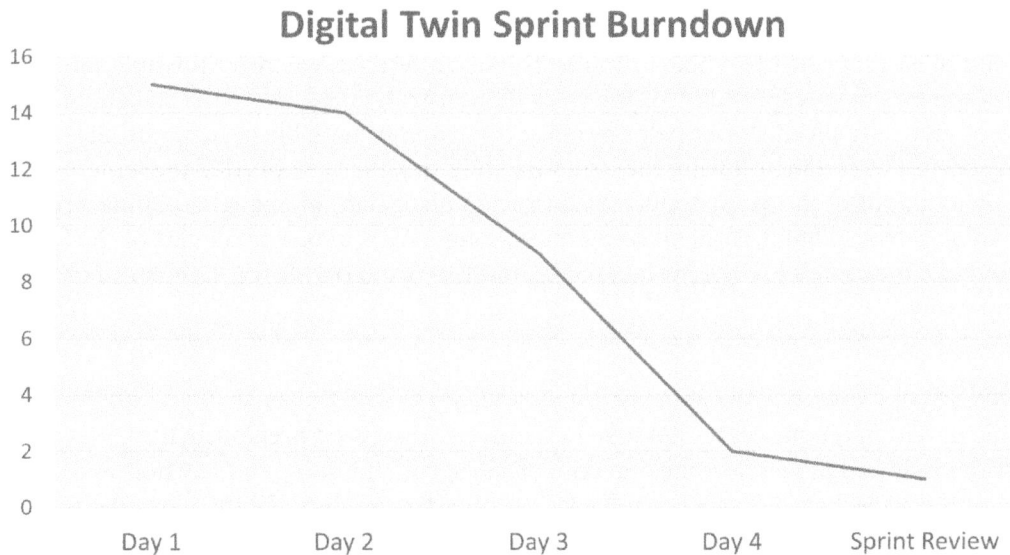

Figure 3.10 – Electronic Scrum board for the Agile methodology

Note

Image source: `http://phdesign.com.au/general/excel-templates-for-scrum-product-and-sprint-backlogs/`

While the daily standup has been described in a generic sense, here it will apply to the WDC scenario as well.

Test cases

Test cases are the scenarios that are used to validate that Sprints are producing work on the stories and epics in a manner that will meet the stakeholder requirements. These test cases can be used by the **Quality Assurance (QA)** team of the users to check and accept the work along the way. The set of conditions or variables used to determine whether a system under test satisfies requirements is created manually from specifications, which are later used to create tests used by the QA team. In the WDC scenario, the test cases will help the stakeholders to validate the progress toward the ARV pilot using the Digital Twin over the Sprints.

Demo and user acceptance

At the end of each Sprint, the whole team meets in a conference, wherever possible, and the development team responsible for the story demonstrates progress to the stakeholders. The use of vertically sliced stories helps to make these demos tangible in nature to the business users. For instance, during the demo for the story, the twin of ARV movement on the second floor of the semiconductor fabrication plant (fab) of Shanghai, China, the team may show the 2D plot of the movement of a single ARV, in one small part of the fab. This would be meaningful to the business SME and they can provide the acceptance or rejection easily.

Iterations

The Agile development process is iterative in nature. As discussed previously, the stakeholder may accept or reject the outcome of the Sprint, the story, or the whole epic at the end of the cycle. Based on such feedback from the stakeholders, the team decides to persevere or pivot as the next step. In the WDC scenario, the team decided to persevere or take it forward for improvements. Their overall business objective was to improve the overall service time at the fab. This in turn would help WDC to improve the throughput and efficiency at the second floor of the fab. Once achieved, this success can be replicated in the entire fab and then in the other WDC locations.

More details about these artifacts and Agile rituals can be found here: `https://www.atlassian.com/agile/scrum/artifacts`.

In this section, we learned about the value of experimentation and iterations, for Digital Twin-related initiatives. The use of established software mythologies such as the Agile Manifesto helps to adopt practices that are likely to provide incremental value and reduce risks. While we used the example in the context of a software application, a similar process can be applied for the convergence of the physical and the digital world where the final solution involves hardware such as sensors and an IoT gateway as well as the software pieces.

In the next section, we will look at ways to arrive at the finalist candidate for the Digital Twin initiatives.

The finalist

After going through the evaluation process of the candidates for building the first Digital Twin, we selected a wind turbine as the asset. Let's look at some of the reasons for the choice of building the Digital Twin of a wind turbine:

- Overall, there is increased focus on renewable sources of energy, to help control the carbon footprint. A wind turbine uses air speed or the wind as fuel for generating electricity.

- A wind turbine is a relatively less complex physical asset compared to a gas generator-powered power plant or a nuclear reactor. Hence, a wind turbine is a better candidate for the first Digital Twin, to keep the complexity lower.

- The Digital Twin of the wind turbine would benefit both the manufacturer/service provider of the turbine as well as the owner/operator, which would often be the utility company. Additionally, the SIs and cloud platform and business software providers will be interested in providing the implementation and technology capabilities. Given renewable energy is commercially feasible, driving efficiency via the Digital Twin of the wind turbine and the wind farm would provide immediate value to its stakeholders.

With the selected asset in mind, for building an industrial-grade Digital Twin, we will look at the planning and prerequisites in the next chapter. In the remainder of this book, we will build the first Digital Twin for the wind turbine, and evaluate it both technically and economically to calculate the ROI. Finally, in *Chapter 8, Enhancing the Digital Twin*, we will extend this to other assets for renewable energy such as a hydroelectric power plant as well as a solar power plant, to provide wider coverage, from a utility perspective, of who may own all such power generation assets.

Summary

In this chapter, we looked at the evaluation process for Digital Twins, from the perspective of different organizations and stakeholders. This provides a framework to analyze the opportunities provided by the Digital Twin and make an informed decision. We looked at the different roles and responsibilities in enterprises around Digital Twin initiatives, including how these roles are being fulfilled. We then looked at the process of experimentation and iterations associated with the development of Digital Twins and related initiatives.

In *Chapter 4, Getting Started with Our First Digital Twin*, we will look at getting started with building the Digital Twin. It will deal with the planning framework, the business process around the Digital Twin, as well as some of the technology and digital platform considerations.

Questions

1. What are the different kinds of enterprises that may be interested in digital twin initiatives?
2. Can you drive efficiency as well as new revenues by using Digital Twins?
3. Give one example of a Digital Twin related to aircraft.
4. What is the use of the RACI matrix in the context of Digital Twins?
5. What is the role of rapid experimentation in the adoption of Digital Twins?

4
Getting Started with Our First Digital Twin

In the previous chapter, we looked at the different organizational perspectives when deciding on your first Digital Twin candidate. The size and type of your company have an impact on your perspective and the specific value drivers that will be important to you in the selection process. We identified the importance of clear roles and responsibilities when embarking on a Digital Twin program. We also described the process of experimentation to determine the finalist for your first Digital Twin.

We also decided on the finalist in our selection process to identify the candidate for our Digital Twin. You should now have a clear idea of the type of Digital Twin that would address your specific organization's needs. We chose a specific finalist in the previous chapter to use as an example for the remainder of this book, but this approach can be applied to any Digital Twin that you may want to start with. However, we recommend that you follow the example as we build it out in the next few chapters.

This chapter will cover the planning framework, how to validate the problem statement and expected outcomes, and the proposed business process for developing your Digital Twin. Finally, we will address some of the technical considerations of and approaches to digital platform selection.

We will cover the following topics in this chapter:

- Planning framework
- Validating the problem statement and outcomes
- Exploring the business process for Digital Twin development
- Factoring in technology considerations
- Exploring digital platforms for Digital Twins

Let's start with a planning framework for your first Digital Twin that builds on the methodologies described in the previous chapter.

Planning framework

Chapter 3, Identifying the First Digital Twin, described an agile development process, which is the approach we suggest when building your first Digital Twin. Agile methods allow you to make quick course corrections as Digital Twins may be new to you and your organization. You probably won't have precise design specifications.

However, it remains essential to follow a structured planning process, even if you are using an agile development methodology. This section will describe different planning perspectives that are important to consider when getting starting with your first Digital Twin.

A project planning framework provides guidance on the different project phases for developing your first Digital Twin. The planning framework for our first Digital Twin has been tailored to be agile as the technical and business impact of Digital Twins is unknown here.

Project planning framework

It is vital to clearly outline what is expected from each stakeholder during the first Digital Twin development. We covered the RACI diagram in *Chapter 3, Identifying the First Digital Twin,* as well as the different RACI roles, depending on the type of organization you are building your first Digital Twin for.

The following diagram shows a project and planning framework for a typical predictive maintenance Digital Twin in the business unit of a large enterprise organization. The five high-level phases apply to any use case or industry when developing your first Digital Twin. Each phase's content and approach may vary slightly, depending on whether this Digital Twin performs a predictive maintenance function, operational monitoring, simulation, or any other specialized capability:

	Phase 0: Pre-project	Phase 1: *(~1-2 weeks)* Project Scoping	Phase 2: *(2-4 weeks)* Project Design/Development	Phase 3: *(1-3 months)* Project Validation	Phase 4: *(on-going)* Project Scaling
Business and Operations Team	• Map the production value chain based on current performance • Define bad actors and system bottlenecks, and identify root causes	• Identify which priority root causes have reference data • Prioritize use cases based on technical readiness and business impact to identify first Digital Twin • Identify value at stake and key success criteria for first Digital Twin	• Design the end-to-end business process and operationalization plan • Ensure that the right team is in place to drive embedding of solution	• Drive orchestration and embedding of the end-to-end process • Validate results and frame key outcomes and success stories	• Ensure that the Digital Twin is fully embedded in the business unit with clear processes • Add features and capabilities based on learning outcomes • Drive scaling and identification of further Digital Twins
IT and Development Team	• Prepare high-level reference architecture for Digital Twin deployment and testing • Prepare high-level security and trustworthiness plan	• Validate data availability and quality for first Digital Twin • Set up platform with the right integration connectors • Align on key success criteria with business	• Design the first Digital Twin with reliability and IT teams • Integrate Digital Twin with IoT and actions (such as work orders) in business systems • Design mechanisms to track use case results	• Improve the tuning of the Digital Twin based on results • Help to drive Digital Twin testing and usage • Build IT capabilities to use and maintain the Digital Twin	• Scale the supporting Digital Twin enabling technologies and cloud infrastructure to support long term use • Provide support services

Figure 4.1 – Project planning framework for a predictive maintenance Digital Twin

We distinguish between the **line of business (LoB)** and **information technology (IT)** roles during these phases while focusing on a key aspect of the Digital Twin's development. The LoB function focuses on the business challenge and engineering analytics to address it. It is also concerned with the operational business process that needs to adapt to support the Digital Twin technology. The IT function focuses on the digital enabling technology that's used to create and operate the Digital Twin throughout its life cycle.

Phase 0 – the pre-project phase

The pre-project phase, as shown in the preceding table, refers to the preparation work that needs to be done, though this is not necessarily part of a Digital Twin project. Reliability engineers, operations managers, and other LoB users often conduct business performance analyses to determine areas to focus on for future efficiency and effectiveness improvements. A bad actor analysis using lean first principles is a typical approach that's used by reliability engineers, as shown in this predictive maintenance example. Bad actor analysis is the formal review process of a plant or factory's operating assets. It uses the **Pareto principle** where, in the case of equipment failures, 20% of the equipment is typically responsible for 80% of failures. The Pareto principle is often referred to as the **80/20 rule** and is used in many industries and applications. The objective of bad actor analysis is to find the 20% of the equipment that causes the most downtime or loss of production and rank them. One ranking mechanism that's used in bad actor analysis is to apply the same Pareto principle to the 20%. It finds the 20% that is responsible for 80% of the original 80% of failures. This means that we now have 4% of the original assessment, which is responsible for 64% percent of failures or downtime.

The LoB function analyzes the overall production value chain and identifies potential system bottlenecks and specific assets or systems, which are referred to as *bad actors*. As mentioned previously, these bad actors often produce the majority of equipment failure incidents. It is a common practice to rank the bad actors in terms of key performance metrics such as throughput or production losses, downtime hours, repair cost, and safety. For a manufacturing line, the main bad actor may be the conveyor system, the second-ranking bad actor may be the robotic assembly arm, and the third may be the wrapping station at the end of the line.

The next step, as shown in the following diagram, is to determine the main failure modes of these top-ranking bad actors. **Formal Failure Mode Effect and Criticality Analysis (FMECA)** is a well-established practice in reliability engineering. For our first Digital Twin, however, we do not require a full-scale FMECA. It is still essential to identify key failure modes based on historical maintenance and operational data, as this ensures that the prototype Digital Twin will demonstrate value during a short duration project validation phase:

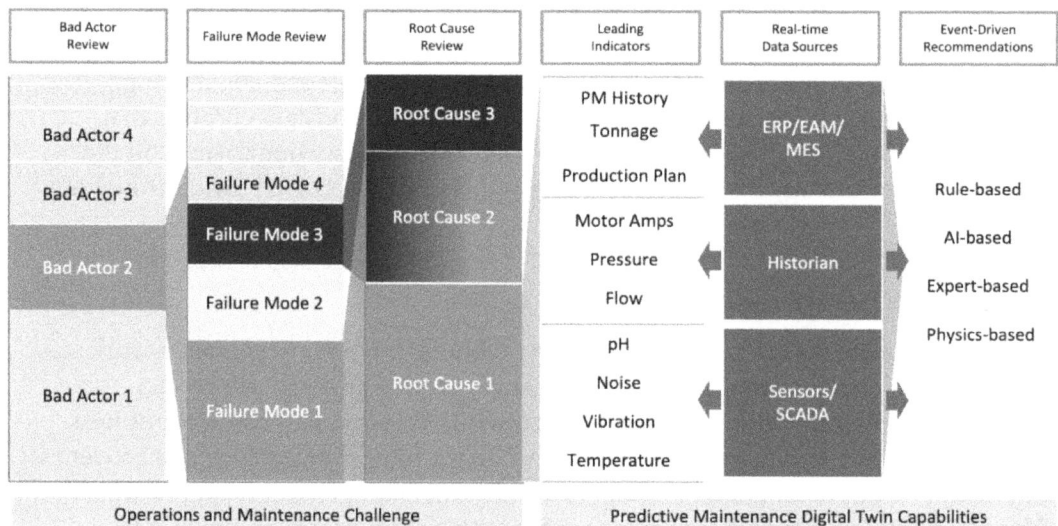

Figure 4.2 – Project planning framework for the predictive maintenance Digital Twin

Once we understand the primary failure modes, we can identify the root causes of these failure modes. This is also a well-established practice in reliability engineering. Still, we will simply identify the leading root causes for the most predominant failure modes for this book. Due to the cause-and-effect relationship that we often see with physical equipment, some root causes may result in multiple failure modes.

The following diagram shows that **Root Cause 2** can create **Failure mode 1** and **Failure Mode 3**. The business impact and nature of the bad actor failure modes will determine the level of analysis, but for this example, we will assume that the LoB function will provide the necessary input for this:

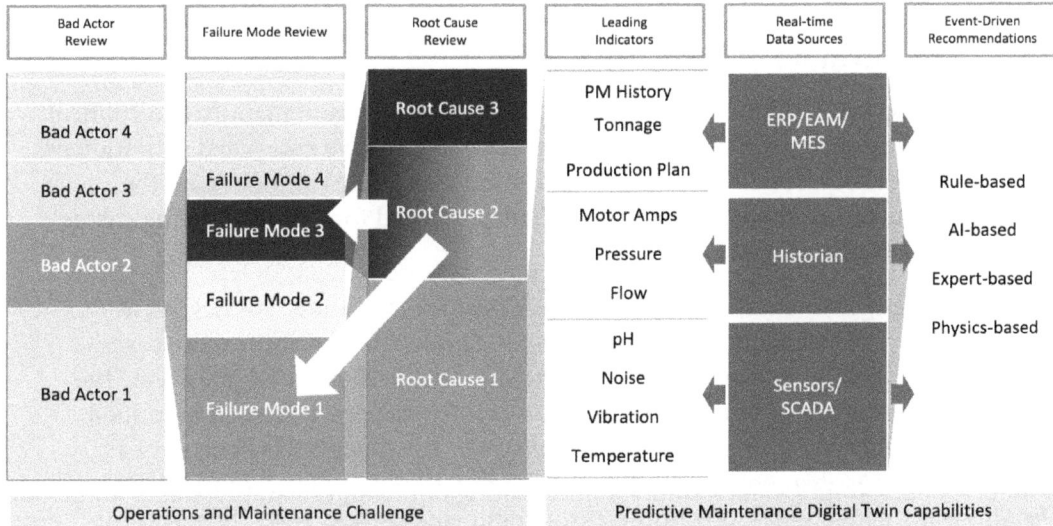

Figure 4.3 – Relationship of root causes and failure modes

The objective of understanding the root causes is to determine if we can identify any leading indicators that could be supported in a Digital Twin, through real-time data and analytics from IoT and sensor devices. These leading indicators can be based on raw sensor data, physics models, and mathematical or statistical models, as described in *Chapter 1, Introduction to Digital Twin*.

These real-time indicators can be established from the **Internet of Things (IoT)**, **Operational Technology (OT)**, and enterprise business systems such as **Enterprise Asset Management (EAM)**, **Enterprise Resource Planning (ERP)**, and **Manufacturing Execution System (MES)** solutions.

This integration requirement to multiple different systems introduces the role of the IT and development responsibilities given in *Figure 4.1*. This is the ideal opportunity to establish a high-level reference architecture that can be used for the first Digital Twin, and then adapted in the future based on the outcomes and learning from this initial project.

It is also recommended to start the governance processes around security and trustworthiness at these early stages and install the discipline for future projects. Digital Twins introduce several new security vulnerabilities and potential attack surfaces. The IT function can use the initial Digital Twin project to assess the impact and identify risk mitigation strategies.

Phase 1 – the project scoping phase

During the project scoping phase, the business and operations team identify and confirm that the lead indicators for the high-priority bad actor assets have associated data sources. It is still important to start with the failure modes and root causes and not with the available data sources. Your first Digital Twin solution should focus on delivering value quickly and, as such, be problem-oriented.

Business and operations teams should complete a business readiness assessment, as outlined in *Figure 1.10* of *Chapter 1, Introduction to Digital Twin*. Prioritize use cases based on technical readiness and business impact to identify the first Digital Twin. The business impact measures also relate to the *value at stake* metrics, which we identified in *Figure 1.9* of *Chapter 1, Introduction to Digital Twin*. The potential business impact measures from the assessment we provided in *Figure 1.10* of *Chapter 1, Introduction to Digital Twin*, include safety, downtime, throughput, quality, and cost. The technical readiness assessment covers the availability of data, the maturity of automation and IT systems, analytics, the proposed deployment environment, and the project management maturity level.

This phase also includes defining the value at stake and the key success criteria for the first Digital Twin. It answers the question, *what does success look like for the first Digital Twin?*

For IT teams, this phase provides the opportunity to assess the data availability and data quality for the lead indicators that the business team identified. Data integration, access, cleanup, and data wrangling can consume more than 50% of project resources and costs for IoT-based projects, based on research by leading analyst firms. The project scoping phase provides the IT team with the opportunity to assess the impact data integration has on the key success metrics of the Digital Twin project.

This is also the phase where we prepare the Digital Twin platform and configure the required data integration connectors within the necessary governance guardrails. Preparing this in advance reduces the risk of creating a Digital Twin that is dependent on data access and may not be available for integration due to technical reasons.

During this phase, a final key point is to ensure that business users and IT are aligned on the **Critical Success Factors (CSFs)** for the first Digital Twin project. A common and shared vision around the specific measurable outcomes or CSFs for the first Digital Twin will ensure a results-based focus for the project.

The next phase focuses on developing and delivering the Digital Twin while preparing the organization to adapt to operational business processes and the way people work.

Phase 2 – the project design and development phase

Digitally enabled projects typically require a change in how people go about routine tasks. Digital Twins, as well as the operational, situational awareness, and decision support that they provide, change the business processes that people traditionally follow. We will cover this topic in more depth later in this chapter.

To ensure that the first Digital Twin is a success, it is essential to identify the team among business users that's willing to embrace technology-based solutions to address business challenges. Operational users in industrial organizations are typically more conservative and skeptical of new or emerging technologies. This is also the phase during the project where a decision is made on what kind of Digital Twin will be built and how it will integrate with design, manufacturing, maintenance, and operational models. Furthermore, the design and development phase provides the engineering team with the opportunity to add additional sensors and data collection points for testing and certification. Substantial planning is involved in the placement and data collection plans for sensor data. Business users bring about the required engineering knowledge and expertise to help plan how to sustain the business value of twins. Selecting the right team will improve your chances of a successful first Digital Twin project.

The IT team will develop or configure the Digital Twin during the design and development phase. This includes integrating real-time input and other metadata and integration to backend business systems. We recommend an agile development approach, as described in *Chapter 3*, *Identifying the First Digital Twin*, using all the artifacts and processes shown in *Figure 3.8*.

The verification steps during the design and development phase provide the necessary governance to ensure the Digital Twin is designed and engineered correctly.

We also recommend that the Digital Twin is configured so that it can automatically track use case results continuously. The initial Digital Twin project is typically used to demonstrate the value based on the CSFs. Automating the reporting on these assists with value tracking during the project validation phase.

Phase 3 – the project validation phase

The project validation phase focuses on measuring the key success criteria set out during the project scope and validating the result of using the Digital Twin. The business team users need to ensure that the business process changes, as described in phase 2, are implemented during the validation phase.

During the business validation process, both the business and IT teams can use continuous CSF monitoring results to improve and fine-tune the Digital Twin's capabilities. This phase will also allow you to understand the support requirements and other business capabilities required to maintain and scale out Digital Twins in the organization.

This phase's outcome is to decide if the Digital Twin has delivered on the initial CSFs and if it is to be continued in production, or if it is the end of the initial assessment. If we have followed the preceding steps, the likelihood of success is exceptionally high, and this will often lead to scaling out the Digital Twin in full-scale production applications.

Phase 4 – the project scaling phase

New requirements and opportunities often emerge during the project validation phase as business users see the benefit of the improved decision support capability. Scaling out could mean providing access to additional users or adding other capabilities and features to address these additional requirements.

The project planning framework used in this example is specific to a predictive maintenance case. Still, the principle applies to any Digital Twin product, and we recommend that you outline the planning framework for your project in a similar way. The single-page summary improves internal communication and provides a clear understanding of the expectations of the different phases.

The project planning framework is supported by a solution framework that explains the business value and scope to business executives who sponsor the Digital Twin project.

Solution planning framework

The proposed solution planning framework has its roots in the **Lean Startup** approach, which was introduced by **Steve Blank** and popularized by **Eric Ries** (`https://hbr.org/2013/05/why-the-lean-start-up-changes-everything`). The Lean Digital Twin is a methodology developed by **XMPro** (`https://bit.ly/idt-ldt`) and is based on the Lean Startup framework, which focuses on achieving the product/market fit of a new product before scaling out.

The **Lean Digital Twin** is an ideal approach when developing your first Digital Twin since the application and use of Digital Twins in organizations is not well defined or understood yet:

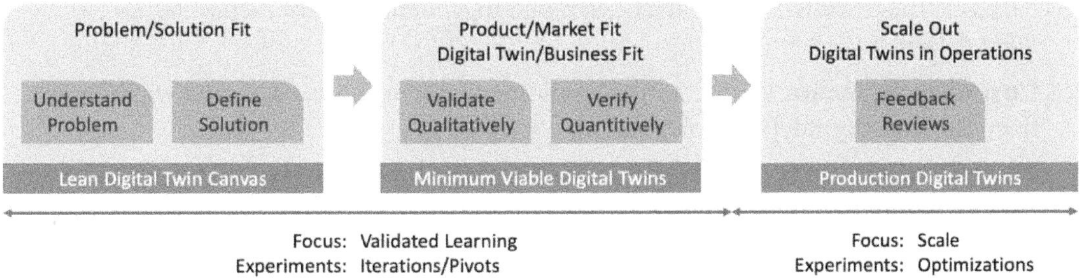

Figure 4.4 – Moving from the Problem/Solution to the Digital Twin/Business Fit

The first part of the lean Digital Twin approach focuses on the Problem/Solution Fit, and the best way to describe this in a simple and easy-to-understand way is by using the **Lean Digital Twin Canvas**.

This is based on the lean canvas that's used in the Lean Startup approach, which describes the business problem, solution integration points, and the business case on a single page that is easy to communicate to a project team and executive sponsors:

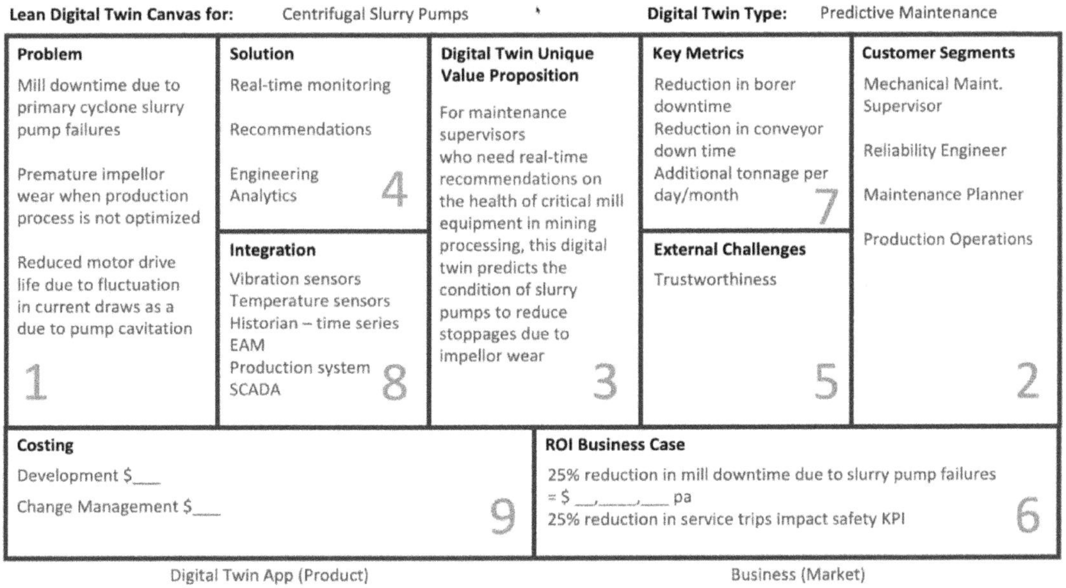

Figure 4.5 – The lean Digital Twin canvas for the slurry pump predictive maintenance Digital Twin

The numbers in the preceding diagram indicate the sequence for completing the canvas during a workshop with the business and IT teams:

1. **Problem**: Describe the top three problems that the first Digital Twin will address based on the prioritization matrix described in *Chapter 1, Introduction to Digital Twin*.

2. **Customer Segments**: Who are the stakeholders and business users that will benefit from the first Digital Twin solution?

3. **Digital Twin UVP**: What makes this Digital Twin different from what you are already doing?

4. **Solution**: What are the top three features that will deliver the key capabilities of the Digital Twin (AI, real time, decision support, and so on)?

5. **External Challenges**: What are the external red flags for the Digital Twin (security, data access, connectivity, and so on)?

6. **ROI Business Case**: How will this Digital Twin deliver the planned *value at stake*, as described in *Chapter 1, Introduction to Digital Twin*?

7. **Key Metrics**: How will the Digital Twin be measured quantitatively?

8. **Integration**: What are the critical integrations required to make it work?

9. **Costing**: What is the projected cost of developing and operating the Digital Twin?

The preceding diagram shows a complete canvas for a slurry pump as part of a predictive maintenance Digital Twin in an industrial mining company. One of this approach's main benefits is that the canvas provides a single-page view of all the critical aspects of interest to executive decision-makers. The template for the canvas is available to download at `https://bit.ly/idt-ldtc`.

The Lean Digital Twin canvas is ideal as a solution planning framework for your first Digital Twin, since it ensures that you have documented the problem statement and visibly clarified the expected outcomes.

Validating your problem statement and assumptions about your first Digital Twin outcomes is a crucial step that should not be overlooked. The first project often creates the lasting perception of a new approach such as Digital Twins in your organization. The second block in *Figure 4.4* describes the approach, similar to the Product/Market validation in the Lean Startup approach. The adapted version of the Lean Digital Twin refers to the Digital Twin/Business Fit, which is used to validate the problem statement and check the expected outcomes.

In this section, we proposed the Lean Digital Twin Canvas as a solution framework for planning the business validation and impact of your first Digital Twin. It is based on the Lean Startup approach, which emphasizes validated learning, and a key aspect of that is validating that we are solving the right problem to deliver the right outcome. We will cover how to validate the problem statement and expected outcomes next.

Validating the problem statement and outcomes

Reviewing the problem statement and expected outcomes is part of the initial phases' validated learning focus, as shown in *Figure 4.4*. It provides us with the opportunity to iterate and pivot toward a successful project continuously.

It is essential to validate the problem that you are solving and the expectation of the business outcomes during each phase of the development life cycle (*Figure 4.1*) of your Digital Twin prototype. The easiest way to do this is to use the lean Digital Twin canvas in a formal review workshop at the end of each phase. You can use this as a checkpoint to ensure that all the stakeholders are still aligned with both the problem and the expected business outcomes.

You should update the canvas with a new version for each phase to provide valuable insights at the end of the project. By doing this, you will be able to evaluate the evolution of the problem statement on the expected business outcomes over the development life cycle. It is a handy tool to present to executives to show the Digital Twin's evolution and development – not just of the technical aspects, but also the business considerations.

Exploring the business process for Digital Twin development

It is essential to define the changes to the business processes and ensure that end users are trained to maximize these new insights from the Digital Twins. We mentioned this in the *Phase 2 – the project design and development phase* section, but this impact must be considered early on during the Digital Twin project's life cycle:

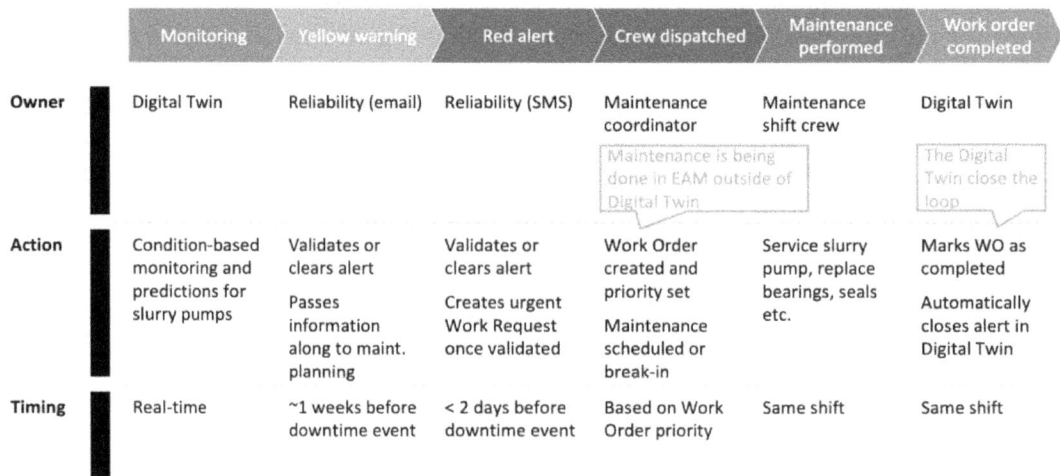

	Monitoring	Yellow warning	Red alert	Crew dispatched	Maintenance performed	Work order completed
Owner	Digital Twin	Reliability (email)	Reliability (SMS)	Maintenance coordinator	Maintenance shift crew	Digital Twin
				Maintenance is being done in EAM outside of Digital Twin		*The Digital Twin close the loop*
Action	Condition-based monitoring and predictions for slurry pumps	Validates or clears alert / Passes information along to maint. planning	Validates or clears alert / Creates urgent Work Request once validated	Work Order created and priority set / Maintenance scheduled or break-in	Service slurry pump, replace bearings, seals etc.	Marks WO as completed / Automatically closes alert in Digital Twin
Timing	Real-time	~1 weeks before downtime event	< 2 days before downtime event	Based on Work Order priority	Same shift	Same shift

Figure 4.6 – Example of business process changes based on Digital Twin inputs

The preceding diagram describes the business process impact of a Digital Twin in the predictive maintenance example for slurry pumps in a mine. This example demonstrates the interaction between the Digital Twin, reliability engineering teams, maintenance planning teams, and the maintenance crews.

It is the responsibility of the Digital Twin delivery team to ensure that existing processes are changed to include new ways of working, especially when it impacts operations and business users that are not working with digital technology solutions regularly.

This may require a formal business process review for a larger-scale project, but we suggest that you map out simple process diagrams for your first Digital Twin, similar to the example shown in the preceding diagram. This will improve the collaboration and communication between various stakeholders and make the changes visible to all the process participants. It is important to review these changes during each phase, but specifically during the validation phase to ensure that the proposed new process improves the overall experience:

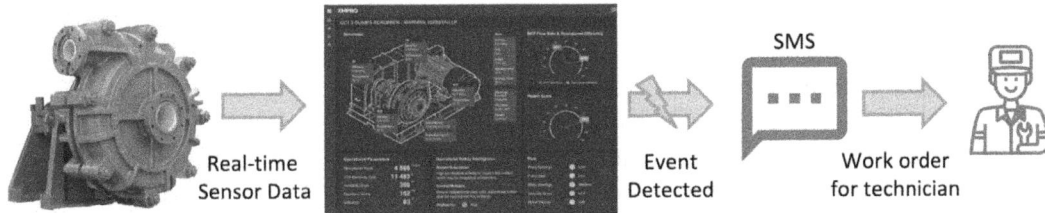

Figure 4.7 – End-to-end business process initiated by a Digital Twin of a pump

The preceding diagram shows a simple, end-to-end business process for a pump where the Digital Twin is receiving real-time data from the physical pump. When the Digital Twin predicts a potential failure, it sends a message to a service technician to initiate the repair. The Digital Twin can create the corresponding work order in the business system, such as an ERP.

Changes to business processes are not the only consideration for your first Digital Twin. Technology decisions that you make at this point may influence the outcome and scale at which you can deploy future projects. Let's address some of those technological considerations.

Factoring in technology considerations

Now that we have a clear understanding of the problem that we want to address with our first Digital Twin, the expected outcomes, the different project phases in a lean and agile development cycle, and the business processes required to support it, we need to address the technical considerations for the first Digital Twin.

To standardize on Digital Twin definitions, interoperability, and how to interact with these Digital Twins, various organizations are working on technology standards to address these challenges. Two notable projects in this area are the **Asset Administration Shell (AAS)**, developed by **Plattform Industrie 4.0** (`https://bit.ly/idt-aas`), and the **Digital Twin Definition Language (DTDL)**, which is sponsored as an open source initiative by Microsoft (`https://bit.ly/idt-dtdl`). In addition to these, there are also standards frameworks for Digital Twins in manufacturing in current development, such as "The Digital Twin Manufacturing Framework," which will be published as ISO 23247.

Both the AAS and DTDL initiatives focus on technically describing and instantiating Digital Twins and have a significant technological impact. At the time of writing, both of these are still developing standards, without sufficient details to help us create fully operational, standalone Digital Twins. Deciding on either of these, or perhaps even your own proprietary approach, is a crucial architectural decision that's influenced by the technology stack in your organization and the level of sophistication that you require in the short and medium term. The benefit of creating your first Digital Twin as a minimum viable product also allows you to test these approaches before deciding on a standard for your business.

To decide on which standard you should use for your first industrial Digital Twin, we will look at the two emerging standards we mentioned previously (AAS and DTDL) at a high level.

Asset Administration Shell

The **Asset Administration Shell** (**AAS**) is the implementation of the Digital Twin for Plattform Industrie 4.0, a network of companies, associations, trade unions, scientific organizations, and governmental entities in Germany. It is developed by the working group for "Reference Architectures, Standards, and Norms" (**WG1**) of Plattform Industrie 4.0 (`https://bit.ly/idt-wgI40`):

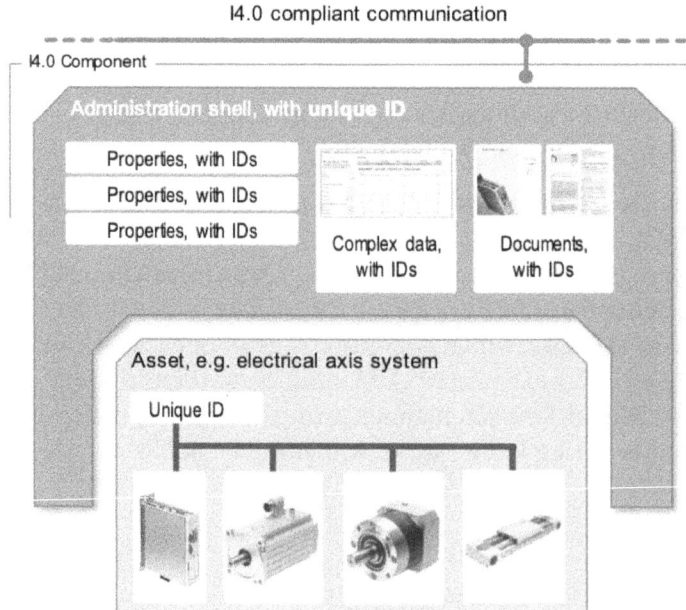

Figure 4.8 – High-level metamodel of AAS: `https://bit.ly/idt-zvei-aas`

One of the reasons for considering AAS for your Digital Twin architecture is the potential library of Digital Twins from product manufacturers that can be used in assembling a composite Digital Twin.

AAS is predominantly associated with the Industrie 4.0 movement, with most activity from European manufacturers and their customers. The technology consideration is primarily around the interoperability with other AAS-based asset Digital Twins.

It is not in this book's scope to provide a full technical evaluation of AAS, but it is a critical technical consideration for standardizing your Digital Twin development in the future. The official technical information is available at `https://bit.ly/idt-zvei-aas`, but we will cover some of the essential decisions for your first Digital Twin here.

One of the technical considerations for Digital Twin development is the format you use to define, create, store, and operate the Digital Twin information models. Standardizing on these efforts will help with interoperability among Digital Twins. It will also reduce the integration effort and make the reuse of models easier to achieve.

Physical assets are central to AAS. The framework is designed to cater to assets, components, information, and sub-models that establish a product hierarchy, somewhat similar to a bill of materials. This is a useful construct for a Digital Twin information model since it needs to operate in the broader Industrie 4.0 ecosystem of suppliers and consumers. It provides a shared understanding of an asset in a machine-readable format, and AAS is a metamodel description of assets and their related data. There are data specification templates for defining concept descriptions for properties and physical units in the AAS framework.

The following AAS serializations and mappings are currently offered. We have also specified their typical use cases:

- XML and JSON for exchange between partners via the `.aasx` exchange format
- **Resource Description Framework (RDF)** for reasoning
- AutomationML for the engineering phase
- The **OPC unified architecture (OPC UA)** for the operation phase

Serialization follows a standardized structure that helps improve collaboration and interoperability. The following diagram shows the metamodel of an asset in the AAS structured approach:

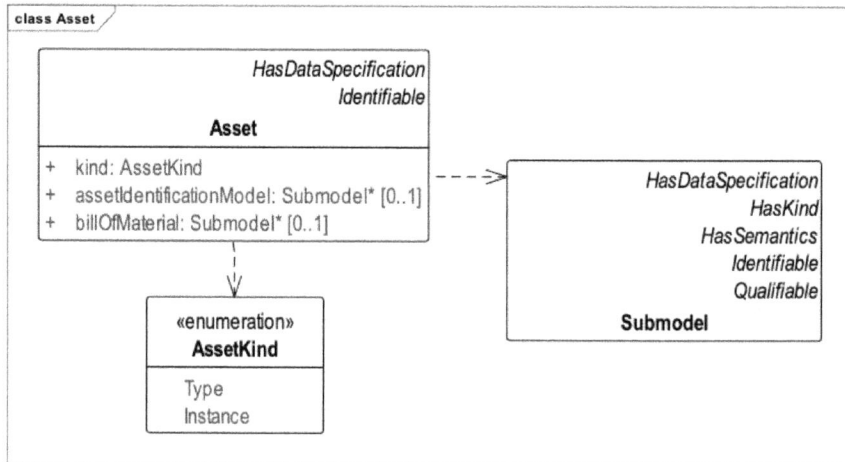

Figure 4.9 – Metamodel of an asset in the AAS structure

The following snippet of XML code shows the structure of defining the asset and its component or sub-model hierarchy in a machine-readable format:

```
. . .
<aas:assetAdministrationShells>
    <aas:assetAdministrationShell>
        <aas:idShort>ExampleMotor</aas:idShort>
        <aas:category>CONSTANT</aas:category>
        <aas:identification idType="URI">http://customer.com/
          aas/9175_7013_7091_9168</aas:identification>
        <aas:assetRef>
          <aas:keys>
            <aas:key type="Asset" local="true"
            idType="URI">http://customer.com/assets/KHBVZJSQKIY
            </aas:key>
          </aas:keys>
        </aas:assetRef>
        <aas:submodelRefs>
          <aas:submodelRef>
            <aas:keys>
              <aas:key type="Submodel" local="true"
```

```
      idType="URI">http://i40.customer.com/
      type/1/1/1A7B62B529F19152</aas:key>
        </aas:keys>
      </aas:submodelRef>
    </aas:submodelRefs>
    <aas:conceptDictionaries />
  </aas:assetAdministrationShell>
</aas:assetAdministrationShells>
. . .
```

This serialization can, in turn, be used to interact with the Digital Twin at an integration level, as well as the visual user representation of an asset, based on the requirements of the use case for the Digital Twin. Open source developer tools have been made available by the Industrie 4.0 community, and the AAS Explorer is a current project whose source code is available at `https://bit.ly/idt-aasx`.

Some Digital Twin-enabling technology vendors provide out-of-the-box support for AAS with visualization and data integration capabilities. The following screenshot shows the implementation of a Digital Twin for a smart factory robot in AAS in a commercial application:

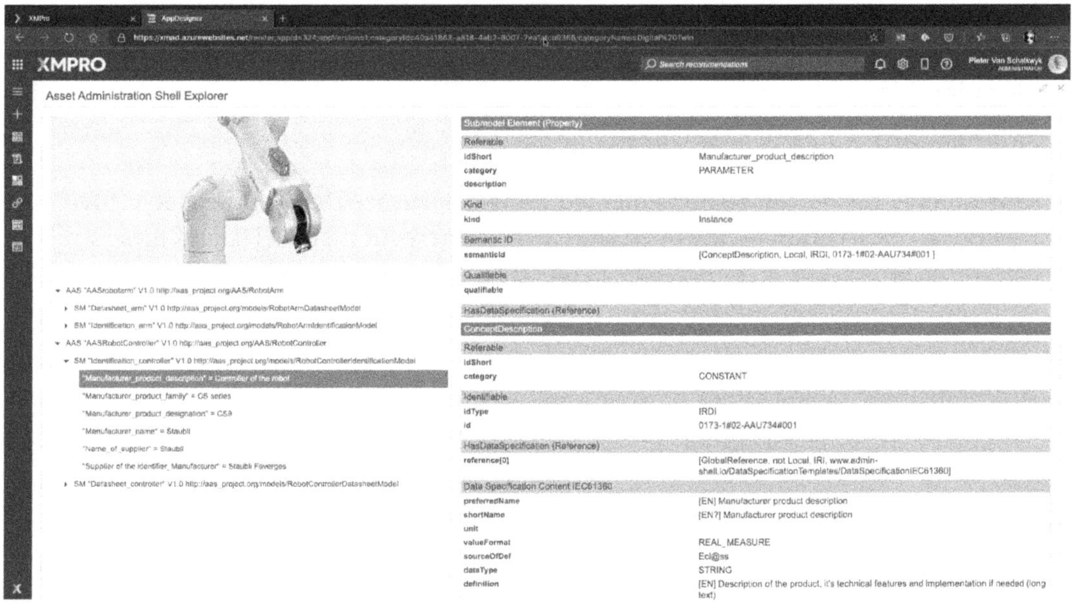

Figure 4.10 – Example of a robotic arm Digital Twin in the AAS definition for a smart factory

Other vendor examples can be found at `http://www.i40-aas.de`.

Another technical consideration is around a standardized data model being deployed and managed in a single-technology environment. This approach makes sense when you are standardizing on a technology stack from a cloud solutions provider. The Microsoft DTDL open source initiative is an approach that supports this technical consideration.

Digital Twins Definition Language (DTDL)

Through its open source initiative, Microsoft developed the **Digital Twins Definition Language** (**DTDL**) as a language for describing models that include IoT devices, device Digital Twins, and asset Digital Twins. Device Digital Twins is the digital representation of a sensor device and includes device information such as battery level and connection quality, which is not normally associated with asset Digital Twins. DTDL uses a variation of JSON, namely **JSON-LD**, which is designed to be used as JSON or in **Resource Description Framework** (**RDF**) systems.

DTDL consists of a set of metamodel classes in a similar approach to AAS. Six metamodel classes are used to define the behavior of DTDL-based Digital Twins:

- Interface
- Telemetry
- Property
- Command
- Relationship
- Component

These metamodel classes can be implemented using a **Software Development Kit** (**SDK**). More technical information on the open source implementation of DTDL and these six classes is available at `https://bit.ly/idt-dtdlv2`.

Note that DTDL can only be deployed on the **Azure Digital Twins** service, which is available in the Microsoft Azure Cloud at the time of writing this book. Organizations that standardize their technology stack on Azure and Azure Services may prefer to use DTDL for their Digital Twin solution deployment. Visit `https://bit.ly/idt-adts` for more information on Azure Digital Twins.

DTDL defines semantic relationships between entities to connect Digital Twins to a knowledge graph that reflects their interactions. It supports model inheritance to create specialized Digital Twins.

The Digital Twin knowledge graph in Azure Digital Twins can be visualized with Azure Digital Twins Explorer (`https://bit.ly/idt-dtdlx`), which shows the relationship between different Digital Twin models. It is a sample application that demonstrates how you can do the following:

- Upload and explore the models and graphs of DTDL-based Digital Twins.

- Visualize the Digital Twin graph with several layouts.

- Edit the properties of DTDL Digital Twins and run queries against the graph.

The following screenshot shows an example of such a knowledge graph based on the DTDL model of a composite Digital Twin. A description of this example is available at `https://bit.ly/idt-dtdlx`:

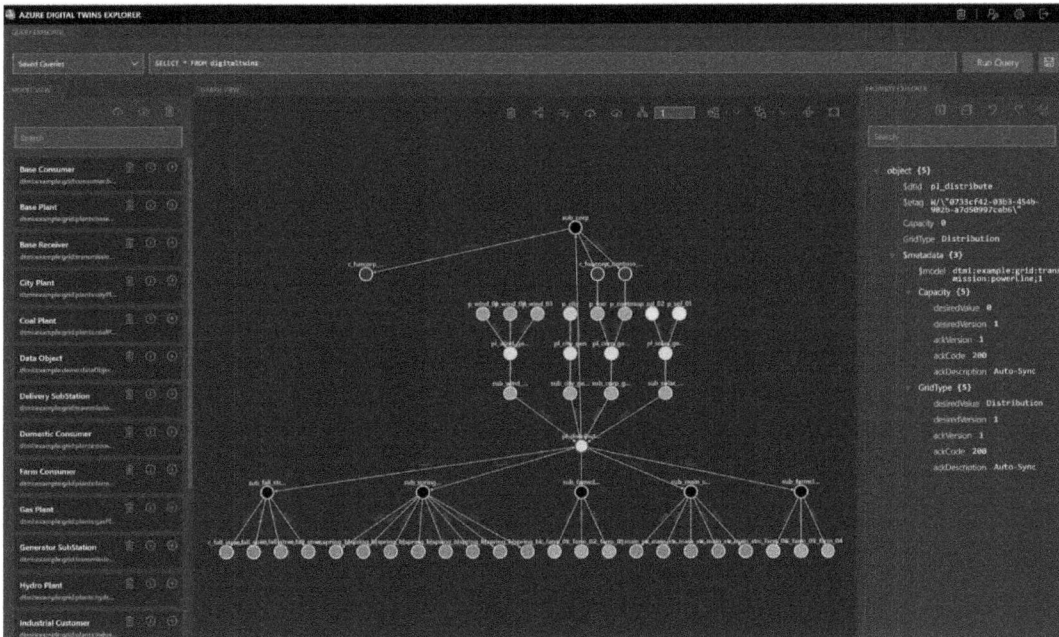

Figure 4.11 – DTDL-based Digital Twin graph in the Azure Digital Twins service

DTDL is currently less complicated than AAS, but it is also limited in its scope and capability. It does not store historical data on the Digital Twin as it only records the current state. If the temperature input from a sensor changes, the current value is overwritten with the new value.

Users of the Azure Digital Twins service with DTDL typically store temporal data in a time series database, and then they use the DTDL asset identifiers and properties to create a historical reference for analysis purposes. This can be done by a developer in Microsoft Visual Studio, or by subject matter experts, such as engineers, in a low-code Digital Twin platform with integration connectors, which provides access to both the Azure Digital Twin and the time series database. An example of an integration connector can be seen in *Figure 4.12*.

These are important technical considerations when deciding on the Digital Twin-enabling technologies that will support your first Digital Twin development. Will the Digital Twin primarily be developed and used by software developers, or is it aimed at business users to create and maintain Digital Twins in your organization? Both are technically feasible options but will require different technological capabilities to support the Digital Twin project's objective.

Here is a DTDL JSON example that describes some of the properties of the centrifugal slurry pump:

```
{
    "@id": "dtmi:com:XMPro:PumpAssembly;1",
    "@type": "Interface",
    "@context": "dtmi:dtdl:context;2",
    "displayName": "Pump Assembly",
    "contents":[
        {
            "@type": "Property",
            "name": "Description",
            "schema": "string"
        },
        {
            "@type": "Property",
            "name": "PumpType",
            "schema": "string"
        },
        {
            "@type": "Property",
```

```
            "name": "MotorRatedPower",
            "schema": "double"
        },
        {
            "@type": more types and properties here
        }
    ]
}
```

The following screenshot shows an example of a low-code application development platform with telemetry data being sent to an Azure Digital Twin and time series insights:

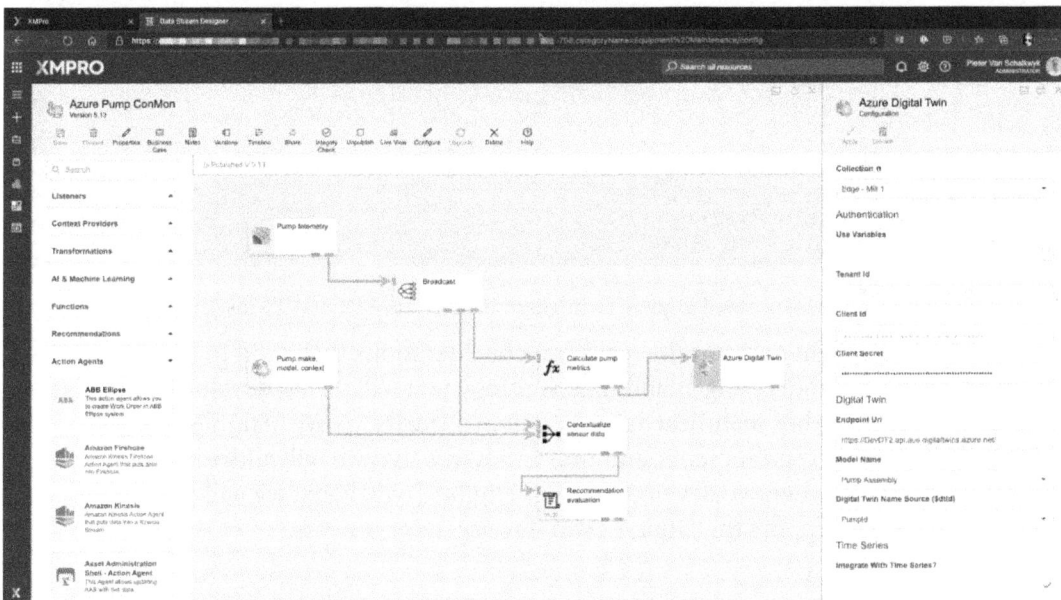

Figure 4.12 – DTDL-based Digital Twin graph in the Azure Digital Twins service

The following screenshot shows how the pump telemetry data from the preceding screenshot, modeled with DTDL, is presented in an end user interface:

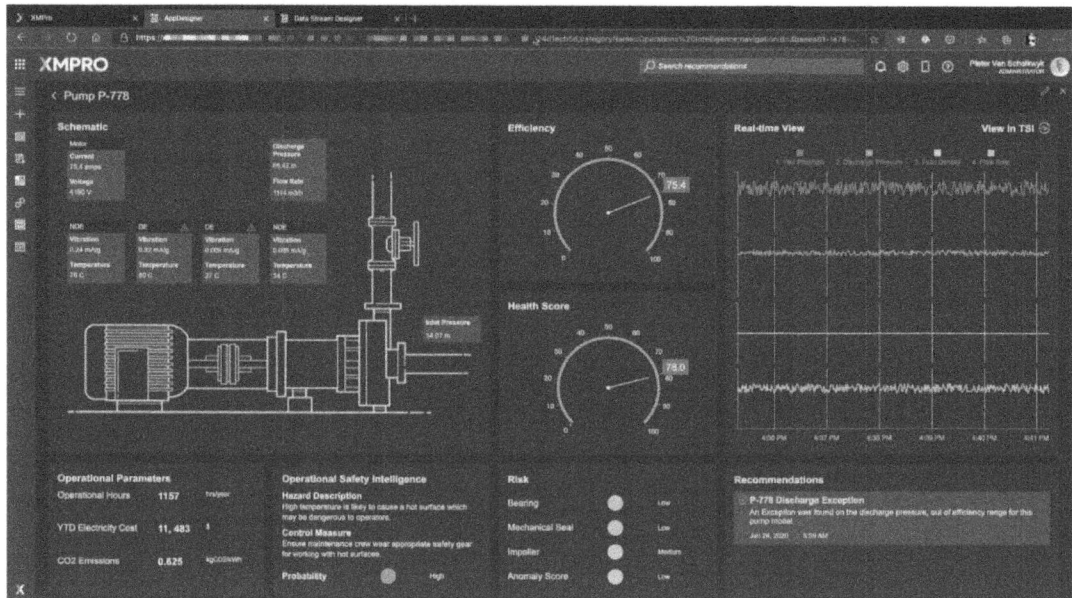

Figure 4.13 – DTDL-based Digital Twin graph in the Azure Digital Twins service

AAS and DTDL highlight some of the technical considerations that need to be addressed when deciding on the underlying enabling technology you will use to develop your Digital Twin. There are many other technical aspects such as security, trustworthiness, remote access, communication requirements, and user interfaces that we will address at a high level later in this book when we develop our first Digital Twin. Next, we will look at the digital platforms that support the Digital Twin development process.

Exploring digital platforms for Digital Twins

Digital Twins require a digital environment to help build and deploy their applications. Digital platforms for Digital Twins often consist of several components that are orchestrated together to provide a Digital Twin-enabling technology stack.

These digital components include the following:

- IoT platforms
- Business Process Management platforms

- Analytics and data platforms
- Application platforms

Let's see how these digital components can be used to create a digital environment for building and deploying these applications.

IoT platforms

IoT platforms typically consist of several capabilities that connect IoT devices to analytics and business applications. Traditional **Operational Technology** (**OT**) platforms connect to proprietary devices and control systems. In contrast, IoT platforms connect to a broad range of IoT devices through open protocols and make the information available to operational and business applications.

IoT platforms support the development of Digital Twins by doing the following:

- Monitoring IoT endpoints and real-time data streams
- Supporting both proprietary and open industry connectivity protocols for connectivity and data transfer
- Enabling physics- and math-based analytics on the IoT data
- Providing edge, distributed, and cloud compute options
- Providing integration through APIs for application development
- Contextualizing IoT data with information from business and operational systems

Some of the key capabilities of advanced IoT platforms include the following:

- Device management
- Data integration
- Data storage and management
- Analytics
- Application development support
- Security and privacy

Combining these capabilities provides the ideal technology foundation for a Digital Twin development project. The objective of a Digital Twin, however, is not just around the real-time sensor or IoT information, but rather around the business outcomes that the Digital Twin drives.

These business outcomes are influenced by the actions that are taken due to the insights gained from the Digital Twin. Changing or adapting business processes, as mentioned earlier in this chapter, is a critical success factor for the long-term value of a Digital Twin.

Some of the representative vendors for IoT platforms include the following:

- Alleantia (`alleantia.com`)
- Particle (`particle.io`)
- Microsoft (`microsoft.com`)
- Relayr (`relayr.io`)
- Thingworx (`ptc.com`)

> **Important Note**
> Please note that this is representative and not an exhaustive list. This has been provided as a reference.

Information from a Digital Twin can either provide decision support for an operational user or be used for process automation to remove the human from the loop. Business process management platforms can address both.

Business Process Management platforms

Business Process Management (**BPM**) platforms for Digital Twins may significantly overlap with IoT platform capabilities, but the focus of BPM platforms is more toward driving the business process or workflow resulting from IoT data. BPM focuses less on IoT device management, connectivity, and communication protocols.

Advanced BPM solutions also provide low-code configuration environments aimed at subject matter experts to help configure workflows, processes, and business rules to actuate or automate actions. This process not only features data from IoT sources but also embeds advanced analytics into running processes to generate insights and situational awareness from the Digital Twin applications.

Some of the representative vendors for BPM platforms include the following:

- Avolution (`avolutionsoftware.com`)
- Boxarr (`boxarr.com`)
- iGrafx (`igrafx.com`)

- QPR (`qpr.com`)

- XMPro (`xmpro.com`)

> **Important Note**
>
> Please note that this is representative and not an exhaustive list. This has been provided as a reference.

BPM platforms deliver the actions from Digital Twins, but the solution may require more of a data and analytics focus to identify the course of action.

Analytics and data platforms

Analytics and data platforms are digital tools that provide advanced analytics capabilities. These capabilities include machine learning, artificial intelligence, and high-fidelity physics capabilities.

These analytics platforms generally rely on IoT platforms for data ingestion from sensors and control systems sources. Additional data management capabilities include historian services, data lakes, and prebuilt analytics libraries for specific equipment types.

Analytics and data platforms are often used in conjunction with BPM or application platforms to visualize and action the outcomes from the analytical insights.

Some of the representative vendors for analytics and data platforms include the following:

- ANSYS (`ansys.com`)

- C3.ai (`c3.ai`)

- OSIsoft (`osisoft.com`)

- Sight Machine (`sightmachine.com`)

- Uptake (`uptake.com`)

> **Important Note**
>
> Please note that this is representative and not an exhaustive list. This has been provided as a reference.

Application platforms

Application platforms are the final category of Digital Twin-enabling technologies that you need to consider when developing and using Digital Twins in your organization. Application platforms are used to create vertically focused Digital Twin solutions in support of existing applications such as **Asset Performance Management (APM)**, **Enterprise Asset Management (EAM)**, and **Operations Performance Management (OPM)**. Digital Twins bring new capabilities to these business applications, and the configuration of Digital Twins is part of the broader application suite of the vendor itself.

Some of the representative vendors for application platforms include the following:

- AVEVA (`aveva.com`)
- Bentley (`bentley.com`)
- GE Digital (`ge.com`)
- IBM (`ibm.com`)
- Oracle (`oracle.com`)
- SAP (`sap.com`)
- Siemens (`siemens.com`)

> **Important Note**
>
> Please note that this is representative and not an exhaustive list. This has been provided as a reference.

The application and use case of your Digital Twin will determine the digital platform capabilities that you require. Validating the business problem of the required outcomes, as discussed earlier in this chapter, is crucial in considering the right digital technology and infrastructure.

This will become more obvious in the next chapter as we start setting up our first Digital Twin prototype.

Summary

In this chapter, we considered the planning frameworks we need before starting our first Digital Twin project. We looked at a project planning framework, which describes the phases involved, and a solution planning framework, which defines the problem that we are addressing, the users that it is focused on, and the expected outcome.

Then, we reviewed how to validate the problem statement and expected outcomes and how this would influence existing and future business processes. We also considered the impact of our technology decisions. Finally, we provided a high-level overview of the enabling technologies and the different types of digital platforms we can use to set up our first Digital Twin in the next chapter.

In *Chapter 5, Setting Up a Digital Twin Prototype*, we will start setting up our first Digital Twin prototype by choosing a Digital Twin platform, deciding on the cloud infrastructure, and initiating the configuration and setup. We will also consider the impact of data and create a solution architecture for our first Digital Twin.

Questions

1. Describe the project phases of your Digital Twin prototype.
2. Can you create a Lean Digital Twin canvas to describe your solution?
3. What are the primary technology considerations for your Digital Twin solution?
4. What do think the benefits of a Digital Twin in your organization will be?

5
Setting Up a Digital Twin Prototype

In *Chapter 4*, *Getting Started with Our First Digital Twin*, we evaluated the planning phase and framework of the Digital Twin journey. We covered the business outcomes expected from a Digital Twin and the process to get to the desired state. We discussed the technical requirements around creating and managing a Digital Twin in an enterprise.

This chapter will cover the steps needed to build a prototype of a Digital Twin. We will begin by evaluating the public cloud and **Internet of Things** (**IoT**) platform considerations, along with the capabilities needed to build a Digital Twin.

We will cover these topics in this chapter:

- Identifying a Digital Twin platform
- Evaluating the public cloud, IoT, and specialty platforms for a Digital Twin
- Configuration and setup
- Data considerations for your Azure Digital Twin
- Solution architecture

Let's start with a discussion on the considerations around a Digital Twin platform, to build on the discussions from the previous chapter.

Identifying a Digital Twin platform

In *Chapter 3*, *Identifying the First Digital Twin*, we looked at the evaluation of a Digital Twin from the perspective of various kinds of companies. The first and second types were large industrial companies, who could be a manufacturer of an industrial asset. Here, we will expand into such considerations from those such as an industrial manufacturer who would be interested in improving a product and providing good maintenance services, over the life of an asset, to its customers or operators of the asset.

The perspective of the asset owner

Let's narrow things down to the energy sector and the manufacturer of wind turbines. Global warming and the use of renewable sources of energy are on the rise. Hence, we believe wind turbines will continue to become an important industrial asset in the energy sector. A **horizontal-axis wind turbine** (**HAWT**), such as the one shown in the following figure, is the most commonly used type of wind turbine. Such a wind turbine can be used as a single asset or as part of a wind farm. An industrial-grade wind turbine could last about 20 years. The wind turbine requires no fossil fuels for the generation of energy as it uses the wind in motion as a source of energy. The wind is the only input to the wind turbine for generating energy, as the sunlight is a source of energy for solar farms. Today, the larger wind turbines can generate 10-20 **megawatts** (**MW**) of energy (see `https://reneweconomy.com.au/germany-gears-up-to-test-20mw-wind-turbines-79007`). Such wind turbines can have a wingspan of 200 meters:

Figure 5.1 – HAWT

A wind farm can contain a small number of turbines to several hundred turbines. Such wind farms can be on land (onshore) or offshore. The following figure shows an offshore wind farm. Such a location generally has winds at the speed of 5-10 **meters/second (m/s)** for effective power generation. The relative position and distance of wind turbines are important to improve the overall energy generation from the wind farm. Likewise, a wind farm is usually located in areas of a sustained flow of wind for the major part of the year or the major part of the day:

Figure 5.2 – Offshore wind farm

As we get ready to understand the requirements for building a Digital Twin of a wind turbine and a wind farm, it is important to understand how the physical layout of wind turbines is done in the wind farm to maximize overall energy generation. The distance between the base of the next turbine and the directional orientation is determined such that one turbine interferes minimally with the flow of wind for the rest of the turbines. Such an effect on wind is called a wake effect. The wake effect can be from different turbines in the same wind farm (wake effect internal) or from neighboring wind farms (wake effect external) (see https://www.wind-energy-the-facts.org/wake-effect.html#). The wake effect is a consideration for future wind farms to be constructed nearby. This is important due to the long life of wind turbines and wind farms. The growth of trees in nearby forests could also impact the nature of wind, over time.

Next, let's look at what kind of fundamental capabilities are needed for the foundation of a Digital Twin solution, such as for wind turbines and wind farms.

Required IoT capabilities

A Digital Twin requires data from an asset to keep the twin current. This helps to build and maintain more accurate twins, which in turn assures better outcomes. These outcomes can be decision-supported for predictive maintenance or can simply arise through better asset utilization. In the last decade, we have seen the growth of several IoT platforms and some of them are geared toward industrial assets. A generic IoT technology stack is shown in the following figure, which depicts the device connectivity to capture and convert the data into a form that can then be communicated to the IoT core platform. Such core IoT often resides in a public cloud platform. Applications, including those for Digital Twins, are often built on top of the IoT platform:

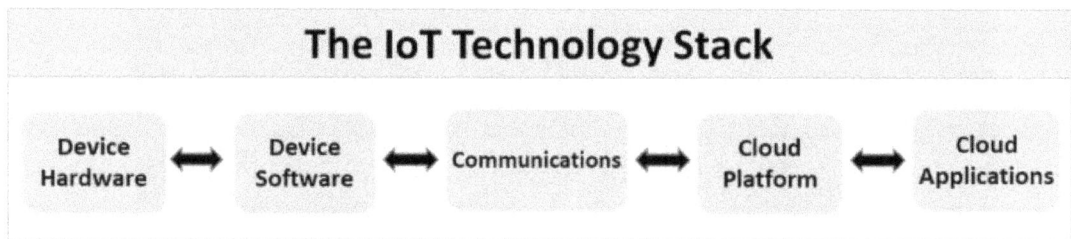

The IoT Technology Stack

| Device Hardware | ⬌ | Device Software | ⬌ | Communications | ⬌ | Cloud Platform | ⬌ | Cloud Applications |

Figure 5.3 – The IoT technology stack

> **Note**
>
> Image citation: Abunahla, H., Gadhafi, R., Mohammad, B. et al. *Integrated graphene oxide resistive element in tunable RF filters.* Sci Rep 10, 13128 (2020). `https://doi.org/10.1038/s41598-020-70041-x`

Let's next look at some of the fundamental capabilities of an IoT platform—namely, the following:

- Ability to gather data from assets, sensors, gateway devices, or third-party sources such as environmental data.

- Ability to securely and reliably transfer data to the data store layer. This activity may require protocol translations and/or encryption of data.

- Handle different types of communication mediums such as wired, wireless, or even satellite communication for remote locations.

- Ability to understand the asset and fleet of assets structure so that data can be mapped to meaningful constructs.

- Ability to analyze the data from the different types of data stores (for example, time series, relational, or unstructured), and apply models and algorithms to generate insights.

- Allow applications for specific purposes to be built on top of the platform capabilities.

Now, when we look at the foundational capabilities required by the IoT platform, we find these are the following:

- Compute

- Storage

- Network

In order to obtain these foundational capabilities in an elastic and agile way, IoT platforms use the public cloud. Due to the distributed nature of the assets in IoT, the compute, storage, network, and connectivity capabilities may be needed in multiple places. Public cloud platforms usually have the concept of regions and **availability zones** (**AZs**) to help meet such requirements. Cybersecurity is taken care of by following secure practices, such as a) limiting remote actuation of a device without going through the control systems in place already and b) by use of data encryption between the edge and cloud, to reduce the chances of tampering with data in motion.

Build versus buy of the capabilities

We looked at the foundational capabilities required for an IoT platform in the prior section. Given that these capabilities exist in any public cloud platform, it could be an easy decision to "buy" this capability from the public cloud rather than "build" it. If we go back about a decade, many large enterprises used to build their own data centers to meet their computing needs and keep their data and **information technology** (**IT**) applications within the company firewall. As public cloud technologies started to mature and strengthened security and compliance, enterprises started to move toward "buying" virtual data center-like capabilities in the public cloud.

When it comes to building a Digital Twin solution (such as a Digital Twin for wind turbines, in our case), a manufacturing company would face a similar build-versus-buy decision. We will break down this decision process by providing details of the current technology landscape at this company, as follows:

- Being a global conglomerate, this company has many applications and databases. These applications have been categorized as a) mission-critical and b) non-mission-critical. Likewise, the databases have been categorized to a) export-controlled/ restricted; b) private; and c) public data.

- The **Chief Information Officer (CIO)** has obtained approval to store applications in the non-mission-critical category and use private or public data in public cloud platforms. This does, however, require that the public cloud provider demonstrates that it meets a certain level of industry standards and compliance requirements.

- Based on the public cloud platforms already approved in the company, options for IoT platforms are available on cloud platforms. The proximity of the IoT platform to the selected public cloud platform for IT applications and databases assures that there is a reduced amount of movement of data in and out of the selected cloud platform.

- A subset of the IoT platforms running on the selected public cloud platform caters to the industrial assets and is not limited to consumer IoT scenarios.

- The company is reducing its footprint of data centers except for its mission-critical applications and data that is highly restricted or export-controlled. However, the company is evaluating a roadmap of public cloud providers to meet their level of performance and compliance requirements, whether this is via the public cloud or hybrid cloud/edge cloud offerings, in the next 2 years.

Based on the considerations here, the company decided to take the "buy" route compared to the "build" route in this case.

Evaluating public cloud, IoT, and specialty platforms for a Digital Twin

Let's look at the considerations for building a Digital Twin solution for a wind turbine. Enterprise computing has been shifting to the public cloud over the last decade, with the industry seeing the emergence of large-scale public cloud providers over this period. According to the *Magic Quadrant for Cloud Infrastructure and Platform Services*, published in September 2020, these are the major providers:

- Microsoft Azure
- **Amazon Web Services (AWS)**
- **Google Cloud Platform (GCP)**
- Alibaba Cloud
- **Oracle Cloud Infrastructure (OCI)**
- IBM Cloud
- Tencent Cloud

Alibaba and Tencent are primarily popular in China, hence, we will not discuss these two platforms here. We will look at the capabilities of commonly available options in the industry today, in the context of a Digital Twin.

Microsoft Azure Digital Twins

Microsoft **Azure Digital Twins** (**ADT**) is part of Azure IoT, an IoT-based Digital Twin platform, as described in *Chapter 4, Getting Started with Our First Digital Twin*. Azure IoT consists of a number of platform services that can be accessed on the edge and in the cloud. Some of these services used to provide the IoT platform include the following ones:

- **Azure IoT Hub**—This is a cloud-hosted, secure bidirectional communications service between IoT devices and an application backend.

- **Azure IoT Central**—This is a **user interface** (**UI**) application to manage devices on Azure IoT Hub.

- **Azure IoT Edge**—This runs IoT edge devices through the containerization of Azure services.

- **Azure RTOS**—This is an operating system for resource-constrained IoT devices and includes an embedded development suite.

- **Azure Time Series Insights** (**TSI**)—Use this to store, visualize, and query large datasets of temporal or time series data.

- **ADT**—This is a **platform-as-a-service** (**PaaS**) capability to create graph-based relationships for entities that describe a model for the entities or things, and their relationships to other entities.

These services are combined in different configurations, based on business and technical requirements, to provide the Azure IoT platform. IoT and Digital Twin applications are developed on the ADT platform through Microsoft developer tools such as Visual Studio and **Visual Studio Code** (**VS Code**).

The knowledge graph in ADT stores entity, relationship, and state information in a single model. *Figure 5.4* shows a high-level perspective of an Azure IoT platform and its services, and where ADT fits in the architecture.

ADT uses **Digital Twin Definition Language** (**DTDL**), which we covered in *Chapter 4, Getting Started with Our First Digital Twin*. DTDL is an open source modeling language, aimed at improving interoperability and reuse of ADT models in different applications and use cases.

You can see an overview of the architecture here:

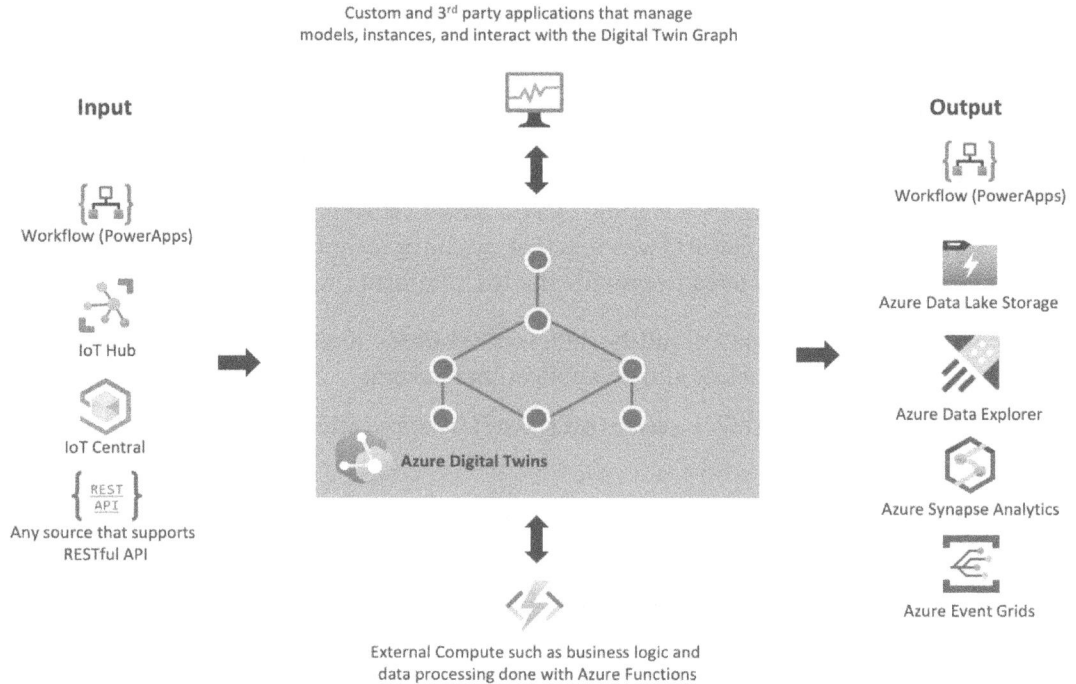

Figure 5.4 – Microsoft ADT in an Azure IoT platform

Microsoft has a broad industry focus with Azure IoT and ADT. This includes verticals such as infrastructure, manufacturing, energy and utilities, oil and gas, and mining at the time of writing this book.

We'll next look at the capabilities of AWS.

AWS IoT platforms

Let's look at the AWS capabilities. AWS started its public cloud offerings as early as 2006. Today, it has a very large share of the market for **infrastructure-as-a-service** (**IaaS**) and PaaS. In late 2015, Amazon announced its AWS IoT offering, starting with AWS IoT Core or Cloud Services for Connected Devices. Other AWS services, such as Amazon **Simple Storage Service** (**S3**), Amazon Kinesis, and so on, could be used along with IoT Core to build IoT applications. AWS IoT platforms provide support for commonly used IoT protocols such as **Message Queuing and Telemetry Transport** (**MQTT**), **HyperText Transfer Protocol Secure** (**HTTPS**), and **low-power long-range wide-area network** (**LoRaWAN**). Enterprises that were already using AWS for IaaS and PaaS and had their enterprise data and applications on AWS started looking at AWS IoT platforms for applications that needed device connectivity and sensor data.

For enterprises that are standardized on a certain cloud platform, it is often the starting point for new cloud capabilities such as IoT and Digital Twins in this case. In some cases, the CIO prefers to have a smaller number of moving parts in the IT and cloud landscape. Often, the process of security and compliance approval for a public cloud provider is a long one, and enterprises try to reduce the number of public cloud platforms in use unless they are open to best-of-breed solutions or have multi-cloud as part of their business continuity strategy. Often, the movement in and out of a public cloud platform incurs data charges and introduces latency between applications.

Amazon's offering for IoT is limited to its IoT platform. Amazon has not built any IoT applications on top of the platform that can be offered as **software-as-a-service (SaaS)**. SaaS offerings or IoT applications are easier to consume by business users, whereas the platform capabilities typically require software professionals and application developers to consume the services via usable IoT applications. Amazon Sumerian provides capabilities around **three-dimensional (3D)** modeling, **augmented reality (AR)**, and **virtual reality (VR)**, which can be used along with the IoT platform to build applications along the lines of a Digital Twin. One such example would be a twin of a manufacturing plant with a 3D view of the equipment and floor plan, for providing training to employees.

Amazon provides a Device Shadow service (see `https://docs.aws.amazon.com/iot/latest/developerguide/iot-device-shadows.html`). This service allows you to create a shadow of a physical device and, for instance, provide the state of the physical device to the applications. However, a shadow is not a dynamic Digital Twin of a physical asset. A device shadow can be stored in a **JavaScript Object Notation (JSON)** file. The information in such a JSON file would be the device metadata, state or version, and any security tokens associated with the device. The applications can interact with the device shadow using **REpresentational State Transfer (REST) application programming interfaces (APIs)**, namely for `GET`, `UPDATE`, or `DELETE` requests or via MQTT messages.

To the best of our knowledge, at the time of writing this book in early 2021, there are no complete Digital Twin services in the AWS platform. However, there are **independent software vendors (ISVs)** who make such capabilities available on top of AWS. One such example is the **Hexagon Digital Reality (HxDR)** platform (see `https://aws.amazon.com/blogs/industries/hxdr-transforming-geospatial-data-in-the-cloud-with-aws-and-hexagon-leica-geosystems/`).

HxDR provides Digital Twin capabilities for building structures on top of AWS. Some of the characteristics of such a Digital Twin solution are outlined here:

- High computational complexity to mix spatial data from physical structures to create a Digital Twin. The ability to grow the computational capacity elastically as the scale and precision of the model grows makes the public cloud suitable for it.

- A high-fidelity Digital Twin requires a lot of data about its physical structures. Storing and making this data available is demanding due to the amount of data. Growth in storage can be on-demand or on the public cloud. HxDR uses AWS S3 for such elastic storage.

- The data may be collected globally, depending upon the problem domain of the Digital Twin. Usually, a public cloud platform has points of presence in multiple locations as well as edge locations.

- The security and sensitivity of the data collected for Digital Twins may require additional security services from the underlying cloud platform.

Vertex is another provider of capabilities for Digital Twins, on top of the AWS platform (see `https://aws.amazon.com/iot/solutions/VertexDigitalTwin/`). Bosch IoT Things on AWS can connect to devices using MQTT and **Advanced Message Queuing Protocol** (**AMQP**) and help to manage Digital Twins (see `https://aws.amazon.com/marketplace/pp/BoschIO-GmbH-Bosch-IoT-Things/B07DTJK8MV`).

In summary, we see that a public cloud provider such as AWS can be used to build Digital Twin capabilities from the ground up using a combination of IoT Core and other services or specialized offerings from ISVs' partners, which can be leveraged to get started. However, Amazon lacks a complete Digital Twin solution of its own.

Let's next explore the capabilities provided by Oracle in this space.

Oracle IoT applications

Let's now look at Oracle's capabilities. Oracle is known for **enterprise resource planning** (**ERP**) and technology solutions that are used by several mid-to-large-sized enterprises globally. When a company is looking for IoT and Digital Twin solutions, the current provider of the ERP and manufacturing applications may influence that decision. Oracle and SAP are the two main global providers of business applications such as ERP, **customer relationship management** (**CRM**), or **human capital management** (**HCM**). Other providers in this space are `Salesforce.com`, Workday, Infor, and so on. Some large and global companies may have a combination of Oracle, SAP, and `Salesforce.com`, either in different lines of business or due to merger and acquisition activities. Oracle's business applications are available via the cloud as SaaS offerings since 2012. Oracle launched its public cloud platform later, and its current offering is called OCI.

Oracle started offering an IoT platform on top of its public cloud a few years ago and further enriched it with IoT applications, which are SaaS offerings (see `https://www.oracle.com/internet-of-things/`). Oracle's IoT Intelligent offerings include the following:

- **Smart Manufacturing/Production Monitoring** —Work in progressing monitoring, maximizing product quality, and preventing unplanned downtime

- **Predictive Maintenance/Asset Monitoring**—Connected assets and connected products

- **Connected Logistics/Fleet and Shipment Monitoring**—Monitoring shipment and warehouse automation

- **Connected Worker**—Worker safety monitoring

Next, let's look at the Digital Twin-related capabilities provided by Oracle. The focus of the Digital Twins is for industrial assets here. The functionality provided by Oracle caters to three different scenarios, outlined as follows:

- **Virtual twin:** This twin is the software equivalent of a physical asset to help simulate the asset for capabilities such as testing and virtual provisioning before connecting physical devices.

- **Predictive twin:** This twin is used to capture the expected behavior of the physical asset and is useful to predict its future state, including the remaining useful life of a machine or its impact on the environment.

- **Twin projections:** This twin is useful for scenario analysis and planning in industrial settings such as smart factories, logistics, **supply chain management (SCM)**, warehousing, maintenance and repair, and delivery-of-field services in asset-intensive industries.

For more details on Oracle Digital Twin implementation, see `https://docs.oracle.com/en/cloud/paas/iot-cloud/iotgs/oracle-iot-digital-twin-implementation.html`.

Oracle provides an IoT digital-twin simulator that allows the simulation of data, alerts, and events from physical assets without connecting to them. Apart from IoT and digital-twin capabilities, Oracle also provides blockchain applications for Intelligent Track and Trace or Intelligent Cold Chain solutions. Such capabilities are very useful in COVID-19-related vaccine distribution to the point of consumption. Oracle allows the creation of a digital thread that can be used to track a product from its design idea all the way to the production use of the asset over its lifetime.

Oracle IoT digital-twin implementation may be suitable for a company using Oracle Cloud ERP applications or OCI for other purposes. In this case, the data and applications will stay on the Oracle cloud. Companies who are running their business applications on other cloud platforms may evaluate the Oracle IoT applications and digital-twin capabilities for their functional requirements.

After looking at offerings from Microsoft Azure, Amazon AWS, and Oracle Cloud, we'll next move to more specialized offerings such as **PTC** (formerly **Parametric Technology Corporation**).

PTC ThingWorx

PTC ThingWorx is an IoT-based digital-twin platform, as described in *Chapter 4, Getting Started with Our First Digital Twin*. ThingWorx is part of the PTC engineering solutions suite of products that includes Vuforia for AR, Windchill for **product life cycle management** (**PLM**), and Creo for **computer-aided design** (**CAD**).

At the time of writing the book, ThingWorx consists of three main components to create Digital Twins (`http://bit.ly/idt-3thingworx`), outlined as follows:

- **ThingModel**—A data model that serves as the foundation for a ThingWorx Digital Twin

- **ThingWorx Composer**—An application development environment to configure models, compose services and logic rules, and manage the system configuration of the ThingModel

- **ThingWorx Mashup Builder**—A UI authoring environment for visualization elements

ThingWorx is a Java-based platform that can be installed locally or deployed on Microsoft Azure or Amazon AWS cloud infrastructure. ThingWorx can run on Microsoft Windows or Linux, based on the requirements of the customer organization. PTC ThingWorx is also available as a hosted PaaS as well as a SaaS solution for customers that do not want to manage the underlying compute infrastructure. The following screenshot shows a sample Digital Twin using PTC ThingWorx:

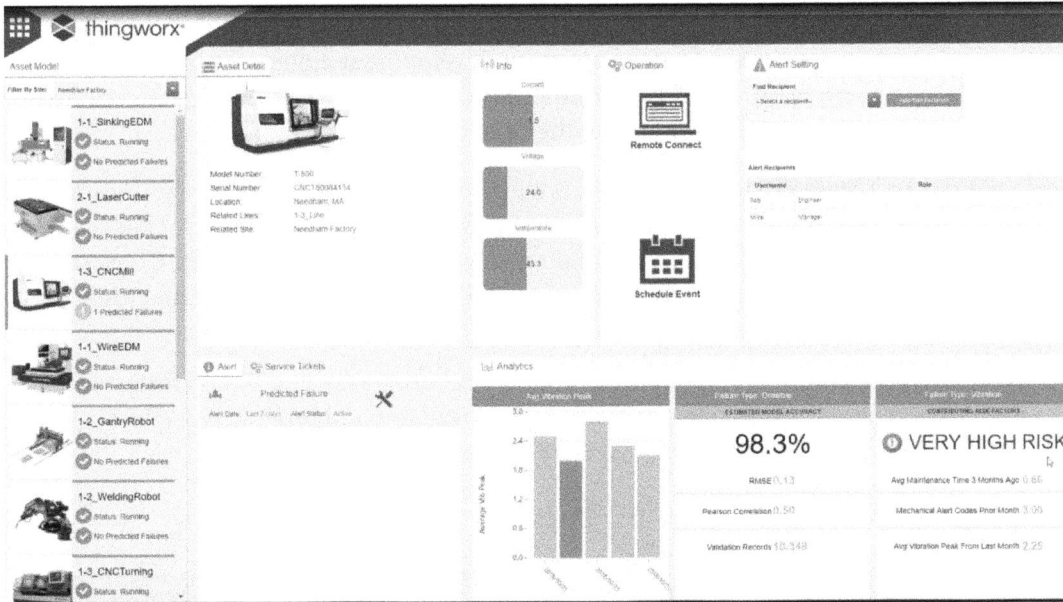

Figure 5.5 – PTC ThingWorx example Digital Twin (courtesy of http://bit.ly/idt-thingworx)

PTC ThingWorx has a broad industry focus that covers all asset-intensive industries but has a high representation of manufacturing customers at the time of writing the book. PTC currently markets a range of PLM and CAD solutions to the manufacturing sector that improves the visibility of ThingWorx in that market segment.

In the next section, we focus on XMPro, which is a niche provider in this space.

XMPro

XMPro is a **business process management (BPM)**-based digital-twin platform, as described in *Chapter 4, Getting Started with Our First Digital Twin*. XMPro is built on the Microsoft .NET Core platform and can be deployed at the edge, in the cloud, or in a hybrid combination of both edge and cloud. See *Figure 5.6* for an example using the XMPro platform.

XMPro is primarily targeted at engineers, scientists, geologists, and other **subject-matter experts (SMEs)** who prefer a low-code application development environment versus a traditional **integrated development environment (IDE)** such as Microsoft Visual Studio. XMPro consists of the following modules at the time of writing the book:

- **XMPro Data Stream Designer**—This is a low-code integration and orchestration environment to connect real-time IoT data with analytics and actions. A Data Stream is a collection of integration and service agents such as Listeners, Context Providers, Transformations, Functions, **artificial intelligence** (AI) and **machine learning** (ML) services, and Action Agents.

- **XMPro App Designer**—This is a low-code visual programming UI to create digital-twin applications. App Designer is also used to configure the workflow logic and business rules for the XMPro recommendation engine.

You can see a sample view of the XMPro platform here:

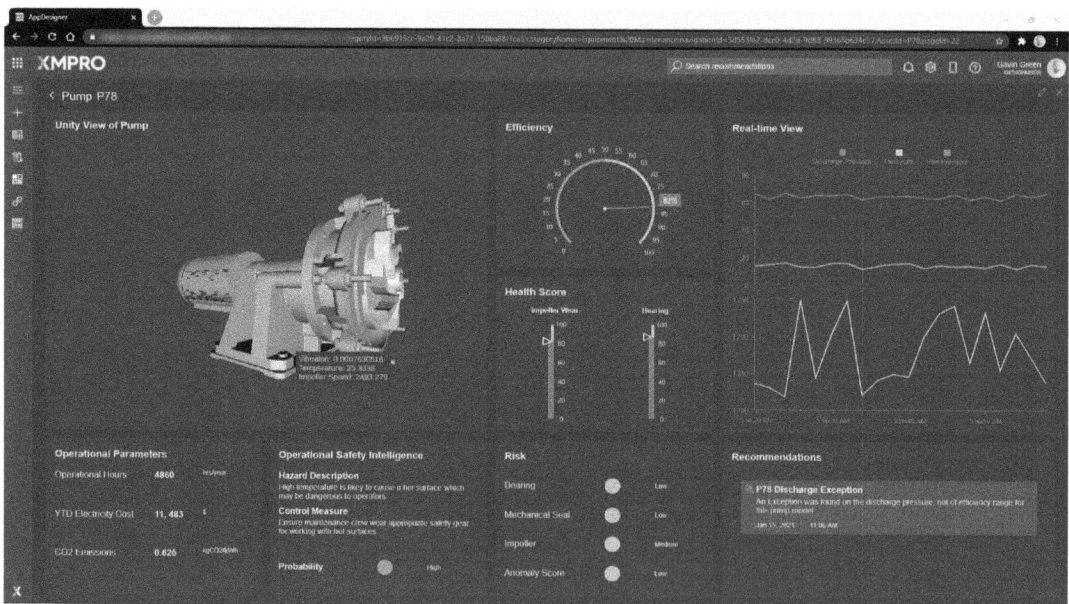

Figure 5.6 – XMPro sample Digital Twin (courtesy of XMPro Inc.)

XMPro focuses on enabling non-programmers in asset-intensive industries such as mining, oil and gas, petrochemicals, and manufacturing, and is also used for supply-chain solutions.

In the previous section, we looked at the capabilities of different cloud-based solutions for IoT and Digital Twins. Such comparative study helps us in the decision process of an enterprise going through its digital-twin journey. In the context of this book, we will use Microsoft ADT for details of the process. This decision is based on a couple of factors, outlined as follows:

- ADT was made publicly available by Microsoft Azure in November 2020, thus making it easy for making use of it for development, testing, or production deployment.

- In our context of the global conglomerate that is building the wind turbine's Digital Twin, the CIO has already selected Microsoft Azure for its enterprise applications.

- The company decided to explore all available options for Digital Twins on Azure first.

- The company also plans to offer the wind turbine's digital-twin capabilities to its customers, such as the owners and operators of wind farms. Based on its market survey, the energy sector did not have any preferred public cloud platform.

In the next section, we will look at the use of Microsoft ADT for building the wind turbine's Digital Twin.

Configuration and setup

Before we can configure our first Digital Twin in Microsoft ADT, we must set up the cloud infrastructure and account on Microsoft Azure. Microsoft provides detailed setup instructions for Azure administrators, but we will start from the perspective of a non-corporate user that wants to set up a free account to build a first digital-twin prototype. The ADT documentation is at `http://bit.ly/idt-azuredocs`.

The first step is to create a free Azure account that will host your ADT service and any other IoT and analytics services that you will need for your first Digital Twin. See the following screenshot for an overview of how to do this:

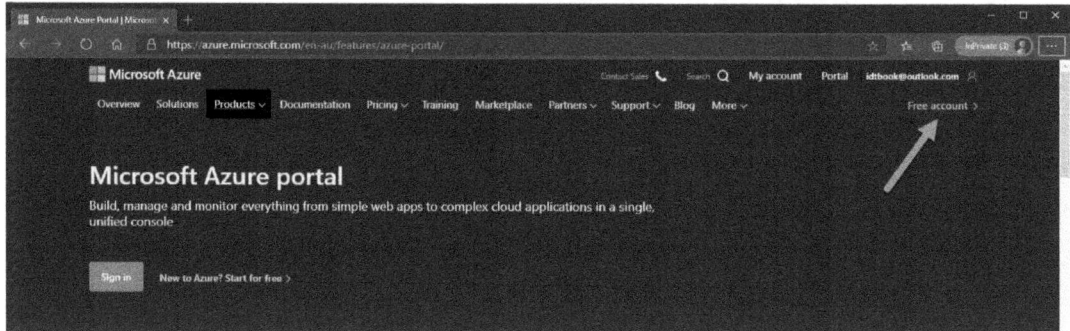

Figure 5.7 – Microsoft Azure portal UI

Once you've created an account, you will be directed to the Azure service portal. This is the central management environment for all Azure services, including ADT, Azure databases, IoT services, and all the other products that Microsoft provides in its Azure product range.

ADT is a PaaS solution that provides the infrastructure to create and use Digital Twins. It is a development environment for Digital Twins that is focused on developers to code Digital Twins. It is not an end user-focused application with a UI for business users to configure Digital Twins. It will require other Azure services in your Azure account to perform these actions.

ADT can be configured through the web-based Azure Portal or in a command line through the **Azure command-line interface (Azure CLI)**. Both approaches are documented in the official Microsoft documentation at `http://bit.ly/idt-azuredocs`. We will describe the portal configuration approach at a high level for the purpose of the book.

The configuration and setup of ADT and the supporting app service to code against is done in five main steps, as illustrated in the following diagram:

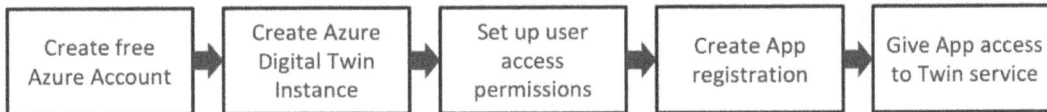

Figure 5.8 – Microsoft ADT resource and application configuration

The first step is to set up an Azure account. Microsoft provides a free account option at the time of writing the book. The second step is to create an ADT resource or service in the Azure account that you've created. The third step is to give yourself user and data access to the ADT resource you created. You can also give others access to your ADT service during this step. The ADT resource that you created requires an Azure app resource to be able to code against the ADT service. We configure the app resource during the fourth step. Finally, in the fifth step, we give the app resource access and permissions to the ADT service.

You can see an overview of this in the following screenshot:

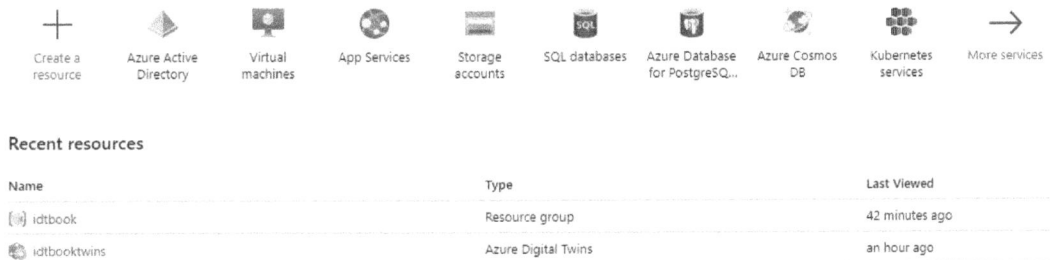

Figure 5.9 – Microsoft Azure portal UI

The UI shown in *Figure 5.9* indicates that you have successfully created your free Azure account and shows a list of services available at the time of writing this book. The next step in our process is to create a new service for ADT. Select the **+ Create a resource** option. A range of existing resources should show, and in the event that ADT is not on the display, you can easily search for it in the search bar, as shown in the following screenshot:

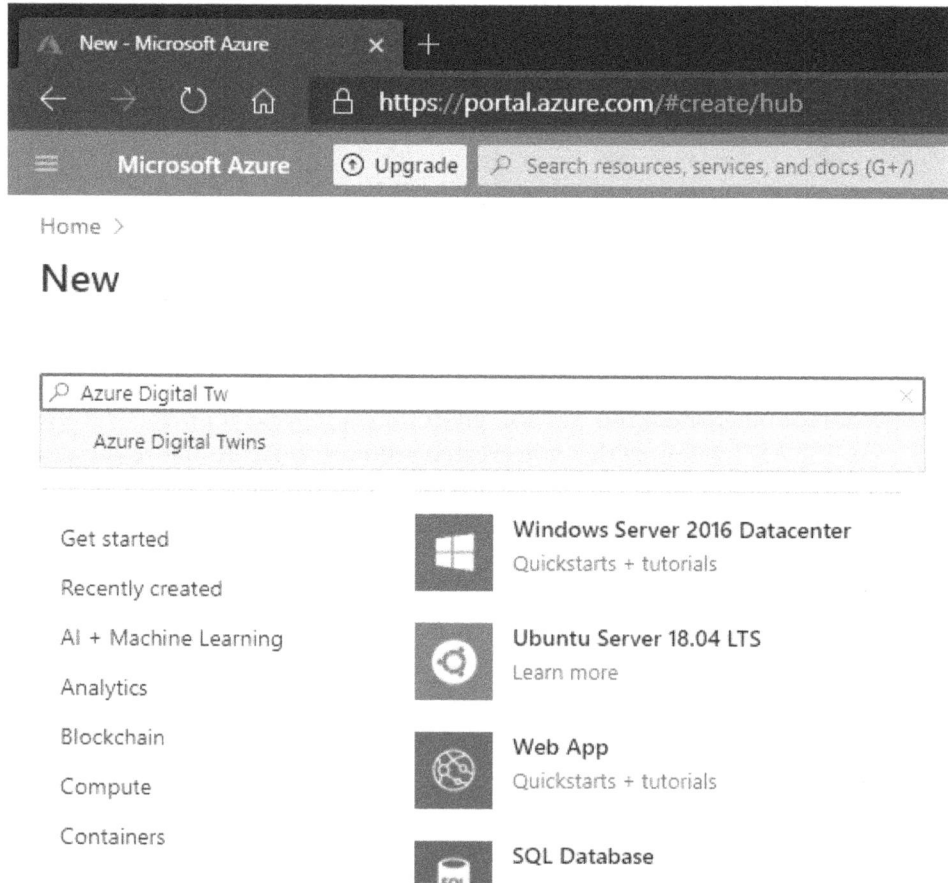

Figure 5.10 – Creating a new Azure resource

Once you've located the ADT resource, click on the **Create** button to start the process of configuring the resource.

Creating the resource has two main components—the first is to choose a subscription that the resource will run in, and the second part is to choose a hosting location and a name for the ADT resource or service.

The following screenshot shows the subscription options, and it is a good practice to name the resource group in an easily identifiable way. For the purposes of building your first Digital Twin, we recommend that you create a resource group for your digital-twin application. You can think of a resource group as a container that holds related resources for an Azure solution. For later reference in the book, we called the resource group `digitaltwinbook`:

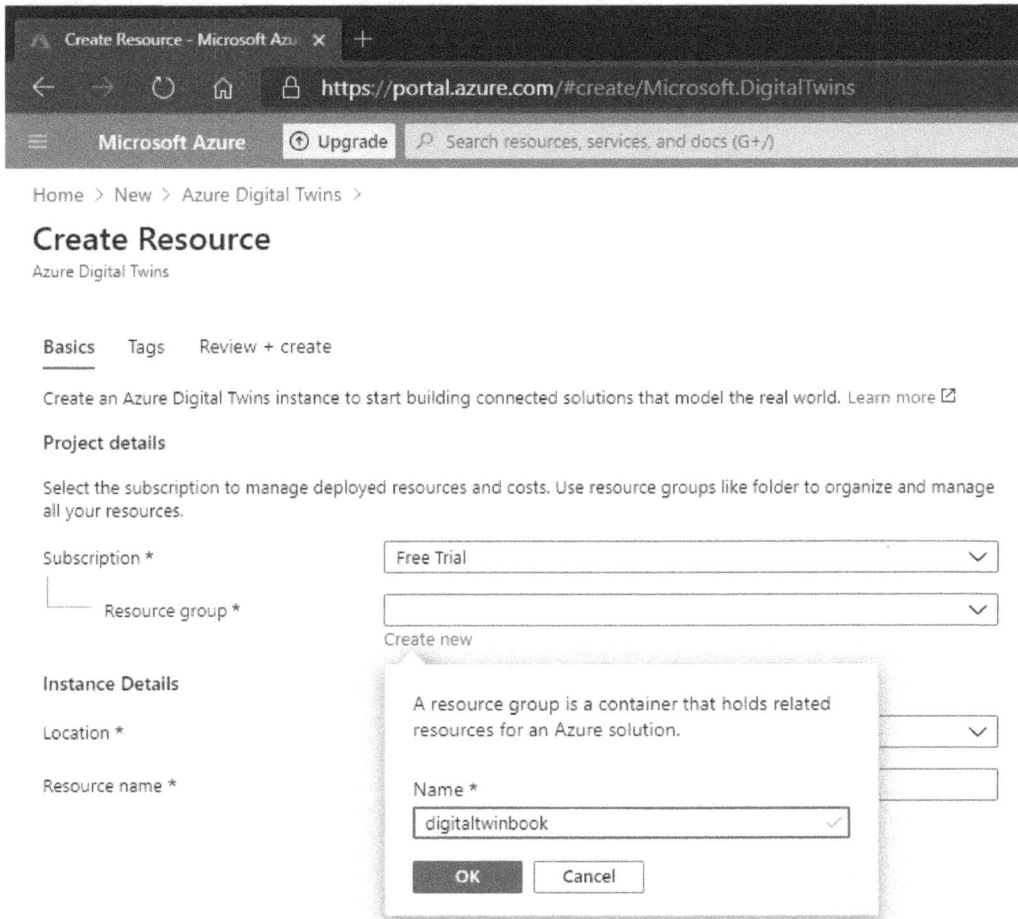

Figure 5.11 – Creating an Azure resource subscription

The second part of the process to create an Azure subscription is to choose a hosting location and name the resources. Hosting locations that provide ADT resources are available from the drop-down list. The decision of a location is most often based on your geographical proximity, to reduce latency. Privacy and data considerations may, however, prescribe your choice if you are in the **European Union (EU)**, for example.

The following screenshot shows the location and name that we chose to use for the Digital Twin that we will configure in *Chapter 6, Building the Digital Twin Prototype*. Clicking on the **Review + create** button will give you the option to review all the settings before the ADT resource is finally created in your chosen subscription and preferred location:

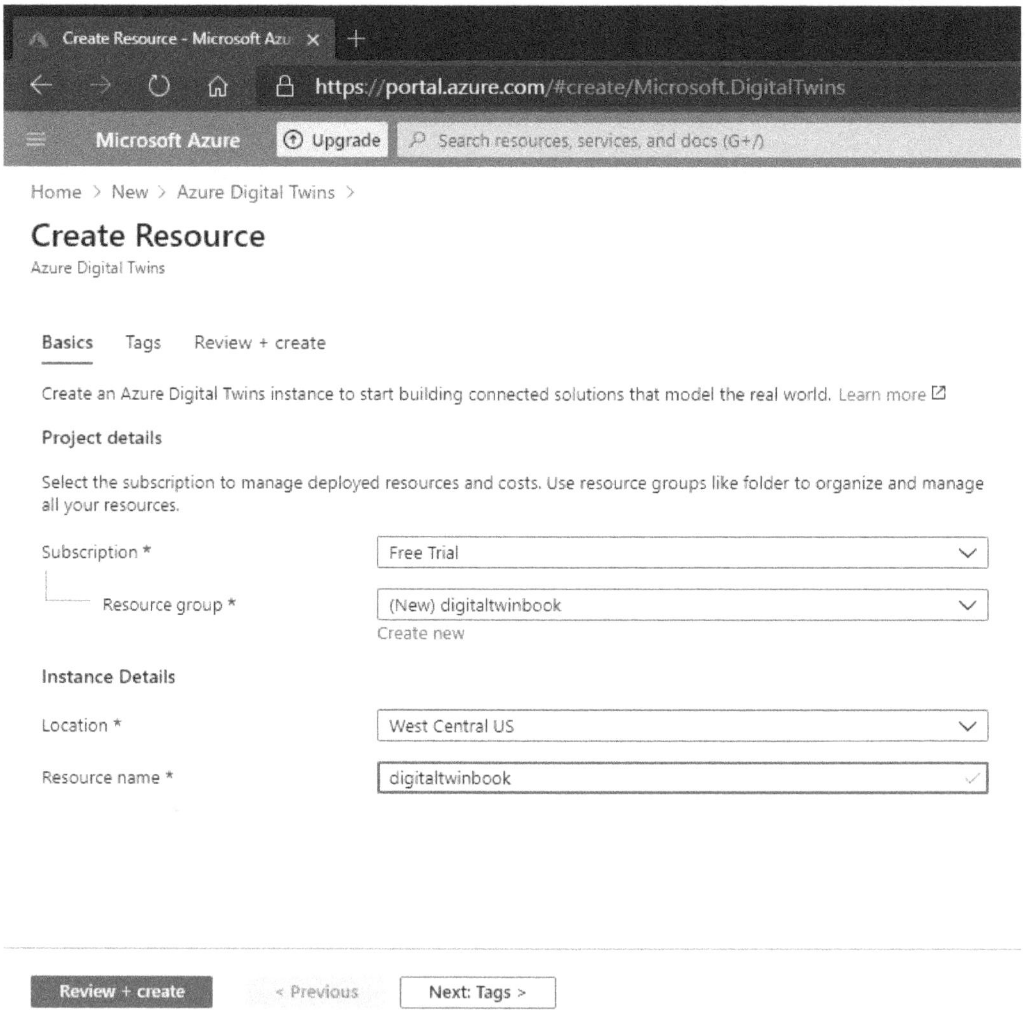

Figure 5.12 – Choose the Azure resource location and name

All the ADT resource information is available in the portal view, as shown in *Figure 5.13*. This concludes the first two steps shown in *Figure 5.8*. The third step is the user access configuration to enable you to access the digital-twin resource when you create your first Digital Twin in *Chapter 6, Building the Digital Twin Prototype*.

Next, we see the successful creation of an ADT resource in the following screenshot:

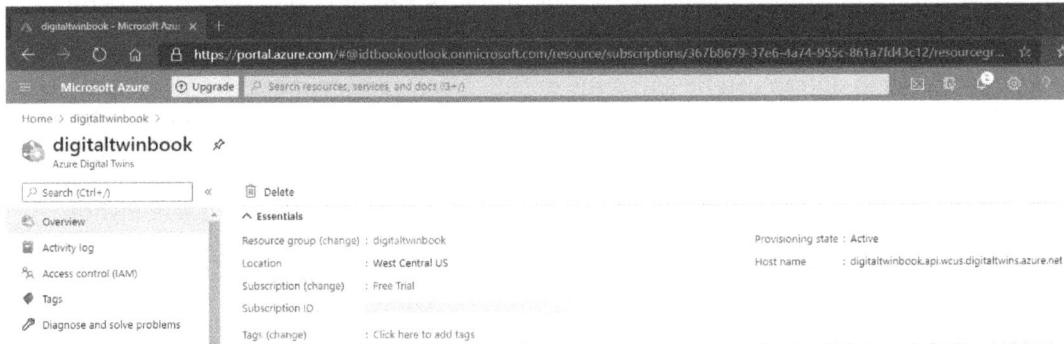

Figure 5.13 – Successful creation of an ADT resource

Select the **Access control (IAM)** option from the left menu and click on **Add role assignments** to open the configuration pane. This will enable you to give your user and credentials access to the digital-twin resource. *Figure 5.14* shows the UI at the time of writing the book.

It is important to set your own login user as the data owner for the digital-twin resource when you set this up in a personal or free account. There may be other governance requirements if you are doing this in your organization's Azure subscription or tenant; however, we recommend that you do the initial prototype in a free account.

You can see an overview of the UI here:

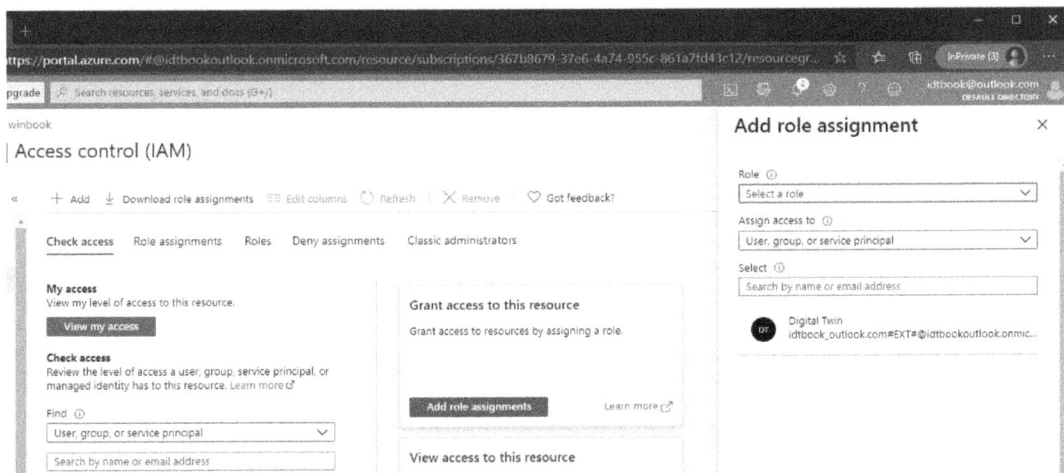

Figure 5.14 – Setting up user access permissions to an ADT resource

Select **Azure Digital Twins Data Owner** from the available options in the **Role** dropdown on the right-hand side of the screen. This option will give you full access and ownership to all the capabilities of the ADT resource, as shown in *Figure 5.15*.

The **Assign access to** option can be left at the default **User, group, or service principal** setting. Select or type in an Azure free account username in the **Select** drop-down field.

Your user will appear as an icon below the drop-down fields. Select your user and save the access rights with the **Save** button on the page, as illustrated in the following screenshot:

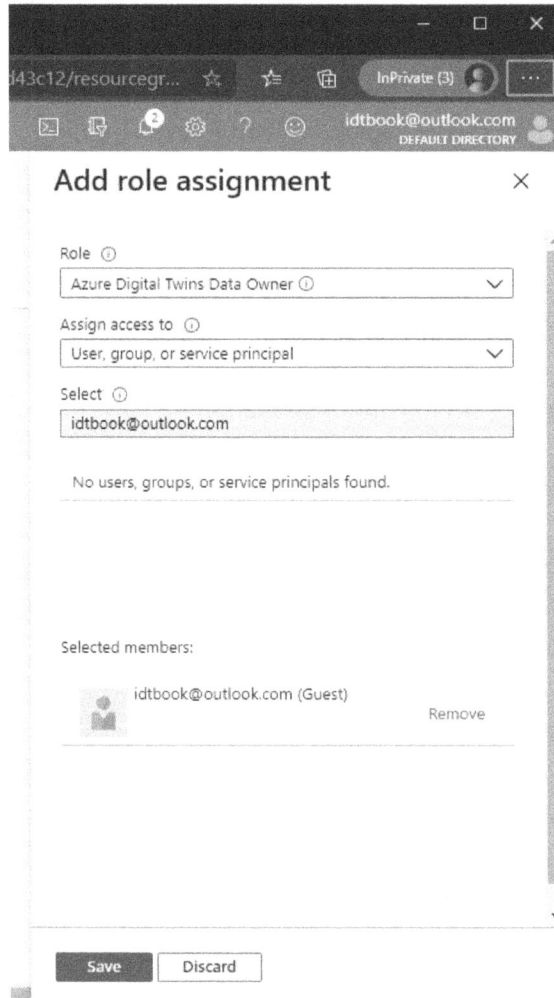

Figure 5.15 – Creating a role assignment for your user in ADT

You have now successfully given your user account access, and this concludes the third step of *Figure 5.8*. Now, have a look at the following screenshot:

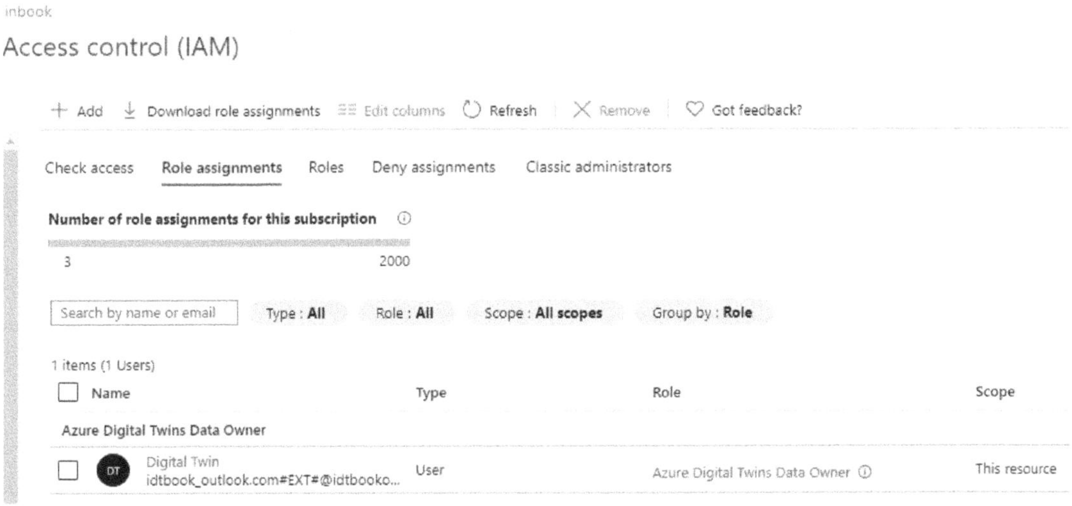

inbook

Access control (IAM)

+ Add   ↓ Download role assignments   ≡≡ Edit columns   ↻ Refresh   ✕ Remove   ♡ Got feedback?

Check access   **Role assignments**   Roles   Deny assignments   Classic administrators

Number of role assignments for this subscription ⓘ

3	2000

| Search by name or email | Type : **All** | Role : **All** | Scope : **All scopes** | Group by : **Role** |

1 items (1 Users)

☐ Name	Type	Role	Scope
Azure Digital Twins Data Owner			
☐ (DT) Digital Twin idtbook_outlook.com#EXT#@idtbooko...	User	Azure Digital Twins Data Owner ⓘ	This resource

Figure 5.16 – User access successfully assigned in ADT

The fourth step in *Figure 5.8* is to create an Azure app that will be able to interact with the digital-twin service.

It is common practice to interact with an ADT instance through an application such as **ADT Explorer** (`http://bit.ly/idt-adtexplorer`) or your own custom application. These applications need to authenticate themselves to the ADT service by using **Azure Active Directory** (**Azure AD**). This means that you need to create an Azure app service in *step 4* of the process in *Figure 5.8*. Once this is complete, the new app servers will be given access and permissions to the Digital Twin, similar to the user access in the previous step.

This is done from the main page of your Azure portal instance or by choosing **Azure Active Directory** from the menu on the left on the screen, as shown in the following screenshot:

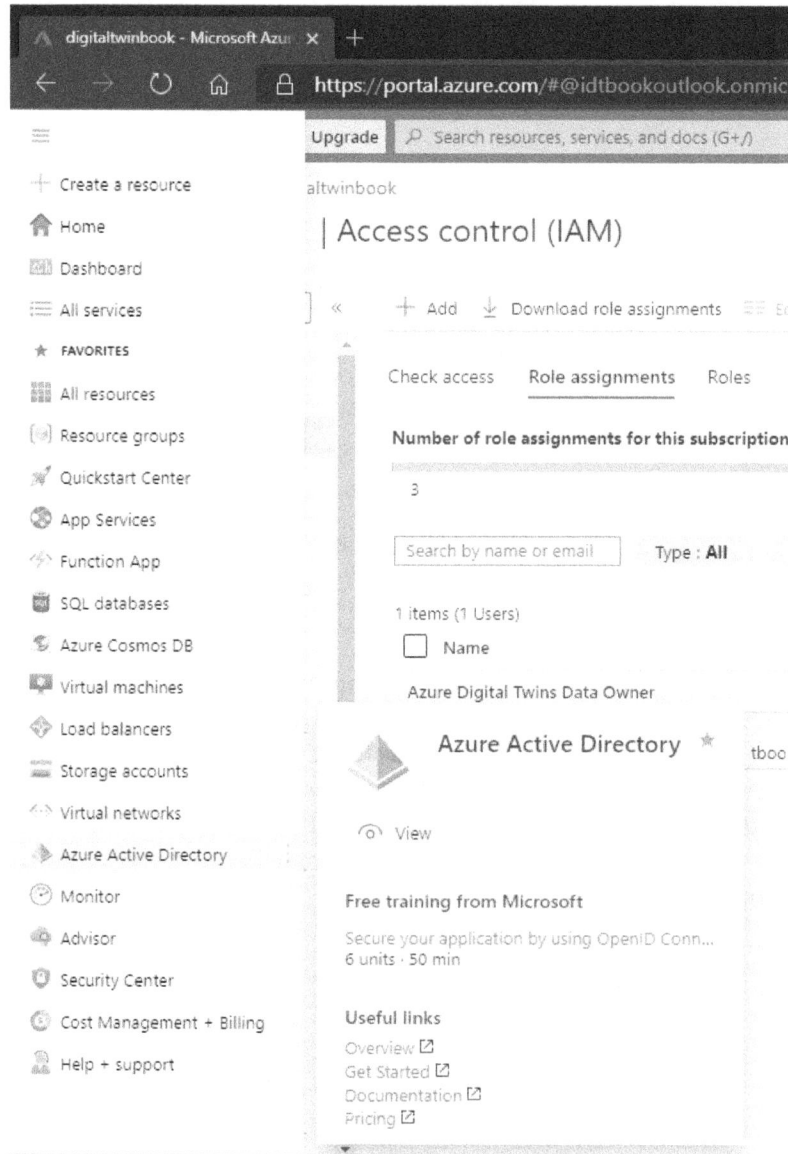

Figure 5.17 – Creating a new Azure AD resource

A screen with app registration options similar to those shown in the following screenshot provides an option to create and manage new applications on Azure. Choose + **New registration** to start the wizard shown in *Figure 5.19*:

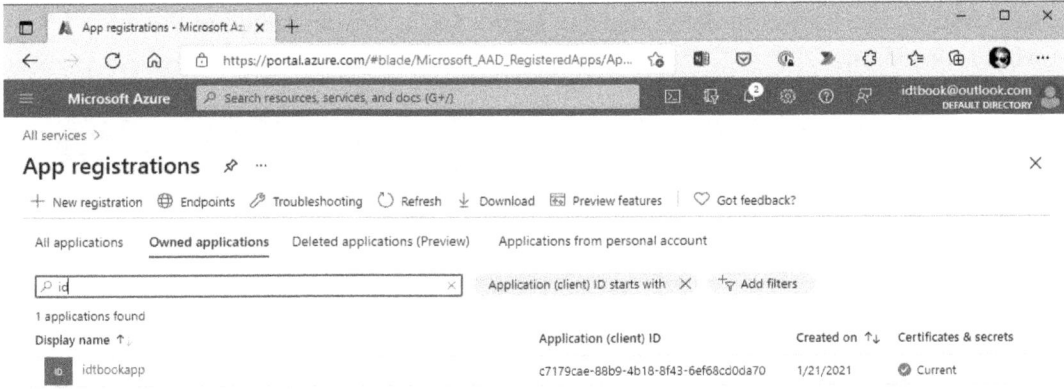

Figure 5.18 – App registrations in Azure AD

Create a recognizable name for your app and continue to register the application with the default settings by clicking on the **Register** button, as illustrated in the following screenshot:

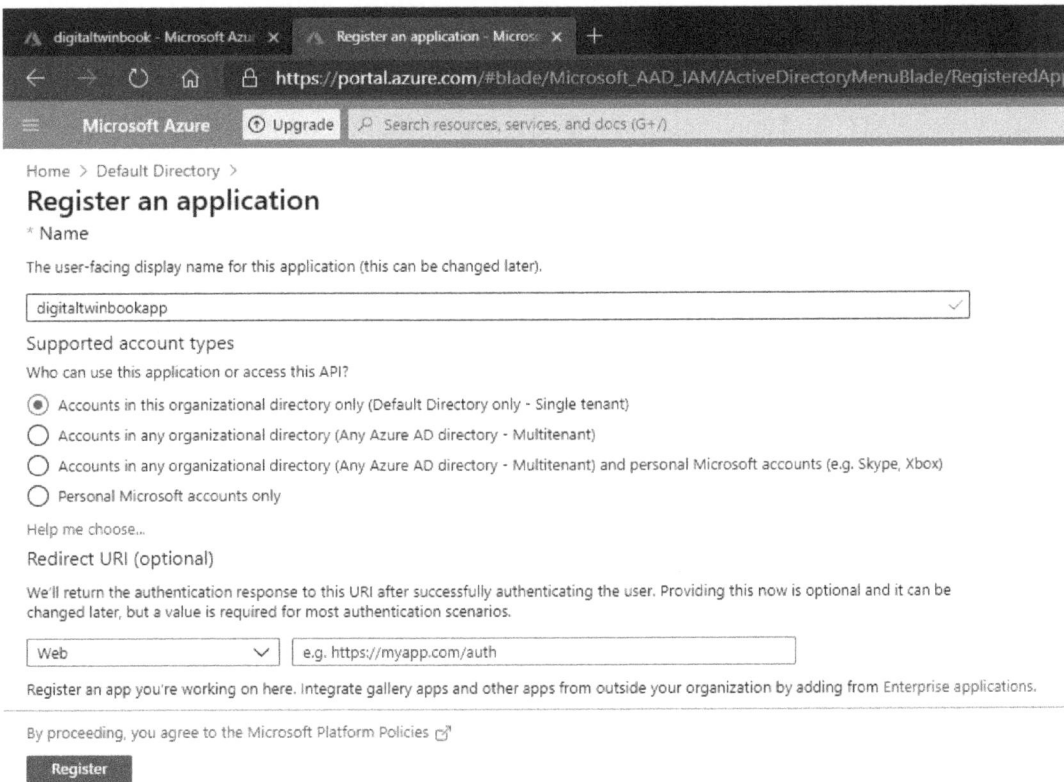

Figure 5.19 – App registration configuration wizard in Azure AD

You have now successfully completed *step 4* in *Figure 5.8*, as demonstrated in the following screenshot:

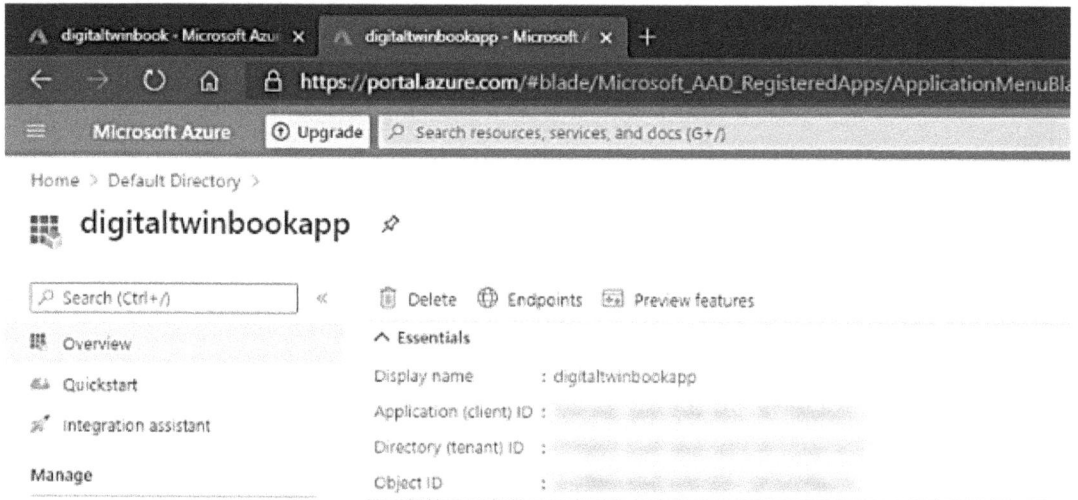

Figure 5.20 – User access successfully assigned in ADT

You now have an ADT and application resource group in your account, similar to that shown in *Figure 5.21*.

The final step in *Figure 5.8* will give your new application resource access to ADT resources. This is similar to the previous step, where we gave you user access. In this instance, we want to give the application the right to read and write information from your ADT resource. We follow a similar approach, but instead of the user account, we will select the new application service that you created, as illustrated in the following screenshot:

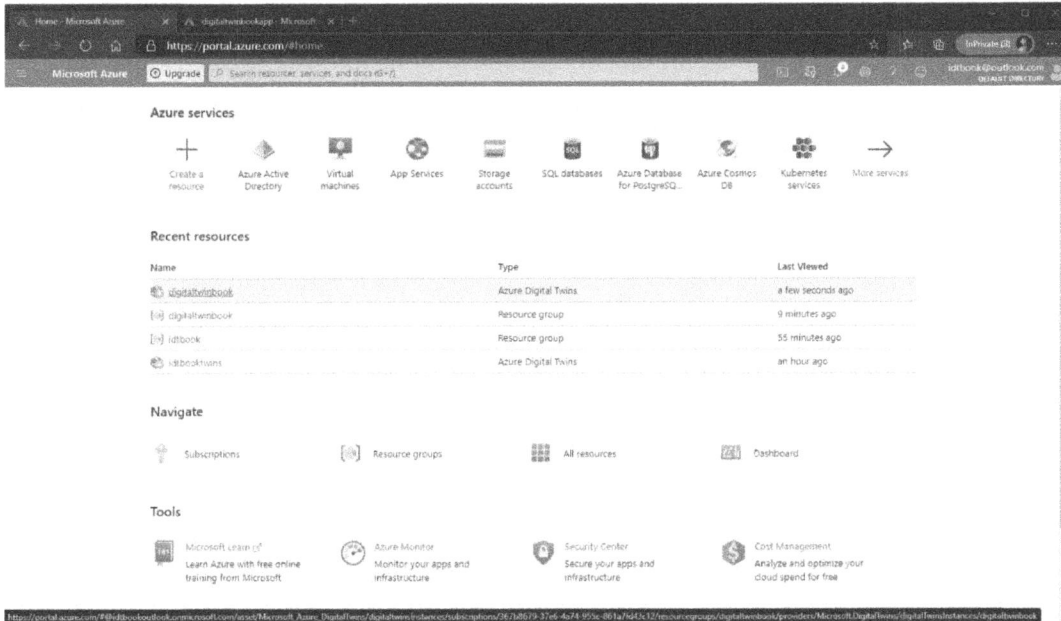

Figure 5.21 – ADT and application resource in your Azure account

Start by clicking on the ADT service on your Azure portal account. In our example, it is the `digitaltwinbook` ADT resource shown in *Figure 5.9*.

Select **Access control (IAM)** from the menu on the left and proceed with the role assignment, similar to *step 3* of *Figure 5.8*, as illustrated in the following screenshot:

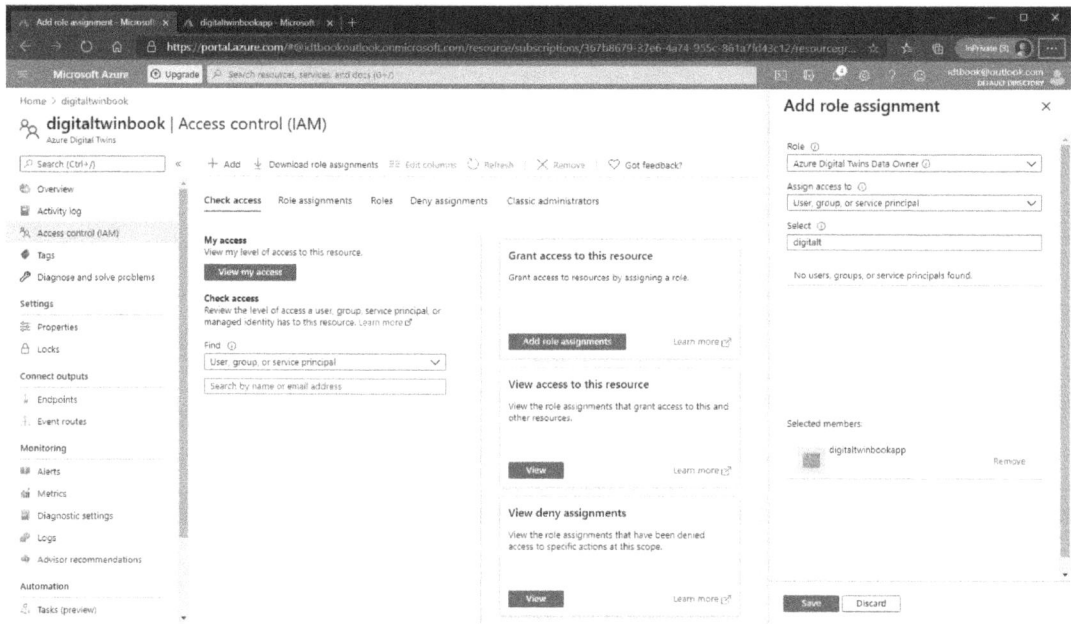

Figure 5.22 – Configuring app access to the ADT resource

We recommend that you assign a data owner role to your application for this application to interact with the digital-twin resource. Select the application instead of your user role in the **Select** dropdown. You may have to type in the name of your application in the search bar if it doesn't appear in the default list.

Check the API permissions of your app to see whether the Microsoft Graph API appears. This API is used by ADT Explorer. If it is visible, this means that you have successfully completed the last step in the configuration of your ADT service process, as illustrated in the following screenshot:

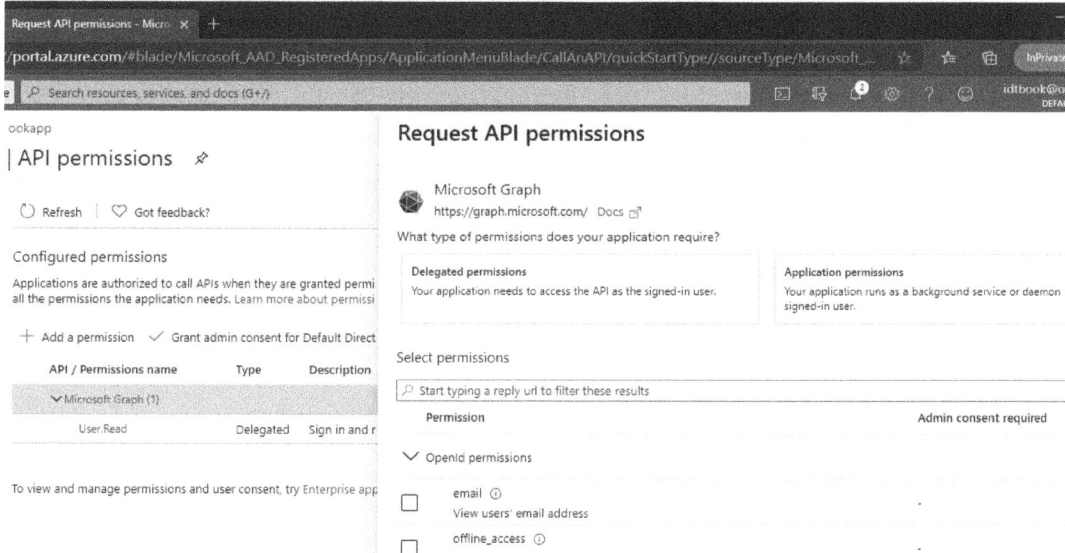

Figure 5.23 – Application access to ADT resource successfully completed

This concludes the configuration of the ADT environment in a free Azure account. We started by creating a free Azure account, creating an ADT resource, and gave our Azure account user access to the ADT service. To interact with our ADT resource, we also created an Azure app with access to the ADT service.

We now have the ability to create our first Digital Twin on the ADT platform. There are, however, two other configuration processes that you may want to follow to install ADT Explorer and Azure TSI.

ADT Explorer is an example application that enables you to view your Digital Twin in a graph-like visualization. ADT Explorer is not an officially supported product by Microsoft at the time of writing the book, even though it is recommended by Microsoft. The sample application as well as source code and installation instructions can be downloaded from GitHub (`http://bit.ly/idt-adtexplorergit`).

The hostname for ADT will be required by ADT Explorer during the configuration to ensure that it is connecting to and visualizing the correct digital-twin service. You will find the **Uniform Resource Locator** (**URL**) in the properties of your ADT service in the Azure portal, as shown in the following screenshot:

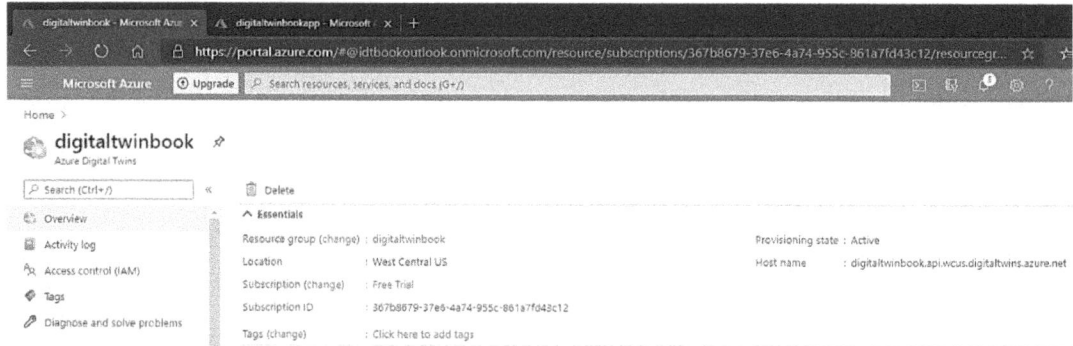

Figure 5.24 – ADT host URL

Configuring Azure TSI is not required at this stage, but it will be used later to store temporal data for our first digital-twin prototype. Installation instructions are available at `http://bit.ly/idt-azuretsi`.

The reasons for using Azure TSI is one of the topics discussed in the next section.

Data considerations for your Azure Digital Twin

In the previous section, *Configuration and setup*, we described the process of setting up the ADT environment that we will use to create our first Digital Twin. ADT provides all the essential services to deploy, configure, and use a Digital Twin, but there are additional considerations around data and processes that require additional capabilities.

The main capabilities of ADT are outlined here:

- An open modeling language to describe all the characteristics and relationships of things or entities
- A live execution environment to deploy this on

ADT collects and stores this data for each instance of an entity and can be depicted as a graph node. It is a snapshot of the data at that point when the ADT entity is created or updated. ADT does not retain any of the historical data for that node on the graph.

Retaining these values for reporting and analysis purposes requires additional storage processes. This can be done through additional Azure services to update Azure SQL, Azure Data Lake, and Azure TSI. These services are not required for the basic configuration of ADT but are practical considerations for deploying and using a Digital Twin in operational use cases.

The nature of the asset and set of problems we want to solve with the Digital Twin will dictate the data elements we would need for building and maintaining the Digital Twin. Let's take the case of a wind turbine. A Digital Twin of a wind turbine can be used to forecast the power generation for certain levels of wind conditions. Likewise, it can also be used to access the physical condition of the wind turbine if it encounters wind blowing harder than expected for a sustained period. For such scenarios, the wind speed, wind gust, temperature, humidity, and related data elements would have to be recorded and used for the Digital Twin. The granularity or how often these data elements are captured would depend on the nature of the parameter—for instance, the wind speed would have to be recorded more frequently than the temperature or humidity in the atmosphere. The previous readings were external to the wind turbine. However, for health monitoring and predictive maintenance of the wind turbine, we will have to collect internal motor temperature, as well as parameters such as viscosity and particulate levels of the oil in the gearbox.

We may often have to deal with the availability and quality of required data for building and maintaining a Digital Twin. The security and compliance requirements at the enterprise might make the data inaccessible, in some cases. This is also tied to the ownership of the data. For instance, in the case of the wind turbine, the company that manufactures the wind turbine has access to the data during the assembly of the wind turbines and any "lab testing" such as physical inspection or **non-destructive** (**NDT**) testing. However, it may not have full access to the supplier parts. Likewise, once the wind turbine is shipped to the owner or the wind farm operator and is in use, the manufacturer may not have any or full rights to the data generated by the operations of the wind turbine.

The analytics system of the digital-twin platform must account for the variability of the data elements available, once the wind turbine is operating in the field. The analytics orchestrations used with the digital-twin data can have rules to handle such scenarios— for instance, if wind turbine data is taken from model A, then substitute vibration by 5 **hertz** (**Hz**) to account for no vibration sensors in model A. In some cases, the operator of the wind turbine may decide not to share certain data elements for privacy or local compliance reasons.

We will highlight the use of different types of data stores for the wind turbine in future chapters as we address the deployment, testing, and evaluation of our first digital-twin prototype. We will further include this in the high-level solution architecture described in the next section.

Solution architecture

Let's look at the high-level solution architecture in this section. In general, the solution architecture provides a reference architecture to solve a given set of business problems. It helps to drive the overall technical vision during the implementation stages. The following diagram shows our business problem statement visually. Our goal is to provide a solution architecture for this problem statement:

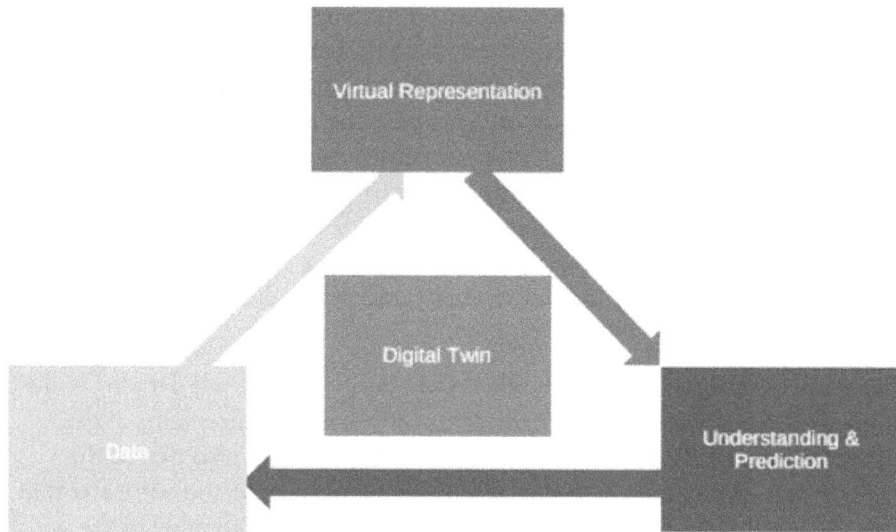

Figure 5.25 – Business problem for the Digital Twin

> **Note**
>
> Image source: Technology Media Telecommunications (TMT), GeoActive Group: `https://blog.geoactivegroup.com/2020/07/digital-twin-apps-in-industrial-markets.html`

We distill the business problem down to the next level, as we evolve the solution architecture, in the following screenshot:

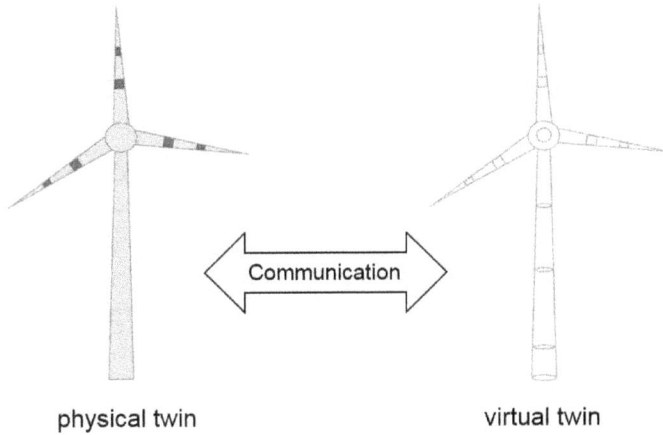

physical twin   virtual twin

Figure 5.26 – Distilling the business problem to evolve the solution architecture

> **Note**
>
> Image source: `http://dx.doi.org/10.18775/iji`
> `ed.1849-7551-7020.2015.52.2006`

As we continue to evolve the solution architecture, we evaluate and make a technology decision. We decided to use ADT as part of our technical solution. In the following screenshot, we show how ADT may fit in a broader enterprise solution architecture:

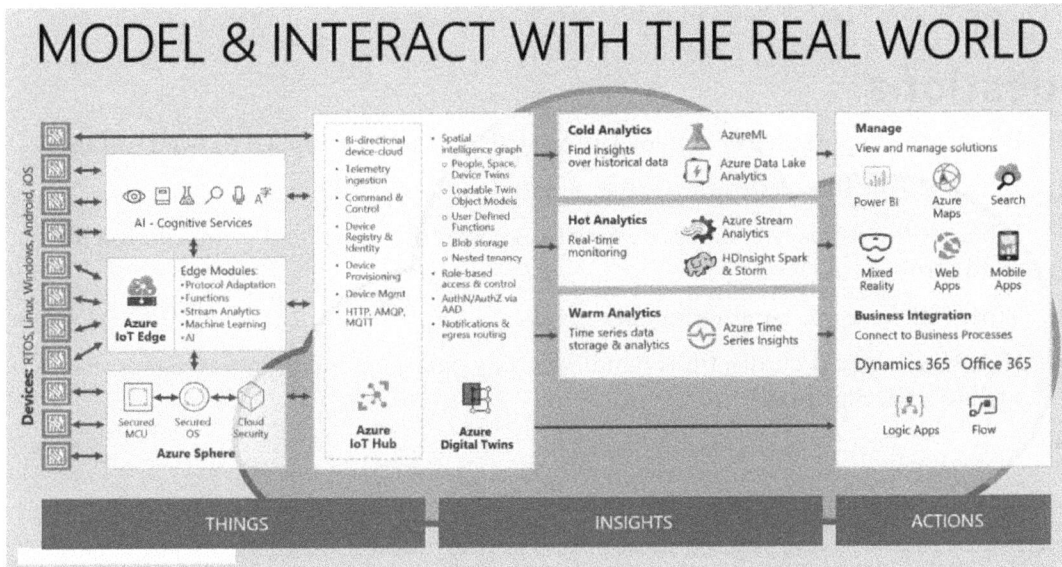

Figure 5.27 – Evolving the solution architecture using Microsoft ADT

> **Note**
>
> Image source: `https://schwabencode.com/blog/2020/03/10/Device-Twins-vs-Digital-Twins-Azure-IoT`

In the next few chapters, we will continue to refine the solution architecture to our specific scenario. Such solution architectures are key to maintain and evolve a full digital-twin solution over its lifetime as it is handed over to future technical and techno-functional experts. Likewise, when a digital-twin solution is sold to external customers, such a solution architecture allows the setup of a customer's instance of the solution that can be further refined in the context of the customer's enterprise landscape.

Summary

In this chapter, we considered the perspective of a global industrial manufacturer of wind turbines. We then described considerations for evaluating and selecting the right platform for setting up and building a Digital Twin. We narrowed it down to Microsoft ADT as the selected platform for the purposes of this book. This got us started to set up the configurations on ADT for our first Digital Twin.

In *Chapter 6*, *Building the Digital Twin Prototype*, we will start implementing the digital-twin prototype in our selected digital-twin platform for wind turbines using ADT. We will further consider practical constraints during the implementation process of the Digital Twin.

Questions

1. What is the importance of a predictive twin? How can it be applied to wind turbines?
2. Why do many IoT platforms use the public cloud?
3. What are the primary business outcomes expected from a digital-twin solution for wind turbines?
4. What is the use of a time series data store?
5. How do analytic orchestrations handle missing data elements from certain assets such as a wind turbine?

6
Building the Digital Twin Prototype

In *Chapter 5, Setting up a Digital Twin Prototype*, we discussed the enablers for building the prototype of the Digital Twin. We looked at the required capabilities of the Digital Twin that can be met by the public cloud and IoT platforms, as the underlying technologies. We further investigated Digital Twin platforms and looked at the configuration and setup details. We discussed the data considerations and the overall solution architecture for the Digital Twin.

In this chapter, we will investigate the development process of the Digital Twin prototype of the identified industrial asset, which is a wind turbine and a fleet of turbines at a wind farm.

Figure 6.1 shows the conceptual view of the Digital Twin of a wind turbine, from the perspective of an industrial user, who will be the beneficiary of the twin.

Figure 6.1 – A conceptual view of the Digital Twin of wind turbines

> **Note**
>
> Image source: Digitalisation in power generation driving performance.
> Available at: `https://www.powerengineeringint.com/`
> `digitalization/digitalisation-in-power-generation-`
> `driving-performance/`

We will cover the following topics in this chapter:

- Development process of our Digital Twin
- Testing framework
- Technical evaluation considerations
- Business validation and understanding

Let's begin with a detailed discussion on the development process for the digital twin prototype.

Technical requirements

In this chapter, we will configure your first Digital Twin prototype. There are sample JSON-based DTDL files for the wind farm example that we use. You can find the code files for this chapter on GitHub at `https://github.com/PacktPublishing/Building-Industrial-Digital-Twin`.

Development process of our Digital Twin

Let's explore the development process of the Digital Twin. This will ensure that we have the skills to undertake such development.

Wind turbine as our Digital Twin prototype

We will use a wind farm as the example of our first Digital Twin prototype. We will focus on a simple model of a wind farm here. Our primary goal is to show how to create the first Digital Twin of the wind turbine in the book, rather than help build expertise on wind turbines or the renewables industry. We will create Digital Twin models and instances for each physical turbine in the wind farm. The Digital Twin models represent the basic elements of a wind turbine, and it is sufficient to address different use cases from a business value point of view.

The perspective for the wind farm and wind turbine Digital Twin is that of a wind turbine manufacturer who is also contracted by the operator to maintain the wind turbines to agreed service levels. Our use case for the Digital Twin in this chapter is limited to the maintenance and operations phases of the wind turbines, as described in *Chapter 1, Introduction to Digital Twin*. In practice, the models will cover the overall life cycle, which includes the design, manufacturing, and commissioning phases of the wind farm and the wind turbines.

The primary use case for the wind turbine Digital Twin in this chapter is a manufacturer that performs predictive maintenance services on its wind turbines while they are with the owner/operator of the asset. The manufacturers have a field service crew that proactively needs to go to the right wind turbine at the right wind farm and perform the right maintenance to prevent the wind turbine from failing, leading to unscheduled downtime or operating at a reduced level of efficiency.

The manufacturer wants to ensure a high first-time fix rate, reduce the number of truck rolls, and limit the field spares that are carried on the service vehicles. In this context, "truck roll" refers to the scenarios where a field service technician for the wind turbine has to be dispatched in their service vehicle, which is often a truck, to a wind farm to carry out services such as installation, reconfiguration, troubleshooting, repairs, or any other form of scheduled maintenance activity. The focus of the Digital Twin prototype in this chapter is an onshore wind farm, as it is more complex and expensive to do this for an offshore installation.

Better management of the wind turbine service activities will improve the yield of the wind farm, leading to a higher level of power generation with increased reliability. It will improve customer satisfaction and reduce the cost of maintenance, with fewer truck rolls. It will further reduce the working capital that is tied up in inventory on the service trucks. These are all key **Value at Stake** measures for a manufacturer who also maintains the assets in operation.

Before we start configuring the wind farm and wind turbines in the Azure Digital Twins instance that we set up in *Chapter 5, Setting up a Digital Twin Prototype*, we will look at wind turbines, their components, and the data that we want to collect to address the needs of our maintenance and operations use cases.

Basics of a wind turbine and a high-level data model

Wind turbines are low-cost producers of renewable electrical energy that convert the wind's kinetic power to electricity. It is regarded as a "clean" energy resource as it uses very little water, it emits no greenhouse gases, and there are no waste products from the generation process.

Figure 6.2 – Wind turbines in southern California, USA

Wind turbines are relatively simple to construct, but wind farms can contain many turbines. This makes it an ideal candidate for our first Digital Twin prototype.

The most common type of wind turbine is configured with a horizontal axis, but turbines can also have a vertical access configuration. Wind turbines are further classified based on their installation. Land-based turbines are classified as onshore, while offshore wind turbines can be deployed miles away in the ocean. Offshore wind turbines have the added complexity of remote access both from a connectivity and a physical access of the field service crew perspective. The offshore wind turbines have to additionally deal with corrosion due to seawater. (See `https://www.materialsperformance.` `com/articles/material-selection-design/2016/03/corrosion-` `risks-and-mitigation-strategies-for-offshore-wind-turbine-` `foundations`.)

We will use an onshore, horizontal-axis wind turbine with a typical three-blade configuration to simplify our first Digital Twin. *Figure 6.3* shows the high-level components of a horizontal-axis wind turbine. We will primarily focus on the overall wind turbine performance, as well as the motor, gearbox, and generator units of the asset. To detect or prevent equipment failure, our maintenance Digital Twin will monitor real-time data from these components. You can extend the Digital Twin with additional models at a later stage to include other components, such as the pitch system, controller, and nacelle.

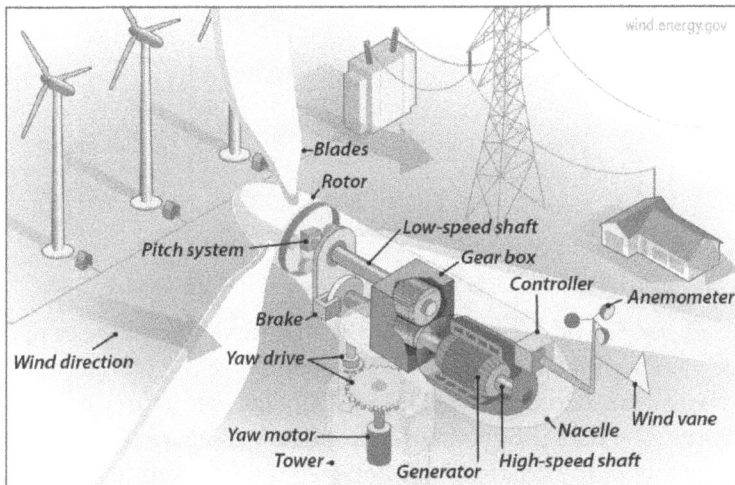

Figure 6.3 – Inside a typical wind turbine

> **Note**
>
> Image source: US Department of Energy: `https://www.energy.gov/eere/wind/inside-wind-turbine`

The Digital Twin model will represent the data elements that we want to store for each instance of a wind turbine in the wind farm. The wind turbine model will also include sub-models that describe the data for the motor, gearbox, and generator. We need to distinguish between the different data types as properties, and the telemetry data that we will receive from the sensors on the wind turbines.

The data model that we use for our first Digital Twin contains all the basic elements to describe the wind farm, wind turbines, and telemetry data.

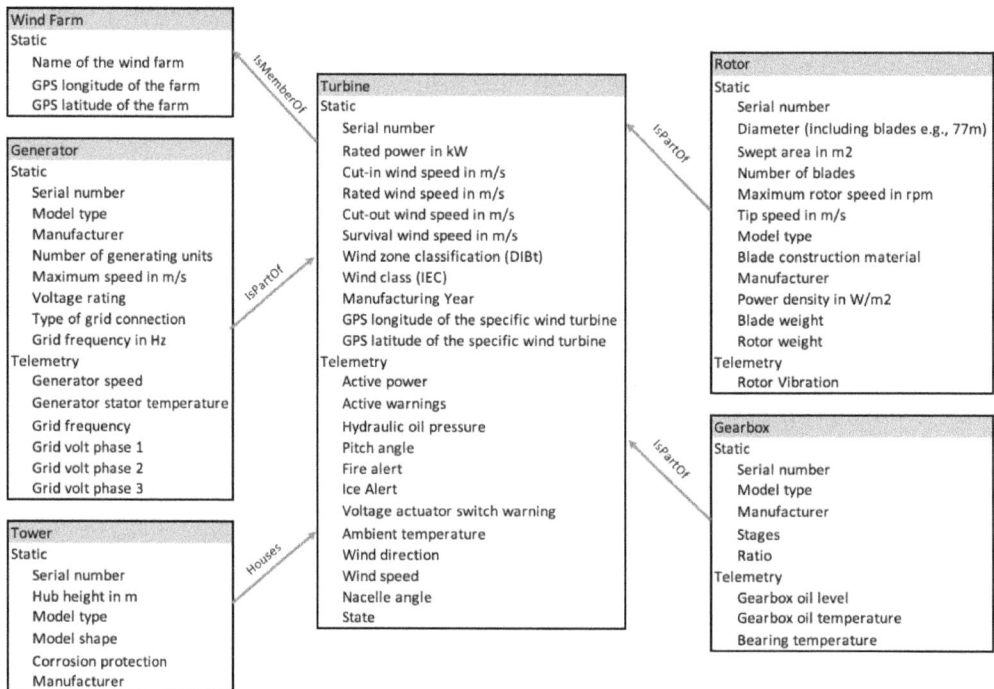

Figure 6.4 – Simple data model for our wind turbine solution

This data model in *Figure 6.4* will be enough for the maintenance use cases in our first Digital Twin of the wind turbine. The next step is to configure the models and sub-models as **Digital Twins Definition Language (DTDL)** JSON files before they can be uploaded to Azure Digital Twins. The data model that we described in *Figure 6.4* contains all the data elements but not any of the relationships between the different models. One of the main reasons for using graph-based Digital Twin services such as Azure Digital Twins is to capture non-hierarchical relationships that may exist between assets.

An example of a hierarchical relationship is that of the wind turbine, which is located at a specific wind farm, and the turbine, which consists of a gearbox, rotor, and generator. There are, however, other non-hierarchical relationships between Digital Twins. An example of this is the proximity of different wind turbines to each other. One of the relationships may be NextTo, which can capture that wind turbine #789 is located next to wind turbine #248.

These relationships and specific characteristics are described in ontologies. The ontology provides the structure for describing categories, properties, and relationships.

In the next section, we will describe how to set up an ontology for our first wind turbine Digital Twin with the corresponding DTDL.

Using an ontology to define Digital Twin models

Figure 6.5 describes the basic steps to create an Azure Digital Twins-based example for the wind turbine prototype.

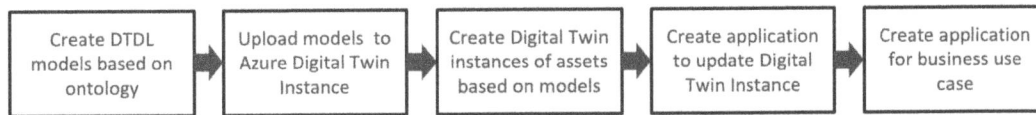

| Create DTDL models based on ontology | Upload models to Azure Digital Twin Instance | Create Digital Twin instances of assets based on models | Create application to update Digital Twin Instance | Create application for business use case |

Figure 6.5 – Process to create and use a Digital Twin

The first step is to create the DTDL models in JSON format that also describe the relationships that are available between the different models and sub-models. The use of DTDL will allow the developers of Digital Twins to describe them in terms of the telemetry or data elements generated by the asset twin, their properties, and the commands they respond to. Overall, DTDL will facilitate the description of the relationship between the twins. This will lead to interoperability of twins from different domains. For instance, a wind farm will interact with energy grids, in the big picture.

These models will then be uploaded to our Azure Digital Twins instance using the **Azure Digital Twins (ADT)** Explorer application. In the third step, we will also use the ADT Explorer to create instances of physical assets based on the models that are now available on the Azure Digital Twins platform. This can be quite a cumbersome and manual process and is not ideal for large-scale deployments. In a production environment, the automation of these activities will be done in your custom digital application or in a third-party solution. In the fourth step, we will demonstrate how to upload information for additional turbine instances in a custom application. In the final step, we will look at how to retrieve the Azure Digital Twins information for our maintenance use case.

The first step is to create our DTDL models based on an ontology and the specific structure of the model file in DTDL, which in turn is based on the **Resource Description Framework** (**RDF**). The RDF nature of DTDL was covered in *Chapter 4, Getting Started with Our First Digital Twin*. There are no specific requirements for the structure of the ontology, but it is recommended that you follow the guidance of *Digital Twins Definition Language-based RealEstateCore ontology for smart buildings* (http://bit.ly/idt-buildingontology), an open source initiative by Microsoft for creating Digital Twins. It provides a very comprehensive description of the ontology and is highly recommended if you want to create more advanced Digital Twin ontologies.

Figure 6.6 provides the proposed simple ontology that we will use for our first wind turbine Digital Twin.

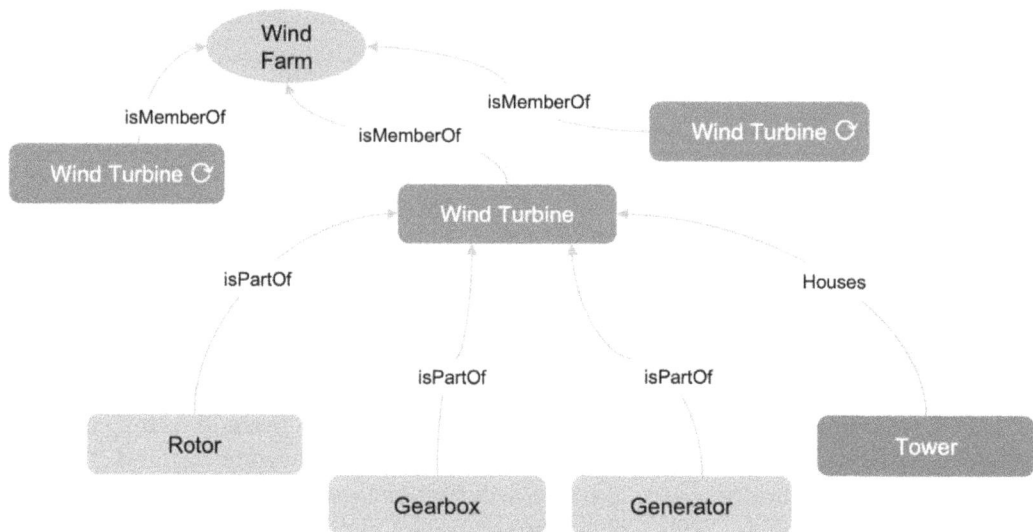

Figure 6.6 – Proposed wind farm and wind turbine Digital Twin

This shows that the wind turbines are "members of" the wind farm. The rotors, gearboxes, generators, and towers are, in turn, "part of" the wind turbine. This is a very basic structure and there are alternative ways of representing this. We will, however, keep it simple for the purpose of configuring our first Digital Twin.

Now that we understand the different relationships between the various models, we can proceed to create those models in DTDL format. Microsoft provides extensive open source DTDL documentation (`https://bit.ly/idt-azuredocs`) for the six metamodel classes that describe the following Digital Twin behaviors:

- **Interface**: Describes the contents (properties, telemetries, commands, relationships, or components)

- **Telemetry**: Describes the data emitted by any Digital Twin that is typically from sensors and synchronized at regular, short intervals

- **Property**: Describes the read-only and read/write state of any Digital Twin, such as the serial number of a component

- **Command**: Describes a function or operation that can be performed on any Digital Twin

- **Relationship**: Describes a link to another Digital Twin and enables graphs of Digital Twins to be created

- **Component**: Enables interfaces to be composed of other interfaces

An example for DTDL for the wind farm is as follows:

```
{
    "@id":"dtmi:com:idtbook:wt:farm;1",
    "@type":"Interface",
    "@context":[
        "dtmi:dtdl:context;2"
    ],
    "displayName":"WT Farm",
    "description":"Wind farm with wind turbines",
    "contents":[
        {
            "@type": "Property",
            "name": "Name",
            "schema": "string"
        },
        {
            "@type": "Property",
```

```
      "name": "GPSLongitude",
      "schema": "double"
   },
   {
      "@type": "Property",
      "name": "GPSLatitude",
      "schema": "double"
   }
 ]
}
```

This is an example of an interface file that does not have any telemetry or relationship data. The typical structure of an interface file is described in *Figure 6.7* and is fully documented at `http://bit.ly/idt-dtdl2`.

Property	Required	Data type	Limits	Description
@id	required	DTMI	max 128 chars	A digital twin model identifier for the interface
@type	required	IRI		This must be "Interface"
@context	required (at least once in the doc)	IRI		The context to use when processing this interface. For this version, it must be set to "dtmi:dtdl:context;2"
comment	optional	string	1-512 chars	A comment for model authors
contents	optional	set of Telemetry, Properties, Commands, Relationships, Components	max 300 contents	A set of objects that define the contents (Telemetry, Properties, Commands, Relationships, and/or Components) of this interface
description	optional	string	1-512 chars	A localizable description for display
displayName	optional	string	1-64 chars	A localizable name for display
extends	optional	set of Interfaces	up to 2 interfaces per extends; max depth of 10 levels	A set of DTMIs that refer to interfaces this interface inherits from. Interfaces can inherit from multiple interfaces.
schemas	optional	set of interface schemas		A set of IRIs or objects that refer to the reusable schemas within this interface.

Figure 6.7 – Structure of an interface file

Microsoft provides a DTDL extension for Visual Studio and the free version of Visual Studio Code (`http://bit.ly/idt-vscodedtdl`).

```
                                   Turbine.json

{} Farm.json      {} Turbine.json ●   {} Rotor.json    {} Gearbox.json    {} Generator.json    {} Tower.json            [] ...

Users > pvs > Downloads > DtdlsWindTurbine > {} Turbine.json > [ ] contents > {} 1
    1    {
    2        "@id":"dtmi:com:idtbook:wt:turbine;1",
    3        "@type":"Interface",
    4        "@context":[
    5            "dtmi:dtdl:context;2"
    6        ],
    7        "displayName":"WT Turbine",
    8        "description":"-",
    9        "contents": [
   10            {
   11                "@type": "Property",
   12                "name": "SerialNo",
   13                "schema": "string"
   14            },
   15            {
   16                "@type": "Property",
   17                "name": "RatedPower",
   18                "schema": "double"
   19            },
   20            {
   21                "@type": "Property",
   22                "name": "FlexPower",
   23                "schema": "double"
   24            },
   25            {
   26                "@type": "Property",
   27                "name": "RatedWindSpeed",
   28                "schema": "double"
   29            },
   30            {
   31                "@type": "Property",
   32                "name": "CutOutWindSpeed",
   33                "schema": "double"
   34            },
   35            {
   36                "@type": "Property",
   37                "name": "SurvivalWindSpeed",
   38                "schema": "double"
   39            },
   40            {

⊗ 0 ⚠ 0                                       Ln 17, Col 28   Spaces: 2   UTF-8   CRLF   JSON  ⚑ ⌀
```

Figure 6.8 – DTDL extension for Visual Studio Code with IntelliSense

The extension provides the ability to create DTDL interfaces from templates. It supports IntelliSense and auto-completion and will validate the syntax of your DTDL file. *Figure 6.8* shows the wind turbine DDL file with IntelliSense and syntax checking.

The DTDL model, in JSON format, for the wind turbine includes additional metamodel classes for telemetry and relationships. It also describes all the data model elements for the turbine that we defined in the *Basics of a wind turbine and a high-level data model* section:

```
{
    "@id":"dtmi:com:idtbook:wt:turbine;1",
    "@type":"Interface",
    "@context":[
       "dtmi:dtdl:context;2"
    ],
    "displayName":"WT Turbine",
    "description":"-",
    "contents": [
      {
         "@type": "Property",
         "name": "SerialNo",
         "schema": "string"
      },
      {
         "@type": "Property",
         "name": "RatedPower",
         "schema": "double"
      },
      . . . (See Github for full json files)
      {
         "@type": "Telemetry",
         "name": "Windspeed",
         "schema": "double"
      },
      {
         "@type": "Telemetry",
         "name": "NacelleAngle",
         "schema": "double"
      },
      {
         "@type": "Telemetry",
         "name": "State",
```

```
      "schema": "string"
    },
    {
      "@type": "Relationship",
      "name": "isMemberOf",
      "displayName": "MemberOf",
      "minMultiplicity": 0,
      "maxMultiplicity": 1,
      "target":  "dtmi:com:idtbook:wt:farm;1"
    }
  ]
}
```

The sub-model for the generator, in turn, contains the relationship with the turbine model, as shown in *Figure 6.4*:

```
{
    "@id":"dtmi:com:idtbook:wt:gearbox;1",
    "@type":"Interface",
    "@context":[
      "dtmi:dtdl:context;2"
    ],
    "displayName":"WT Gearbox",
    "description":"-",
    "contents": [
     {
      "@type": "Property",
      "name": "GearboxSerial",
      "schema": "string"
     },
     . . . (See Github for full json files)
     {
      "@type": "Relationship",
      "name": "isPartOf",
      "displayName": "PartOf",
      "minMultiplicity": 0,
      "maxMultiplicity": 1,
```

```
            "target":  "dtmi:com:idtbook:wt:turbine;1"
        }
    ]
}
```

The DTDL JSON files for the wind farm, turbine, and its components are available
to download in the GitHub repository for the book at `https://github.com/`
`PacktPublishing/Building-Industrial-Digital-Twin`.

It includes the following files:

- `Farm.json`

- `Turbine.json`

- `Rotor.json`

- `Gearbox.json`

- `Generator.json`

- `Tower.json`

In the next section, we will upload the model files to our Azure Digital Twins instance
using the Azure Digital Twins Explorer application.

Uploading models to the Azure Digital Twins instance

In *Chapter 5, Setting Up a Digital Twin Prototype*, we configured the Azure Digital Twins
service and suggested that you set up Azure Digital Twins Explorer. ADT Explorer is
an application that enables you to view your Digital Twin in a graph visualization. ADT
Explorer is not an officially supported product by Microsoft at the time of writing, even
though it is supported by Microsoft as open source. It is not recommended for large-
scale deployments but provides the basic capabilities that we require to build our first
Digital Twin. The sample application, source code, and installation instructions can be
downloaded from GitHub (`http://bit.ly/idt-adtexplorergit`).

Log in to your free Azure service that you configured in *Chapter 5, Setting Up a Digital Twin Prototype*, before starting the ADT Explorer application.

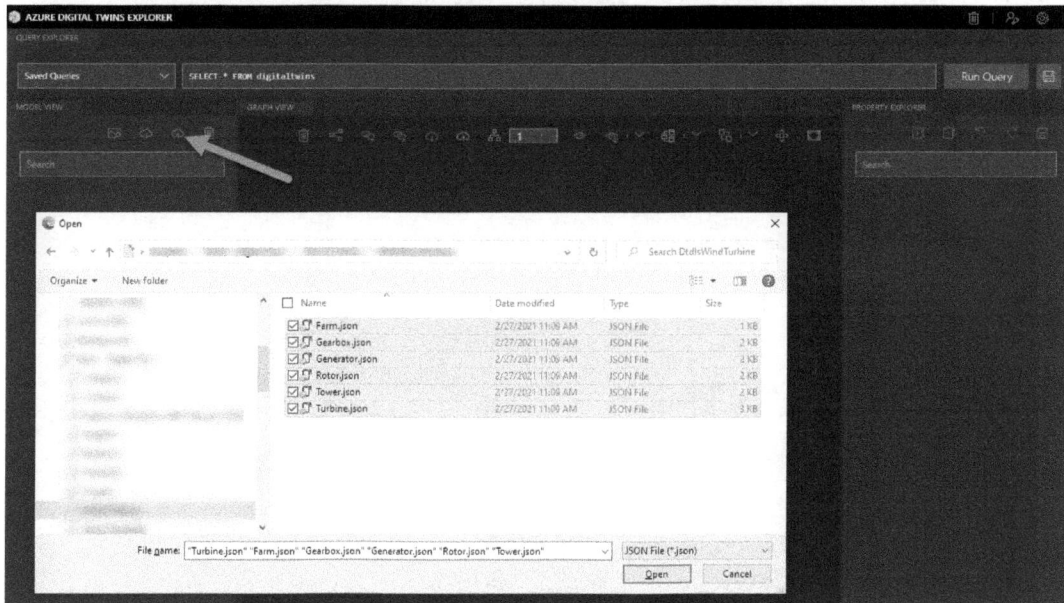

Figure 6.9 – Upload DTDL JSON files with Azure Digital Twins Explorer

Select all the wind farm and wind turbine models and sub-models and upload them to ADT Explorer, as shown in *Figure 6.9*. This will create the model files in your Azure Digital Twins service that you configured in *Chapter 5, Setting Up a Digital Twin Prototype*.

The models are now available in the model repository on the left, as shown in *Figure 6.10*.

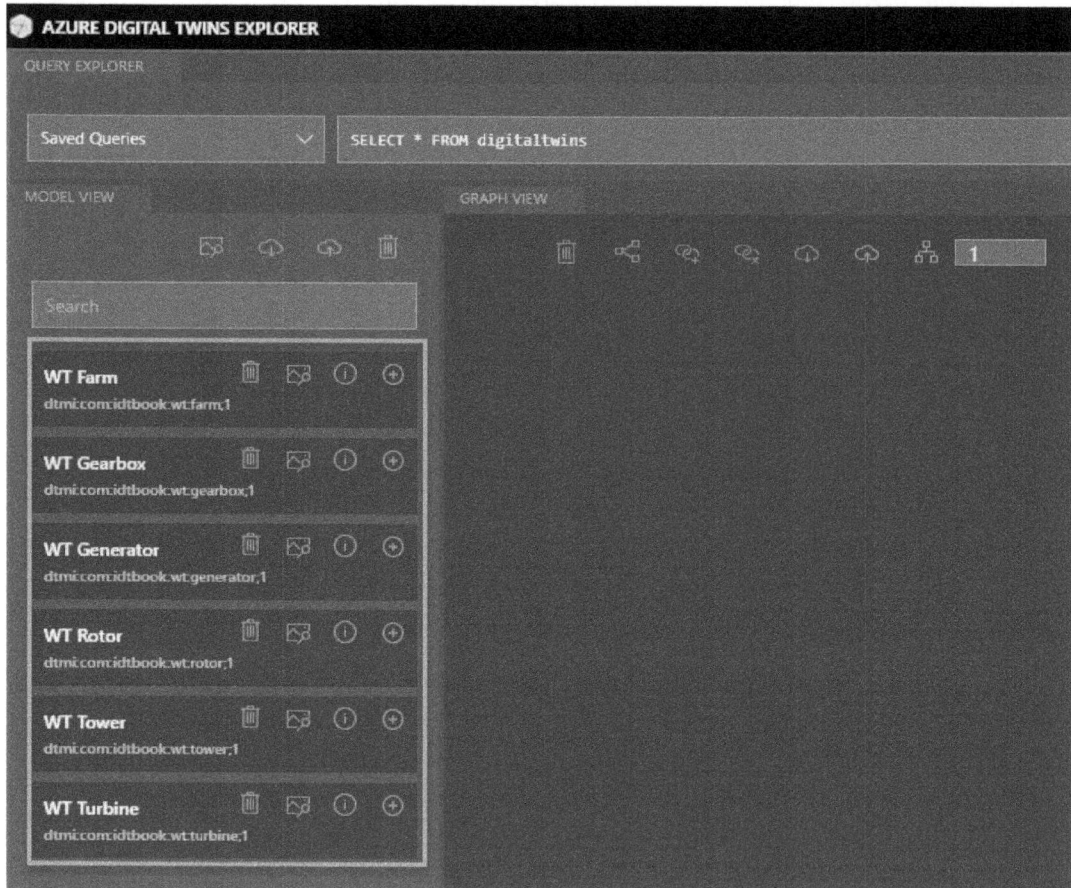

Figure 6.10 – DTDL models available for use in Azure Digital Twins

The next step in the configuration of our first Digital Twin, as shown in *Figure 6.11*, is to create Digital Twin instances for our physical wind turbines. These instances will each be based on the Digital Twin models that we now have in the Azure Digital Twins service.

Configuring Digital Twin instances for the wind farms and turbines

A wind farm can contain hundreds and even thousands of wind turbines. The Jiuquan Wind Power Base in China has about 7,000 wind turbines (see `https://www.power-technology.com/features/feature-biggest-wind-farms-in-the-world-texas`).

One of the primary benefits of the Digital Twin software design approach is the ability to have a single Digital Twin model and several thousand Digital Twin instances. A change to the attributes in the model will make the attribute available to all the thousands of applicable instances. Digital twin applications can be developed to address specific business needs based on the information architecture in the Digital Twin model.

To create the first wind farm Digital Twin instance, select the + button next to the **WT Farm** model (see *Figure 6.11*) and proceed to give the instance a unique name. This name will be the unique identifier or ID for the instance of the physical twin and cannot be changed later. This can be a serial number, an asset number, or any unique descriptor. For the purpose of the book, we will use `windfarm1` as the unique name.

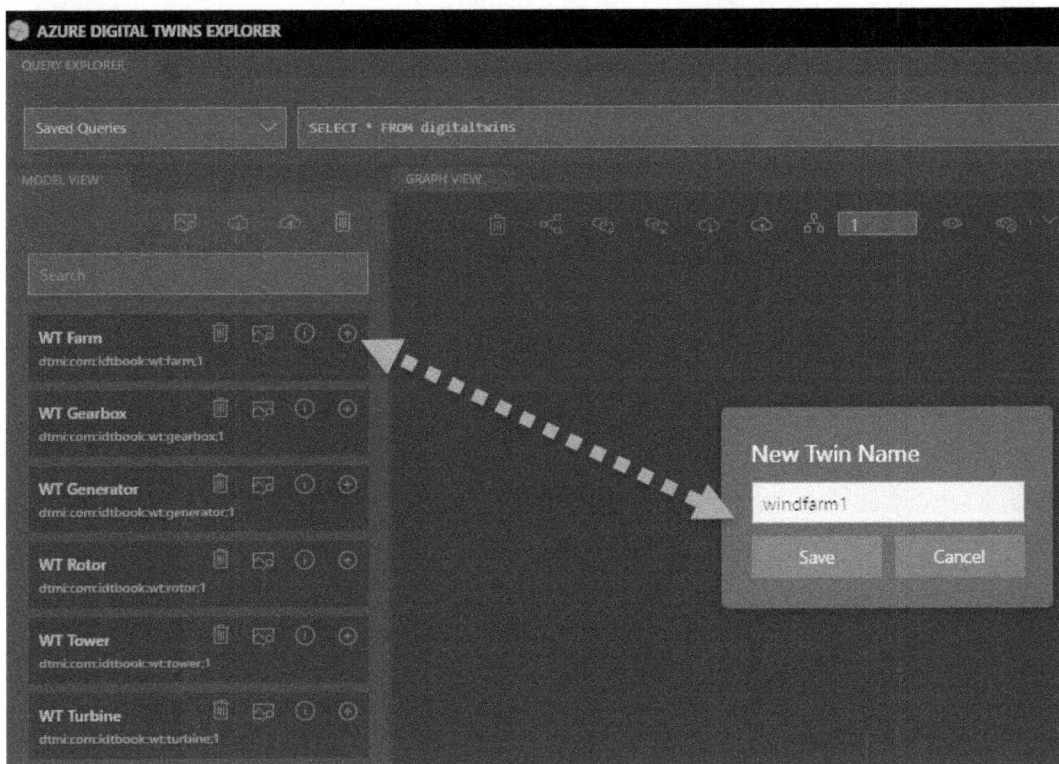

Figure 6.11 – Create a unique instance for a specific wind farm

Save the twin name, and the first instance of a wind farm will be created based on the wind farm DTDL model and the unique `windfarm1` ID.

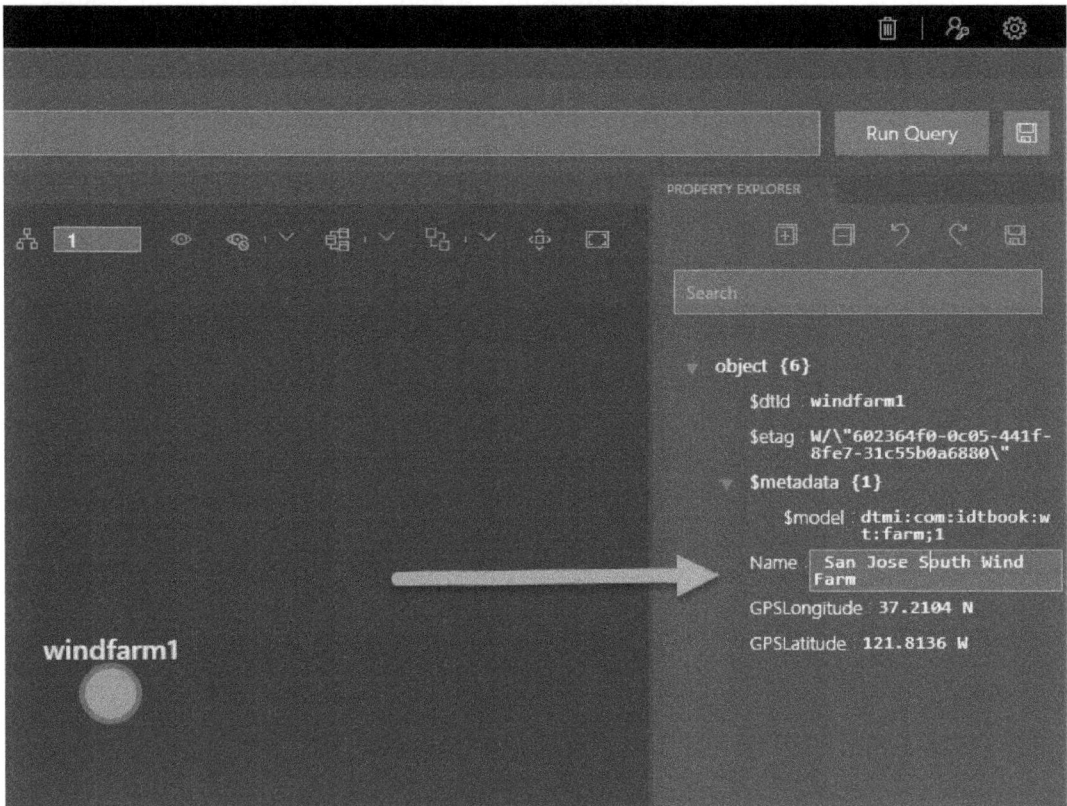

Figure 6.12 – Update instance-specific Digital Twin values

You can edit the properties and edit the information for this instance in the right-hand property explorer pane, as shown in *Figure 6.12*. This will update the instance with that value in the field. We can update the name of `windfarm1` to `San Jose South Wind Farm`. The `$dtid` ID will remain unique and cannot be edited, but the values of the properties can be changed through ADT Explorer. `$dtid` is the instance ID, like the primary key in a relational database table.

Next, we proceed to create a wind turbine instance in a similar process for the WT Turbine model and update the specific instance data. When we have the instances for both the wind farm and the first turbine, we can proceed to link these instances with the relationship option in the top bar.

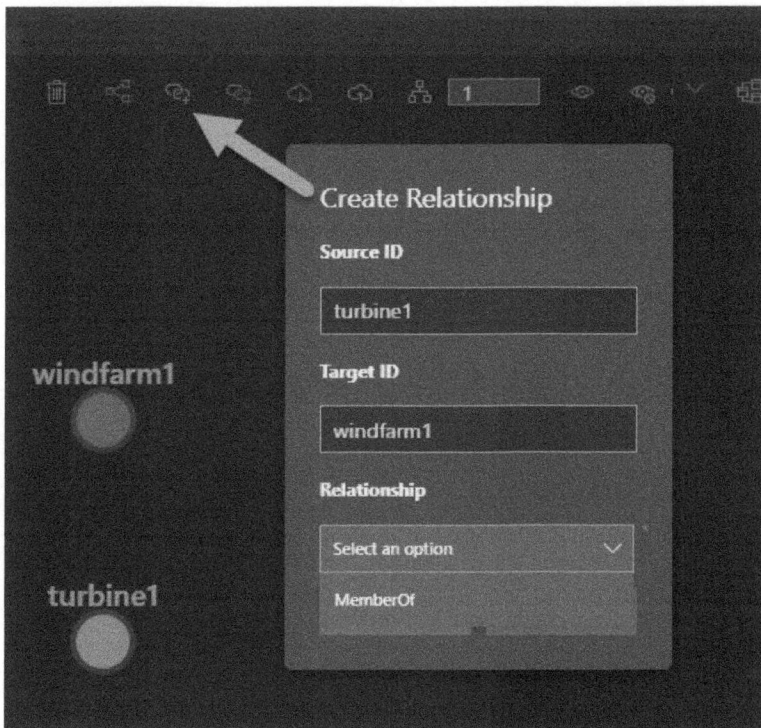

Figure 6.13 – Set the relationship between two instances

First, select the turbine, then select the wind farm and click on the relationship icon on the top bar, as shown in *Figure 6.13*. This will open a dialog box with a dropdown of all the types of relationships that you defined in the DTDL model. In this instance, we only have the **MemberOf** relationship available. Saving this will create an arrow between the two instances with a description on the arrow of the relationship. Proceed with setting up instances for additional turbines and creating unique instances for each component: rotor, gearboxes, generators, and towers. Also update the properties and values for each instance of the turbines and components.

The final model for three wind turbines in a specific wind farm should resemble the nodes and relationships in *Figure 6.14*.

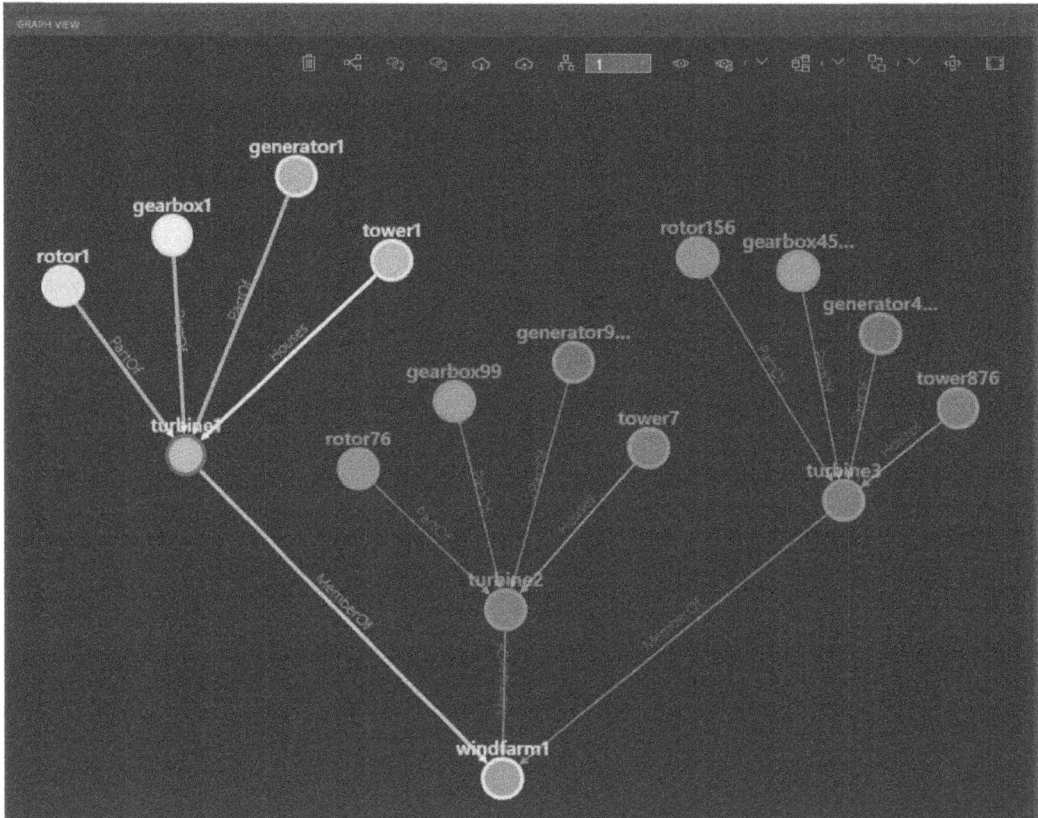

Figure 6.14 – Create a unique instance for a specific wind farm

You have now successfully created an Azure Digital Twin with models and instances for the wind farm, turbines, and its components. You can now use SQL-like queries to interrogate the instances.

The graph in *Figure 6.14* shows that **rotor1**, **gearbox1**, **generator1**, and **tower1** are part of **turbine1**. In this example, the numeric indicators of the components are aligned, which seldom happens in practice. An example of **turbine3** with **rotor156**, **gearbox457**, **generator4213**, and **tower876** is a better reflection of a real-world configuration.

It is quite a tedious task to capture all the instances manually. Just imagine loading 7,000 wind turbines and their components manually; it will certainly result in human data capture errors. A graph with hundreds or thousands of nodes is not the best user experience for manual navigation and data capture. We also notice that the telemetry fields cannot be updated from ADT Explorer as this is typically streaming data from sensors.

Azure Digital Twins services and DTDL provide an environment for application developers to interact with Digital Twins and create solutions to specific business challenges. Our maintenance use case is a typical example of such a business challenge that can be solved using the Digital Twin.

The application allows the testing of the Digital Twin development done in the prior section of this chapter. Let's next focus on the testing phase.

Testing framework

The next step in *Figure 6.5* is to create an application to provide maintainability and scalability over a large number of wind turbine instances and to pass real-time telemetry data to the Digital Twin. This adds ease of use to the framework, for real-life scenarios.

Creating an application to update the Digital Twin prototype in code

Azure Digital Twins (ADT) is a **Platform as a Service (PaaS)** solution aimed at developers to create sigital twin solutions. For the purpose of the book, we will address two typical development personas. The first is a software developer that has the necessary coding skills to develop a solution by using the APIs and SDKs of ADT. At the time of writing the book, the ADT APIs and SDKs can be accessed in .NET, Java, JavaScript, Python, and Go.

The second persona is that of a subject-matter expert such as a reliability and maintenance engineer in the wind farm. The subject-matter expert has technical skills, but typically does not have the formal software development skills to create applications from scratch.

The remainder of the section will focus on the formal software development approach to creating an application to update the wind turbine model.

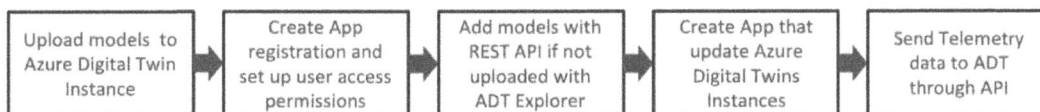

Figure 6.15 – Process for creating a custom-coded solution to update Azure Digital Twins

Figure 6.15 shows the process for creating a custom-coded solution to update ADT. Step one of the process should have been completed in the previous section of the book. It is recommended to have the models in ADT, as well as one or two instances to test your application as you develop it. These instances of the twin represent the specific wind turbines.

The second step is similar to the app registration process in *Figure 5.20* in *Chapter 5, Setting Up a Digital Twin Prototype*. In this instance, we will create an app with a recognizable name, such as `digitaltwinapp`. Provide app access to the Digital Twin resource similar to the process in *Figure 5.23* in *Chapter 5, Setting up a Digital Twin Prototype*.

The custom application that uses the ADT API and SDK will now be able to access the ADT service in Azure in the same way as ADT Explorer can access the ADT services. The APIs and SDKs provide the capabilities for the final three steps in *Figure 6.14*. Using the APIs and SDKs requires software coding skills and access to an **Integrated Development Environment** (**IDE**) such as Visual Studio, Visual Studio Code, or any IDE that supports your programming language of choice. We will use the .NET programming platform and Visual Studio or Visual Studio Code, which is available for free from the Microsoft website.

The Azure Digital Twins APIs and SDKs are well documented at `http://bit.ly/idt-adtapisdk`. The data plane APIs are of specific interest in our custom application as they will create and update the Digital Twin instances and send telemetry data to the Digital Twin instances. The APIs provide access to the Digital Twin models, instances, and event routes. They also enable a developer to programmatically query the models and instances. A detailed list of API operations is available at `http://bit.ly/idt-apioperations` and it is maintained by Microsoft as new operations are added.

Application examples are available at `http://bit.ly/idt-adtapisdk` and a basic Create Twin Instance example in C# is as follows:

```
string twinId = "turbine2";
var initData = new BasicDigitalTwin
{
    Id = twinId,
    Metadata = { ModelId = "dtmi:com:idtbook:wt:turbine;1" },
    // Initialize properties
    Contents =
    {
        { "SerialNo", "YF568" },
        { "RatedPower", 1500 },
    },
};
await client.
CreateOrReplaceDigitalTwinAsync<BasicDigitalTwin>(twinId,
initData);
```

Microsoft provides a full tutorial to code a client app at `http://bit.ly/idt-tutorialapp` for developers who want to create Azure Digital Twins applications with real-time telemetry data. It provides comprehensive source code, and the link is also listed on the GitHub page for this book. It demonstrates all the steps and actions to create an application that creates Digital Twins models and instances and updates them with telemetry data. This addresses the three last steps in *Figure 6.15*.

As a developer, you will now have successfully created Azure Digital Twins models and instances and updated the Digital Twins with telemetry data in a custom application. *Figure 6.16* shows the additional wind turbine instances that were read from a database and added to ADT through a custom-developed application.

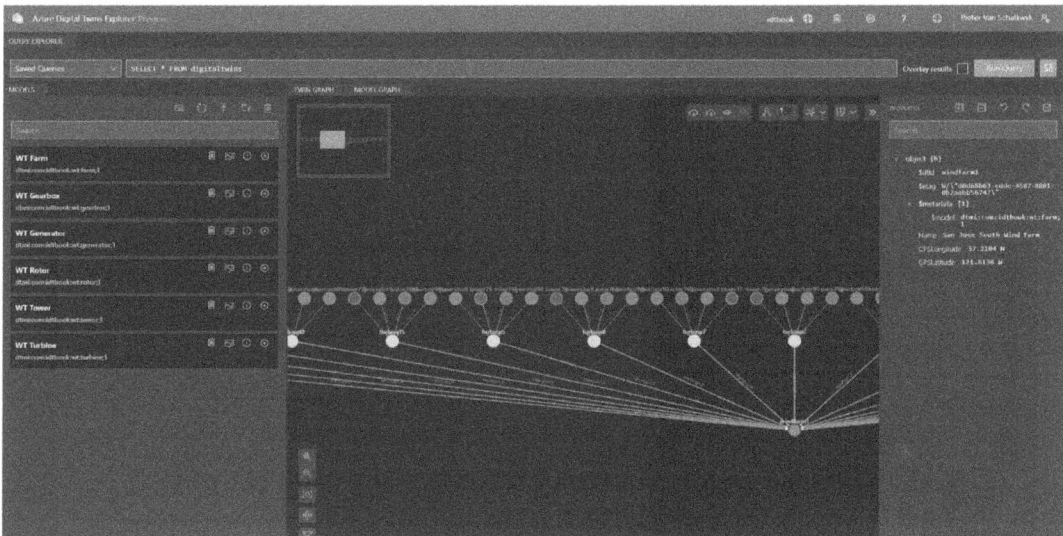

Figure 6.16 – Multi-turbine example

Creating an application, as the last step in the process in *Figure 6.15*, to view or use the model will follow the same process as described. Another approach is to view the Azure Digital Twin in a **business intelligence** (**BI**) or visualization application such as Microsoft Power BI. This approach also requires programming skills, similar to the requirements for creating the ADT application.

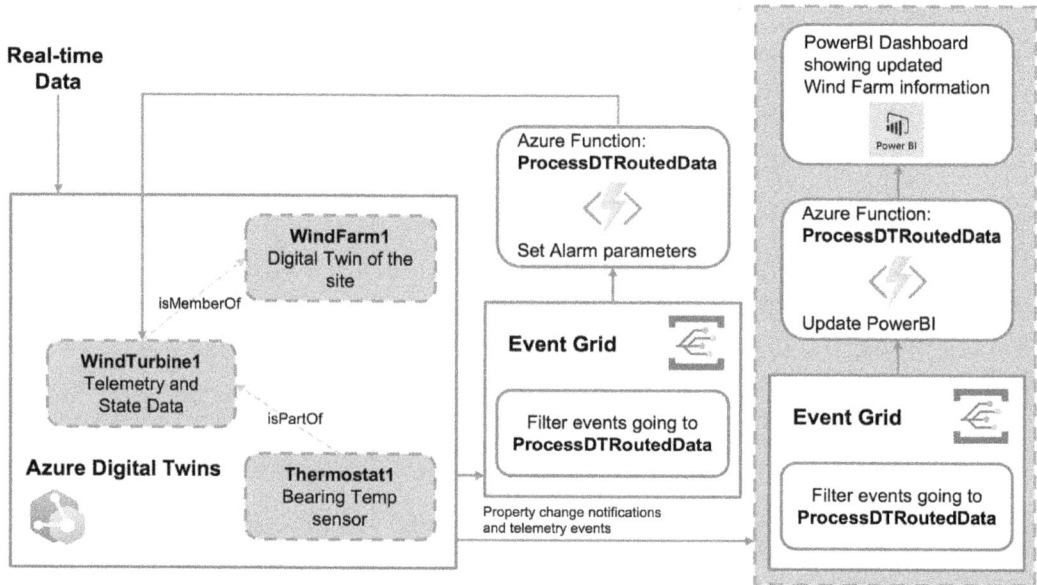

Figure 6.17 – Create a Power BI dashboard to view your Digital Twin

Figure 6.17 shows a possible approach to show ADT information on a Power BI dashboard. It follows a similar development approach as described in this Microsoft tutorial on updating a map service from Azure Digital Twins: `http://bit.ly/idt-connectmaps`. The sample code provided in the GitHub repository for the book includes an Azure function to take the ADT from an event grid and update a Power BI dashboard file as shown in *Figure 6.18*.

A Digital Twin application differs from an IoT application in the sense that the Power BI application will receive updates from the Digital Twin instances, rather than from individual sensors for the different telemetry points. It acts as a proxy between the state and telemetry updates and the business application. You can create different Power BI dashboards from the single event update service. You can also create multiple applications that are updated from the ADT service without reading from individual sensors each time.

The ADT service also differs from traditional relational databases in the sense that it does not create a new transactional row of data every time it is updated. It overwrites the previous instance state values with new state values. The instance is always a snapshot at a specific point in time of the state of the Digital Twin instance. It requires additional programming to persist data, such as telemetry time series data in a **time series database** (**TSDB**) such as Microsoft Time series Insights or InfluxDB.

The Power BI dashboard shown in *Figure 6.18* is used to monitor the operation of the turbines on the wind farm. It is also used to plan maintenance services based on the condition of the turbines from the telemetry readings.

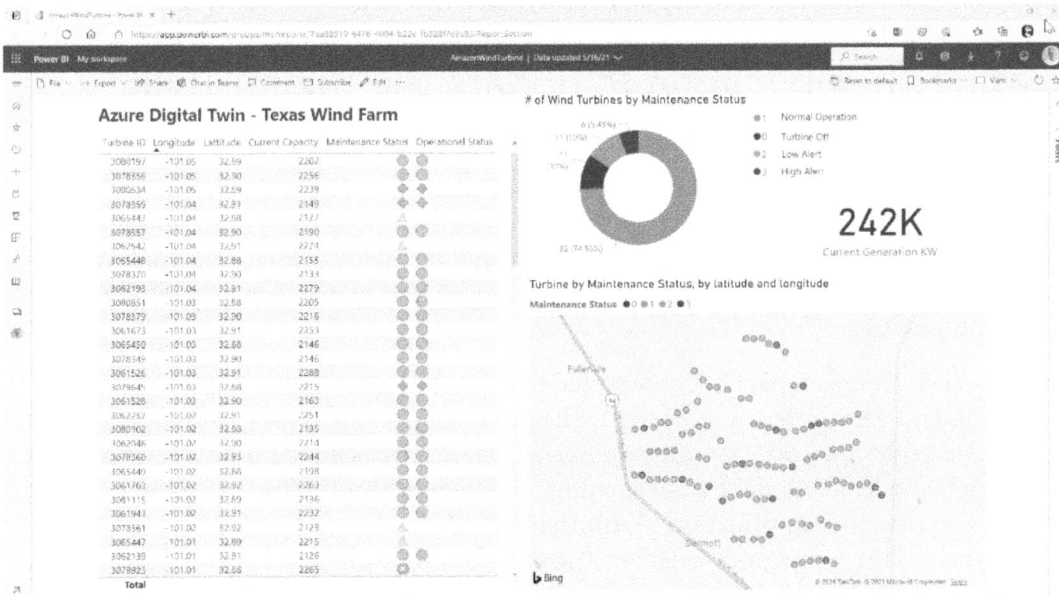

Figure 6.18 – Power BI dashboard example for our wind farm

We have now created an Azure-based Digital Twin as our first Digital Twin prototype application. It is a custom-coded application that can create new ADT models, instances, update telemetry data from IoT sensors, and view the Azure Digital Twins in applications such as Power BI. This approach provides a great deal of flexibility to skilled programmers who can create a wide range of specialist Digital Twin applications. Willow Inc. (`https://www.willowinc.com/posts/under-the-hood-willowtwin-x-azure-digital-twins/`) is a great example of Azure Digital Twins applications in the construction industry.

The challenge with this approach is that subject-matter experts and operational Digital Twin users who are not skilled developers cannot use the ADT service without the assistance of a developer. No-/low-code application development tools that are aimed at these subject-matter experts address the challenge, but it reduces the flexibility of the applications developed on these platforms. Applications on no-/low-code platforms need to stay within the boundaries of the platform. There are multiple no-/low-code applications on the market that can be used, but XMPro is a Microsoft .NET Core-based no-code platform with native support for Azure Digital Twins.

In the next section, we will provide a brief overview of creating a similar application to the coded solution described in this chapter in the XMPro no-code environment.

Creating an application to update the Digital Twin prototype in no/low code

In the previous section, we described the process of creating your first Digital Twin of a wind farm by coding the solution in an IDE if you have the necessary programming background and skills. This approach gives you the full flexibility of a custom application that is developed to address the unique requirements of your use case, but it does require programming skills.

A no-/low-code approach may be more suited to subject-matter experts with limited coding skills and who prefer to compose applications using a visual programming approach. Recently, low-code development technologies have been the center of attention as a means to accelerate digital transformation. The analyst firm Gartner recently predicted that **low-code application platforms** (**LCAPs**) will grow by 23% during 2021 (see `https://www.gartner.com/en/newsroom/press-releases/2021-02-15-gartner-forecasts-worldwide-low-code-development-technologies-market-to-grow-23-percent-in-2021`). The industrial giant Siemens purchased Mendix for $700 million in 2018 for such LCAP capabilities. Oracle APEX is another example of an LCAP; see `https://apex.oracle.com/en/platform/low-code/` for more information.

There are several no-/low-code solutions to choose from. Here, we will use XMPRO to demonstrate the configuration process using a no-/low-code platform that has native support for Azure Digital Twins. We will recreate the wind turbine Digital Twin solution in XMPRO to demonstrate how the two approaches differ for the maintenance and field service use case. XMPRO provides a free 120 days trial license for readers of this book at `https://xmpro.com/idtbooktrial`.

A no-/low-code platform provides less flexibility than a custom solution, but it decreases the development time of a solution such as the maintenance and field service application by a factor of 10 or more.

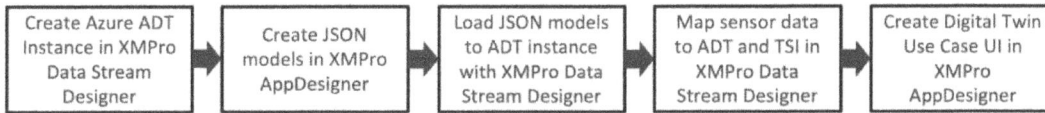

```
┌─────────────────┐   ┌─────────────────┐   ┌─────────────────┐   ┌─────────────────┐   ┌─────────────────┐
│ Create Azure ADT│   │                 │   │ Load JSON models│   │ Map sensor data │   │Create Digital Twin│
│ Instance in XMPro│──▶│ Create JSON     │──▶│ to ADT instance │──▶│ to ADT and TSI in│──▶│ Use Case UI in  │
│ Data Stream     │   │ models in XMPro │   │ with XMPro Data │   │ XMPro Data      │   │ XMPro           │
│ Designer        │   │ AppDesigner     │   │ Stream Designer │   │ Stream Designer │   │ AppDesigner     │
└─────────────────┘   └─────────────────┘   └─────────────────┘   └─────────────────┘   └─────────────────┘
```

Figure 6.19 – Low-code approach to building our first Digital Twin on ADT

Figure 6.19 shows the high-level steps of creating the Digital Twin application on a no-/low-code platform.

The first step is to create the Digital Twin resource in the free Azure subscription, as shown in *Figure 6.20*. This is similar to the process described in *Figure 5.9* of *Chapter 5, Setting Up a Digital Twin Prototype*. It still requires Azure portal access to configure user access rights, as described in *Figure 5.9*.

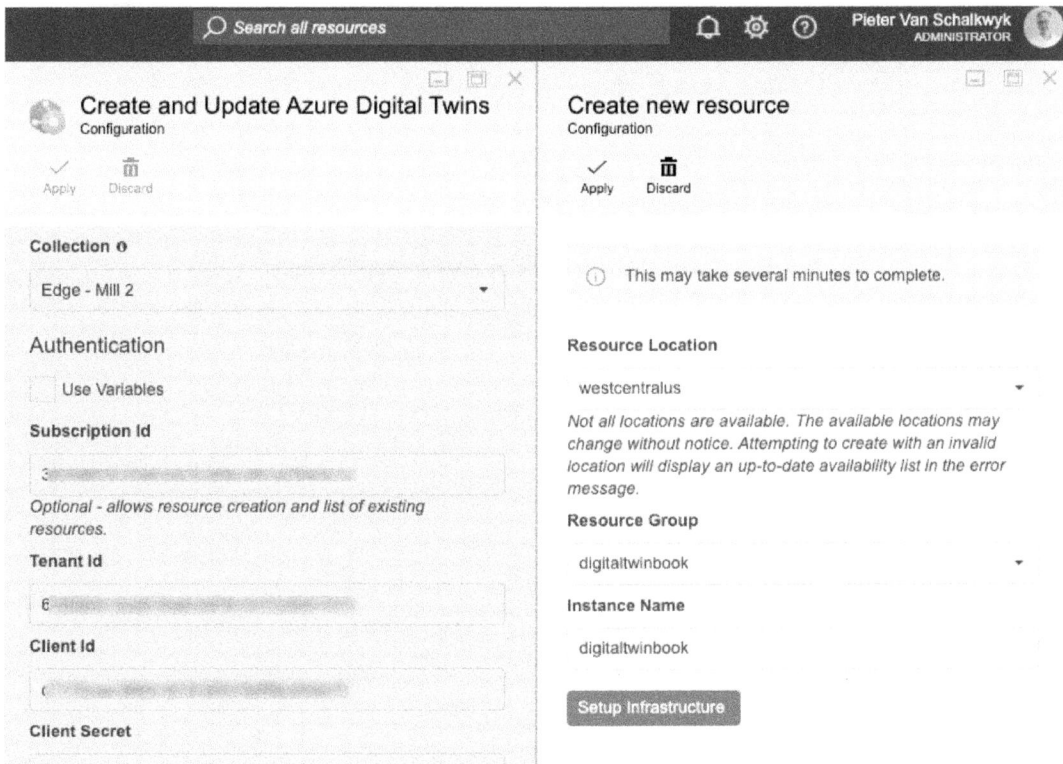

Figure 6.20 – Create an ADT instance from within the no-/low-code platform

The next step in the process in *Figure 6.19* is to create JSON models for each of the components of the wind turbine, including the rotor, gearbox, and generator. *Figure 6.21* shows an application for creating a DTDL JSON file in a no-/low-code page that is more aimed at an end user to define the properties of, for example, the wind turbine in this instance.

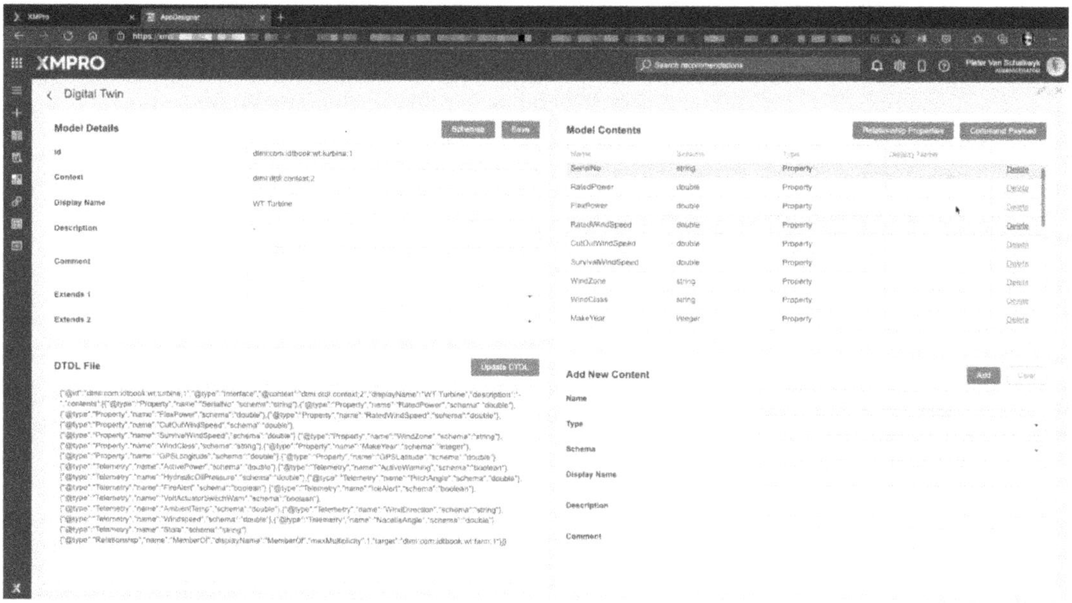

Figure 6.21 – Create JSON models in XMPro App Designer

The form creates the JSON file that we can then upload in the next step of the process in *Figure 6.19*. The XMPRO Azure Digital Twins connectors shown in *Figure 6.22* provide an upload function that automatically loads the Digital Twins models in ADT.

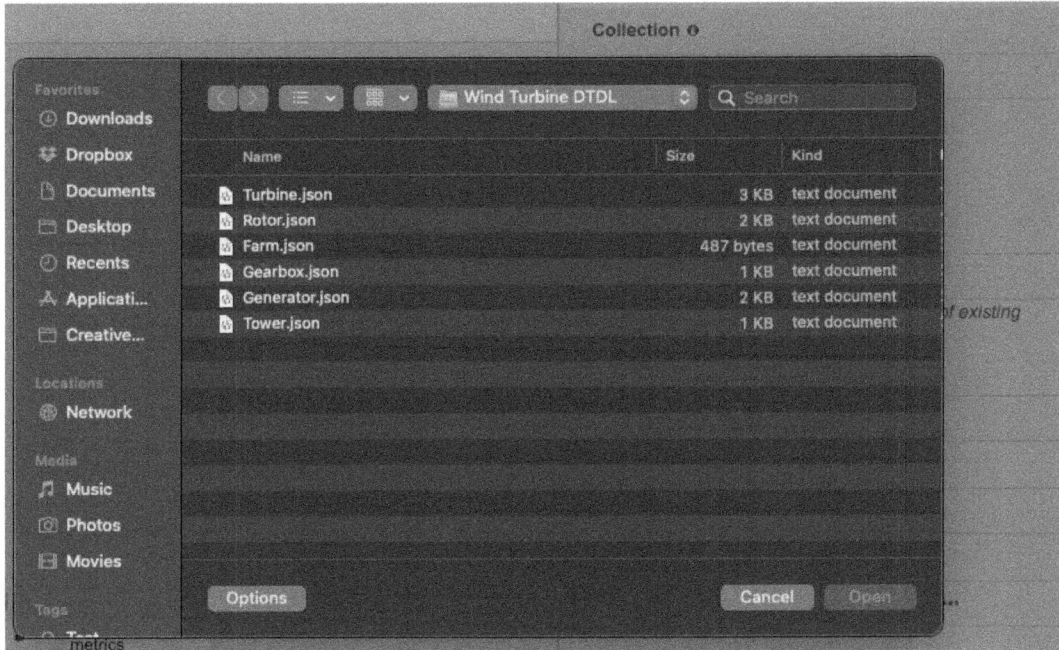

Figure 6.22 – Load JSON models to our ADT instance with XMPRO Data Stream Designer

The fourth step in *Figure 6.19* is to map the sensor data from either real-time telemetry or simulated values, as shown in *Figure 6.23*, to the property and telemetry fields in ADT.

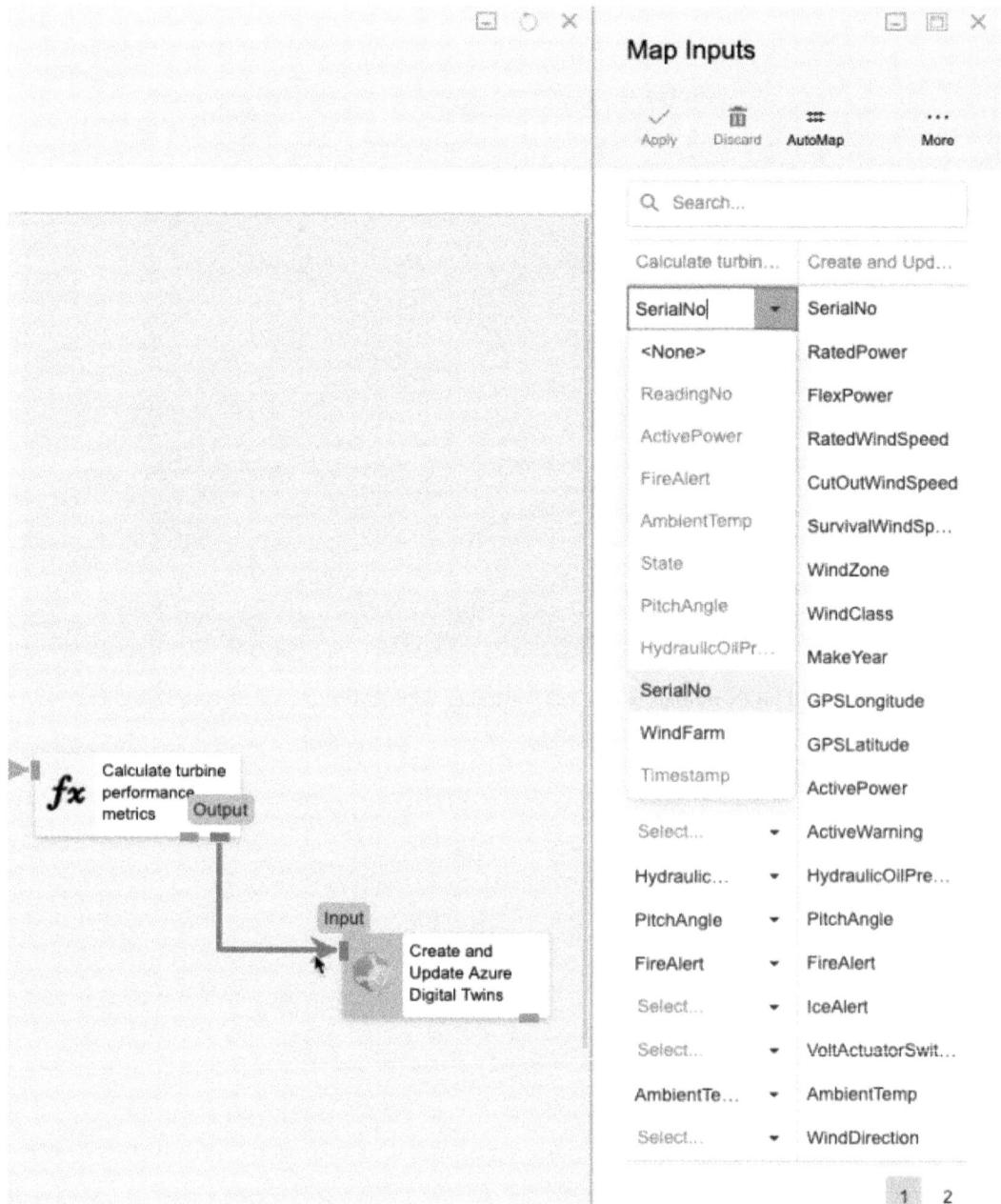

Figure 6.23 – Map sensor data to ADT and TSI in XMPro Data Stream Designer

The final step is to create a visualization for the maintenance and field service application in the drag-and-drop visual design in the no-/low-code platform.

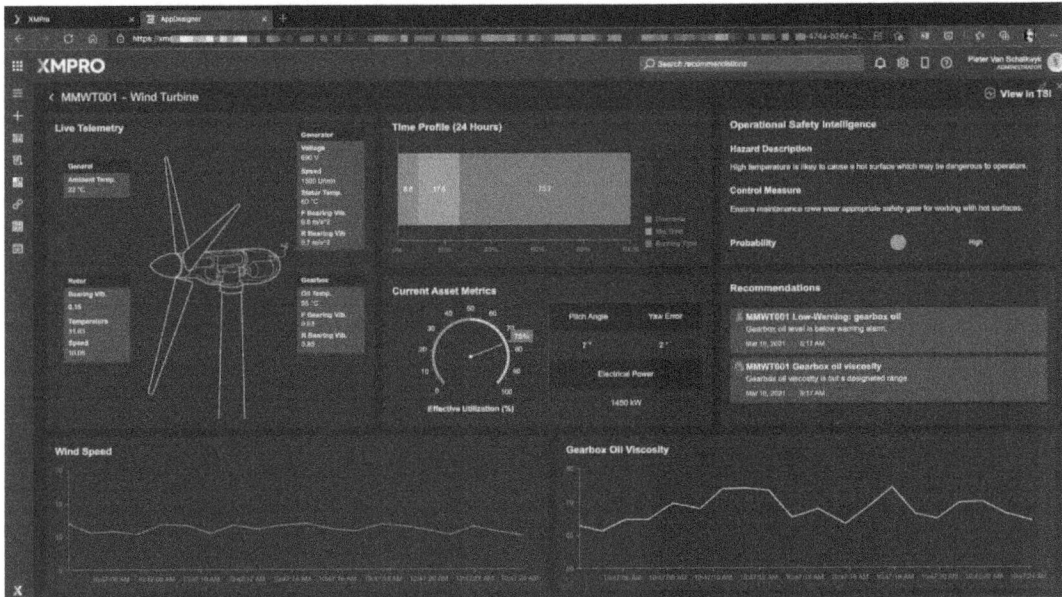

Figure 6.24 – Create Digital Twin Use Case UI in XMPro AppDesigner

Figure 6.24 shows an example of a wind turbine Digital Twin with real-time telemetry for condition monitoring. The platform also allows for the creation of analytics-based recommendations based on real-time telemetry data. The analytics for the recommendation can be based on engineering calculations from condition monitoring telemetry, machine learning models that receive real-time telemetry input, or business rules that are configured for the specific application.

This example shows a recommendation rule based on the observed gearbox oil level from a decision tree. This can be used to plan maintenance and provide feedback to the wind turbine manufacturer on gearbox oil consumption.

In the next section, let's focus on the technical evaluation of the Digital Twin process.

Technical evaluation considerations

Our Digital Twin is expected to reflect the current condition of our physical asset, which is a wind turbine in a wind farm. In our case, we ensured that the DTDL of the different sub-assemblies of the wind turbine contained the data elements necessary for our goal, which is predictive maintenance of the wind turbine when operating in the farm. Referring to *Figure 6.25*, we can see attributes such as the gearbox oil level, the oil temperature, and the bearing temperature are captured in the DTDL elements for the gearbox.

```
30 ▾    {
31          "@type": "Property",
32          "name": "Manufacturer",
33          "schema": "string"
34      },
35 ▾    {
36          "@type": "Telemetry",
37          "name": "GearboxOilLevel",
38          "schema": "double"
39      },
40 ▾    {
41          "@type": "Telemetry",
42          "name": "GearboxOilTemp",
43          "schema": "double"
44      },
45 ▾    {
46          "@type": "Telemetry",
47          "name": "BearingTemp",
48          "schema": "double"
49      },
```

Figure 6.25 – Example data elements of the wind turbine's gearbox

Figure 6.24 shows the ability to visually display attributes such as the gearbox oil viscosity via the visualization application of the Digital Twin over a specific time interval. Since gearbox oil condition monitoring is a common practice in the industry for wind turbines, this helps to connect the dots between the Digital Twin application and a meaningful parameter for the business user.

The Digital Twin application can provide a view of the wind turbine at a point in time in a **monitoring and diagnostic (M&D)** center such as the one shown in *Figure 6.26*. Such M&D centers are generally used by the service organization of the manufacturer to maintain the entire fleet of its wind turbines, which are under warranty or service contracts.

Figure 6.26 – Industrial M&D/command center

> **Note**
>
> Image source: `https://commons.wikimedia.org/wiki/`
> `File:Elite_ISI_Command_Center.png`

The M&D center generally combines information from the Digital Twin as well as other enterprise and third-party data sources, as shown in *Figure 6.27*. The combined information is displayed in a way that makes it easy for the analyst to consume the information. Often, M&D centers are run by the manufacturer of the industrial equipment and provide monitoring service to the operators of the wind farm.

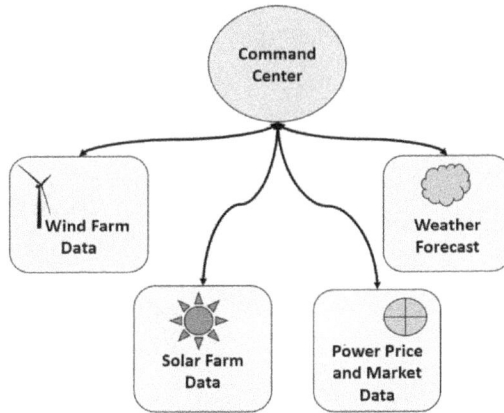

Figure 6.27 – Industrial M&D/command center

When we do the technical evaluation of the Digital Twin, we must consider the integration with the systems at the M&D center. The data from different systems may have different levels of granularity; for instance, the weather forecast, such as wind speed and temperature, may be hourly, but the telemetry data from the wind turbine may be recorded every second. The data integration at the M&D center would have to handle such complexities.

Next, let's at look at the business validation considerations of the Digital Twin of the wind turbine.

Business validation and understanding

According to a wind energy publication from July 2013, titled *Monitoring wind turbine gearboxes*, more failures have been observed in the gearbox than in the other sub-assemblies in the wind turbines. According to the US **Energy Information Administration** (**EIA**), the expected lifespan of a wind turbine is about 20-25 years. The gearboxes are designed for about 20 years, but most have experienced a shorter life. The gearbox is also one of the most expensive sub-assemblies in the wind turbine. It can be as much as 13% of the cost of the wind turbine. The repair and replacement process of the gearbox is complex, as it is located at a great height and leads to long downtime. *Figure 6.28* shows a view of the gearbox in a wind turbine. The oil in the gearbox protects the pitch gear, open gear, and yaw gear.

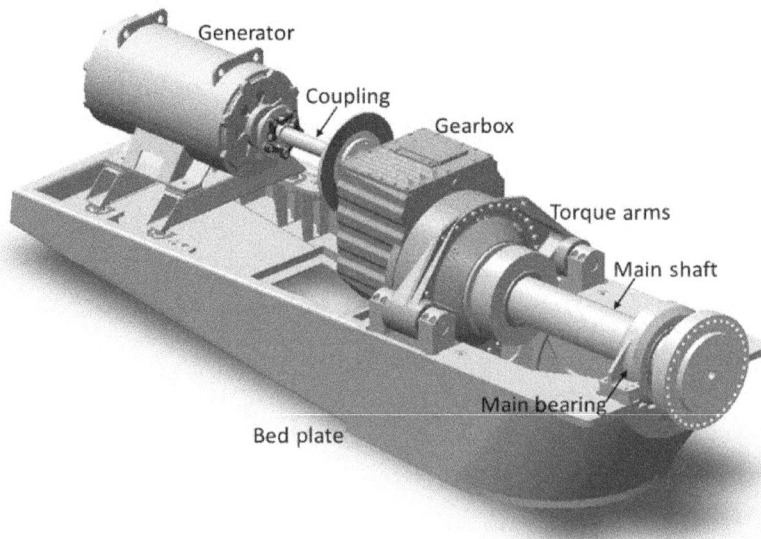

Figure 6.28 – Wind turbine sub-assemblies

> **Note**
> Image source: Keller, J., Guo, Y., Zhang, Z., and Lucas, D.: Comparison of planetary bearing load-sharing characteristics in wind turbine gearboxes, Wind Energ. Sci., 3, 947–960, `https://doi.org/10.5194/wes-3-947-2018`, 2018

One of the common causes of failures in the bearings of wind turbines is **white etching cracks (WEC)** as these bearings are subjected to a high degree of force and torque. WEC is one of the leading causes of reliability issues in the bearings of wind turbines. WEC causes structural changes in the bearings' material below the surface. The resulting cracks eventually extend to the surface of the bearing, when they are under stress, leading to failures of the bearing. Proper lubrication maintained by monitoring the condition of the gearbox oil can help to reduce the incidents of WEC in wind turbine bearings. The condition of the oil has a key role in the overall reduction of the friction and wear and tear of the moving parts in the gearbox. According to a publication by ExxonMobil, the average age of wind turbine farms is 7 years in 2020. Based on an average 5- to 10-year manufacturer warranty on wind turbines, this topic of field maintenance is very timely and relevant from a business standpoint.

Historically, the monitoring of the gearbox oil was carried out in offline mode by sampling the gearbox oil. A sample of oil taken from the wind turbines was sent to the laboratory for analysis, examining properties such as the viscosity and ferrous and non-ferrous particle levels. The Digital Twin of the wind turbine, along with the telemetry, can facilitate the online monitoring of the condition of the oil. The sensors can record the temperature and derive the oil viscosity continually.

During the business validation phase, the **subject-matter expert** would look at the initial estimates of the economic impact of the Digital Twin on the **operations and maintenance (O&M)** cost of the wind turbine or the whole wind farm. The SME would also look at how trustworthy the Digital Twin is to be able to make such O&M budgetary decisions over time.

Next, let's look at some real numbers in this context. According to Shell, the industry spends about $8 billion per year on wind farm maintenance globally (see `https://www.shell.com/business-customers/lubricants-for-business/sector-expertise/power-industry/wind-power/true-cost-of-wind-turbine-maintenance.html`). Each gearbox failure incident costs the operator between $300K and $500K. According to our research, the cost of changing the gearbox oil for an average wind turbine is about $8,000. The gearbox may hold anywhere from 200 to 800 liters of oil. On average, the gearbox oil change of a wind turbine is done every 36 months based on scheduled maintenance.

Over the 20-year average life of a wind turbine, 6-7 oil changes are required. If the condition-based maintenance using a Digital Twin reduces it by 1 that is 5-6 oil changes over the usable lifetime of the wind turbine, which will reduce the maintenance cost by $8,000 per wind turbine just on this expense item. In addition, it can reduce the incidents of downtime due to gearbox failure. Apart from health monitoring and predictive maintenance, the Digital Twin can also contribute to the optimization of the wind turbine, leading to an increase in the energy generation level of the whole wind farm.

In this section, we looked at the business validation of the Digital Twin of the wind turbine.

Summary

In this chapter, we demonstrated how to build a Digital Twin of an industrial asset, which in this case is a wind turbine. We made use of DTDL and Microsoft Azure Digital Twins to build the Digital Twin. We discussed how a developer can make use of the PaaS capabilities exposed via ADT. We further showed the need for an application to be built on top of ADT for the business persona. We used Power BI and XMPRO Data Stream Designer to showcase these scenarios. Then we looked at the technical and business validation of the Digital Twin for wind turbines.

In *Chapter 7, Deployment and Value Tracking*, we will start to look at considerations for the deployment of Digital Twins for wind farms at a production level.

Questions

1. What is the role of DTDL in building the Digital Twin using ADT?
2. Why do we need to look at the sub-assemblies of the wind turbine to build the Digital Twin?
3. Why is predictive maintenance of gearbox critical for wind farms?
4. How can we store historical telemetry data from the asset in ADT?
5. How can we evaluate the business outcomes expected from the Digital Twin solution for wind turbines?

7
Deployment and Value Tracking

In *Chapter 6, Building the Digital Twin Prototype*, we covered the development of a wind-farm Digital Twin that consists of many wind turbines, each with its own Digital Twin. The Digital Twin application was configured using the Visual Studio **integrated development environment** (**IDE**) on the Microsoft **Azure Digital Twins** (**ADT**) service. The Visual Studio IDE approach is for programmers who want to build advanced Digital Twin applications on the ADT service. We further demonstrated this using a no-code application development platform aimed at **subject-matter experts** (**SMEs**) who want to create Digital Twin applications without coding. We further assessed the testing, technical evaluation, and business validation of our first Digital Twin.

This chapter will focus on the deployment and scaling of the solution in an operational environment. This will help to provide a structured approach, from initial experimentation with a Digital Twin to a target state where it delivers business outcomes. This is important as often, experimentations with emerging technologies such as **Internet of Things** (**IoT**) and Digital Twins are not productized, due to various complexities involved, in the full life cycle. We will continue with the wind farm and wind turbine example and demonstrate the following deployment steps:

- Functional testing of the Digital Twin
- Pilot rollout

- Full deployment
- Value proposition and tracking

In the first part of this chapter, we will assess how the Digital Twin addresses the functional requirements initially set in *Chapter 6, Building the Digital Twin Prototype*.

Functional testing of the Digital Twin

Functional testing is standard practice in developing software applications, and creating Digital Twin solutions is no exception. For Digital Twins, however, we recommend functional testing of both the Digital Twin infrastructure and the Digital Twin application.

In *Chapter 5, Setting Up a Digital Twin Prototype*, we created models and instances of a wind farm and wind turbines as your Digital Twin prototype solution. Testing the functionality and integrity of the models and ensuring that they are correctly deployed is the first step of functional testing of a Digital Twin. Once we've confirmed that our Digital Twin infrastructure is working effectively, we can test the actual Digital Twin applications configured in *Chapter 6, Building the Digital Twin Prototype*.

Let's look at the test framework next.

Testing the Digital Twin infrastructure

Your wind-farm Digital Twin prototype was configured on the ADT **platform as a service (PaaS)**. It is one example of an **integration PaaS (iPaaS)** for Digital Twin infrastructure. We will continue with that example as we describe the first step in the functional testing of your Digital Twin prototype.

The purpose of the infrastructure functional test is to ensure that the platform components are correctly configured. This functional test will eliminate incorrect platform configuration as a potential reason for failing the actual application functional test.

We propose the testing sequence shown in the following diagram for the infrastructure functional test:

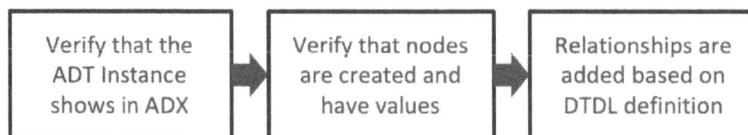

Figure 7.1 – Functional testing Digital Twin infrastructure

The first step in the sequence is used to check if the Digital Twin configuration and access control are correctly configured in Microsoft Azure. The functional test is done by accessing your Digital Twin through **ADT Explorer (ADX)**.

This test aims to show that we can access a Digital Twin instance of our wind farm in ADX that displays the different models on the left pane and a graph in the middle pane. If there is any issue with the underlying infrastructure or access rights, we would not successfully display our Digital Twin instance. The following screenshot shows a typical error message:

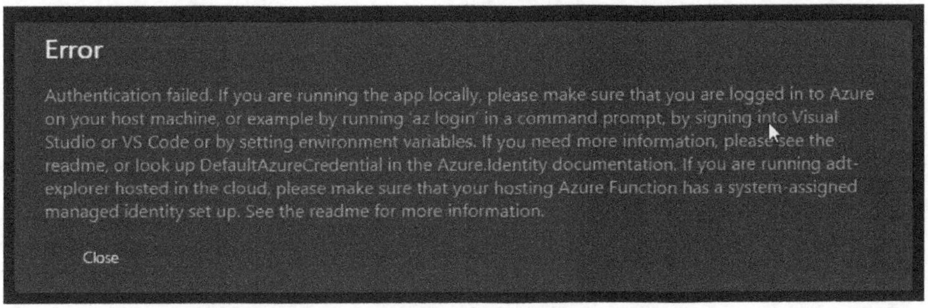

Figure 7.2 – Access rights error message in ADX

The following screenshot provides an example of a successful test that shows both the models and the instances on the Azure iPaaS:

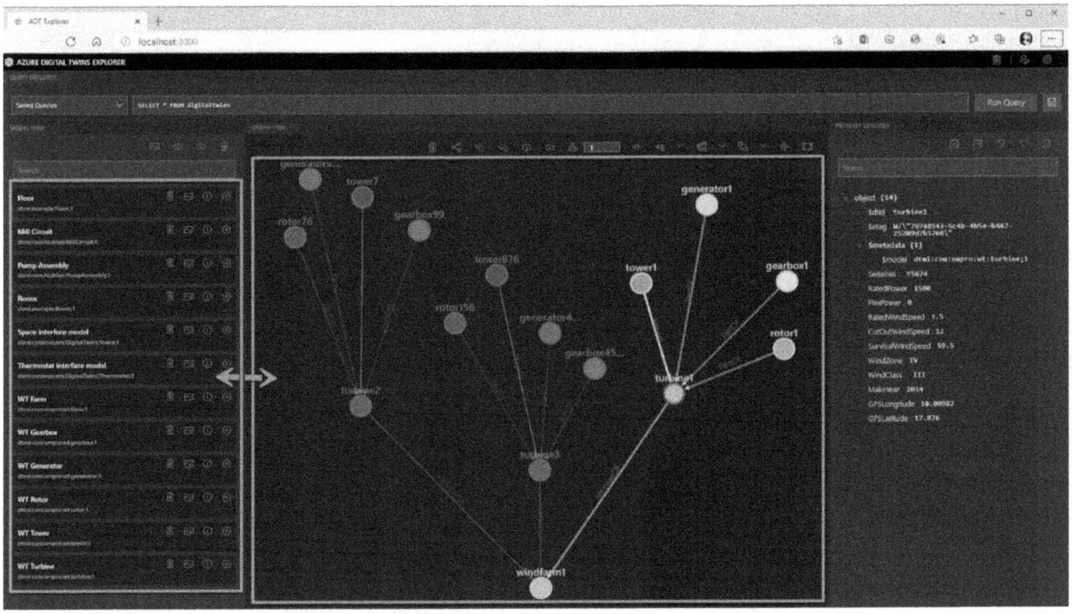

Figure 7.3 – Functional testing of Digital Twin infrastructure

The second step of the infrastructure functional test in *Figure 7.1* checks that nodes are created with the correct values in the property fields. The following screenshot provides an example of a successful turbine node and its associated properties:

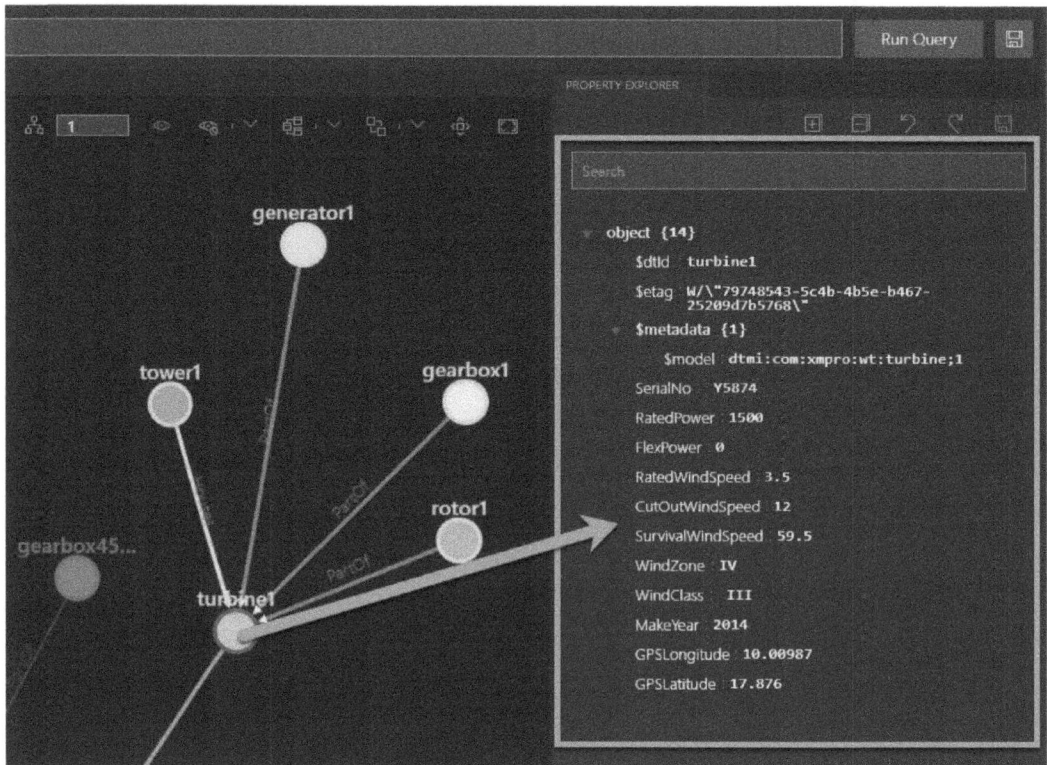

Figure 7.4 – Functional test for nodes and values

If this information is not correct, then there is a likelihood that the **Digital Twins Definition Language** (DTDL) model files contain invalid information or are structured incorrectly. It may also indicate that the data ingestion service on your application is not passing data through to the Digital Twin instance. In such a case, we suggest that you revisit the configuration steps in *Chapter 6, Building the Digital Twin Prototype*.

The final step of the infrastructure functional test in *Figure 7.1* is to check that the relationships are correctly configured. ADX provides a visual, graph-based interface that makes it easy to see the various relationships defined in the multiple DTDL models. The relationships between these models are critical to the success of the Digital Twin instances, and testing this as part of the infrastructure functional test ensures that the underlying graph functionality is correctly deployed.

Each relationship is named on the arrow that connects the nodes, as shown in the following screenshot. If you can see node relationships, this means your iPaaS services are correctly configured, and it concludes the three infrastructure functional tests outlined in *Figure 7.1*:

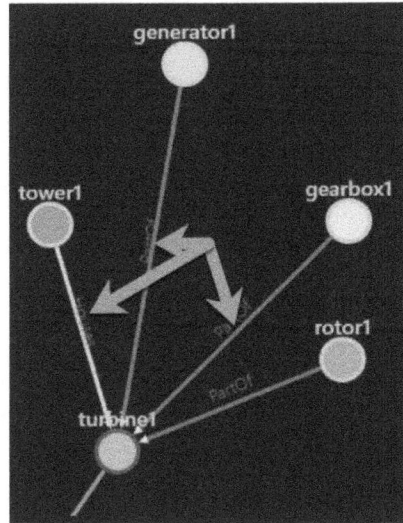

Figure 7.5 – Functional test for relationships

You can proceed to the functional testing of your Digital Twin application once you are satisfied that the infrastructure components for your Digital Twin model and instances passed the infrastructure functional tests.

Testing the Digital Twin applications

Let's next look at the details for testing the Digital Twin application of the wind turbine.

Testing a coded solution developed in Visual Studio

Functional testing for Digital Twin applications follows a more traditional software development testing approach, especially if the application is a coded solution designed in an IDE such as Visual Studio. The functional testing requirements will be dictated by the Digital Twin use case characteristics, such as the following:

- Criticality of the Digital Twin application
- Security and safety requirements
- The complexity of integration to other systems and Digital Twins

- Level of autonomy and automation of control in the Digital Twin

- Accuracy of data and recommendations

The application functional tests for a coded Digital Twin application are based on best practices for complex system development. The objective of functional testing of software is to validate the application to the initial functional specification of the Digital Twin. Functional testing tests each stated function by providing input and verifying the output against the functional specification of the Digital Twin application. The most common functional tests are outlined here:

- **Unit testing**—A software testing method whereby individual units of source code are tested by the developer to confirm the unit of code performs as expected.

- **Smoke testing**—Initial or preliminary testing to determine if a software build is stable enough for further **quality assurance (QA)** testing.

- **Sanity testing**—A surface-level testing method when new modules or code are added to decide if the application is stable enough for further development cycles before full functional testing.

- **Integration testing**—Individual modules or components are combined and tested as a group. This method is highly recommended for composite Digital Twins where modules from different discrete Digital Twins need to interoperate to deliver the required function of the Digital Twin.

- **White-box testing**—A method for testing the Digital Twin application whereby the tester has full knowledge of the internal structure and code of the digital twin solution.

- **Black-box testing**—A method for testing the Digital Twin application whereby the tester has no knowledge of the internal structure or code of the Digital Twin solution.

- **User acceptance testing** (**UAT**)—This is a method for testing where by the end user of the Digital Twin application tests the solution to determine if it can be accepted or not.

- **Regression testing**—This is a software testing method to verify that code changes have not adversely affected existing functionality. Partial or full re-execution of previous test cases identifies code that regressed.

It is not in the scope of this book to explain each of these testing methods in detail, as this is a well-defined software discipline with many great resources available.

Unit testing is a test that is typically done by the developer of the Digital Twin application. Unit-testing scenarios for the Power BI-coded solution that was introduced in *Chapter 6, Building the Digital Twin Prototype,* requires the developer to test each functional area of the Digital Twin. The functional areas for the example solution used in that chapter are shown in the following screenshot. Each block on the diagram is tested individually for scenarios where the code would most likely break, starting with ADT, then the event grids, and finally, the Power BI **user interface** (**UI**), as shown here:

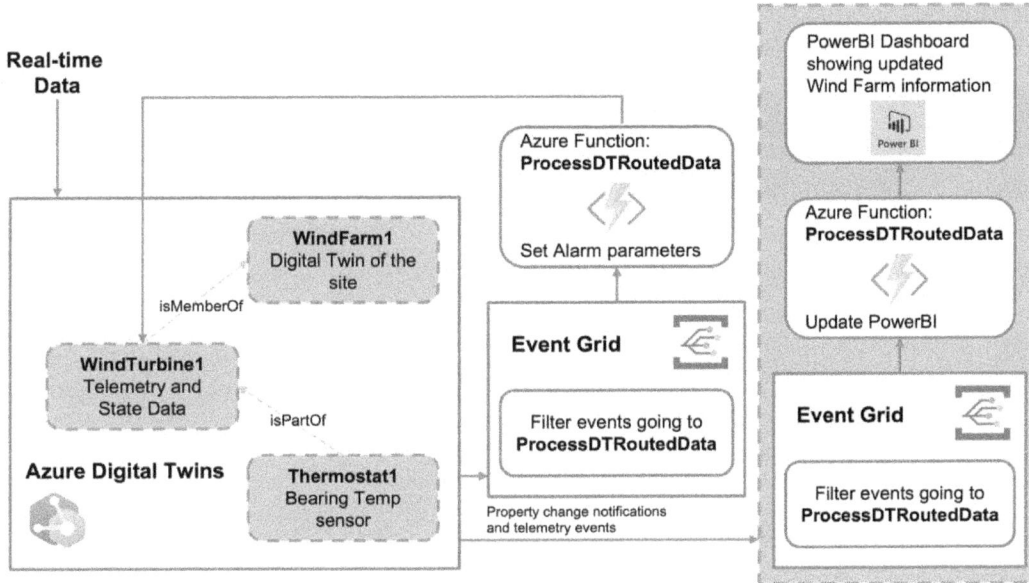

Figure 7.6 – Unit testing a coded Digital Twin

A black-box test, in contrast, is done by the QA team, who evaluate the expected output without understanding the code behind the solution. This would, for example, be evaluating the results on the Power BI end-user interface by varying input values with both expected and unexpected input values.

A Digital Twin solution that is created in a no-code environment follows a similar functional-testing approach. The major difference is that we cannot perform unit testing at the code level but rather at the functional blocks in the no-code environment.

Testing a no-code Digital Twin platform solution

A no-code application development platform provides an end-user configuration environment with limited coding capabilities. This is aimed at SMEs who understand the business requirements of a Digital Twin application but do not have software development skills.

Unit testing of a Digital Twin application in a no-code environment is limited to scripts or models such as external models—for example, a failure prediction model in Python. No-code application development platforms typically make provision for embedding or calling external models, such as the aforementioned Python prediction model. Unit tests can be applied to the models or scripts but not on the core Digital Twin application.

The functional testing of the Digital Twin application is often limited to integration testing and black-box testing. The following screenshot demonstrates integration and black-box testing on the wind turbine Digital Twin that we created with XMPro in *Chapter 6, Building the Digital Twin Prototype*:

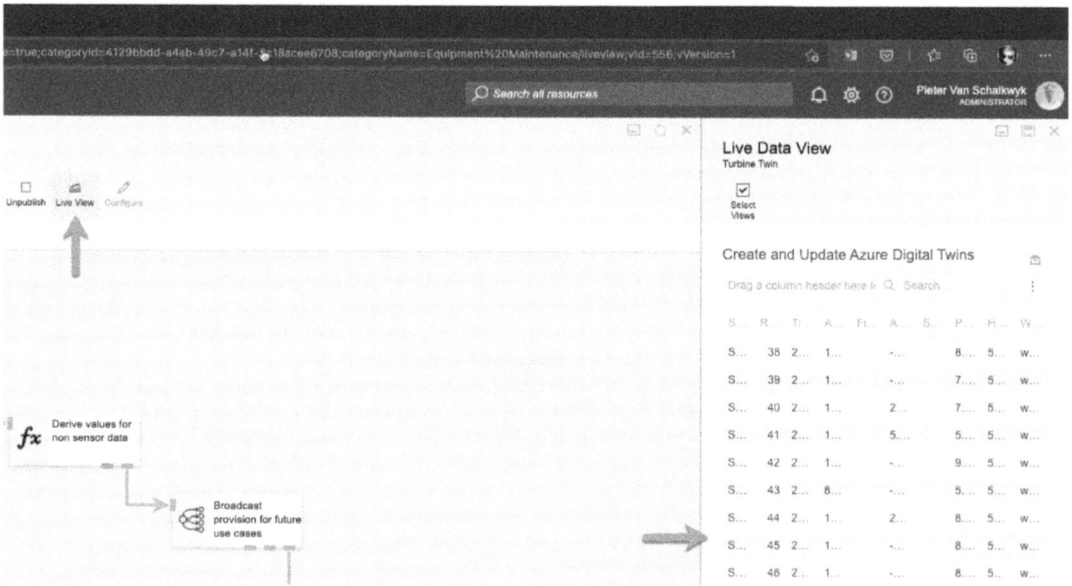

Figure 7.7 – Integration and black-box functional testing in no-code application development

The **Live View** tab on the top menu opens a pane on the right side of the application that shows the data values in the last block of the data flow when the data stream is published. It provides a simple, functional test view of the data flowing from integration sources and any manipulation of the data along the way. This view is ideal for black-box functional tests. The pane with that data can be expanded to clearly show the values, as shown in the following screenshot:

Figure 7.8 – Expanded Live View data

UAT provides the opportunity to test user interaction with the Digital Twin application, checking valid outcomes of the solution logic and performance on different infrastructures such as desktop browsers, mobile devices, and **augmented reality/virtual reality (AR/VR)** hardware. The following screenshot shows an example of UAT on a desktop browser and a mobile browser:

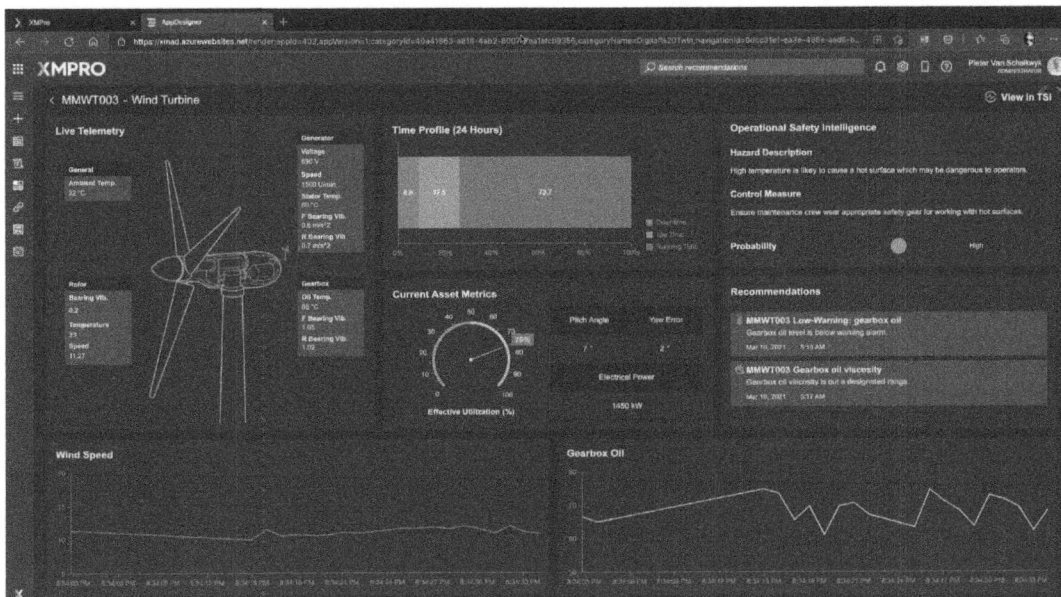

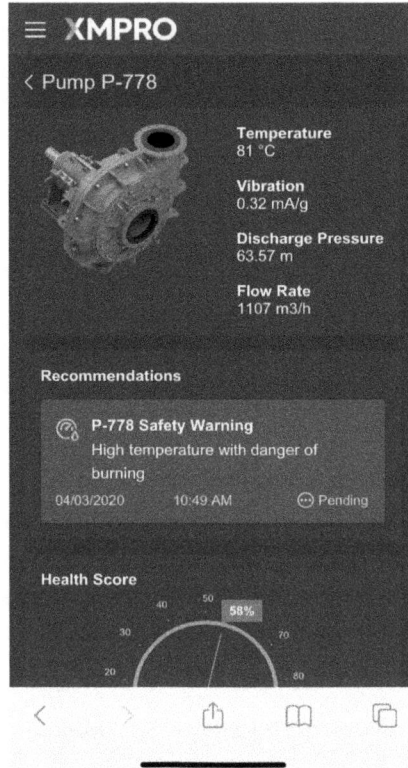

Figure 7.9 – UAT on desktop and mobile browsers

In this section, we outlined a typical approach for functional tests on your Digital Twin prototype. The specific test you conduct for your Digital Twin prototype will depend on the code or no-code approach that you followed to create your solution.

Once we have completed both the infrastructure and application functional testing, we are ready for a pilot rollout of our Digital Twin prototype.

Pilot rollout

Digital-twin projects follow a typical evolution that starts with proving concept through prototyping, piloting, and then full-scale deployment. Each of these phases serves a specific purpose along the journey of creating a successful Digital Twin solution.

The following screenshot shows the evolution from concepts to full deployment and how the scope evolves along the journey:

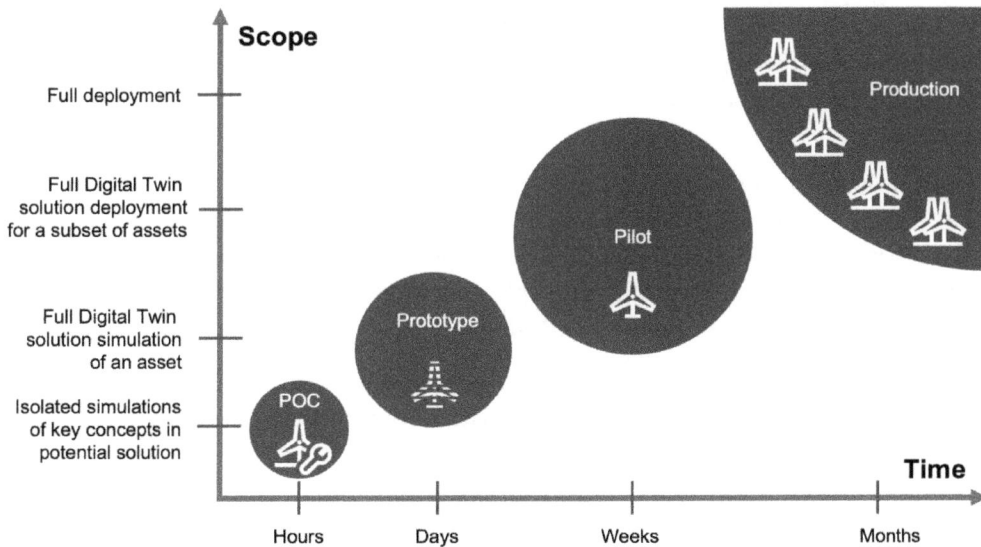

Figure 7.10 – Evolution from concept to full deployment

During the initial **proof-of-concept** (**POC**) phase, the objective is to demonstrate the viability of specific technological or design components. This phase verifies the suitability of using these concepts in developing a production system and serves as a decision point or gate to determine if a specific solution can move to the prototyping phase. In the case of our wind turbine example, we may use a POC to determine if the data that we receive from our sensors is sufficient to create a **machine learning** (**ML**) model for predictive maintenance.

Chapter 6, Building the Digital Twin Prototype, focused on configuring the Digital Twin prototype of a wind farm that supports several wind turbines. The prototype is a complete model of the overall solution, using simulation data to demonstrate critical capabilities. It brings together several POC elements into the configuration of the Digital Twin.

Once we have successfully created and tested the prototype, we can move to a pilot implementation of a Digital Twin application. The scope of a pilot rollout will be determined by the availability of a pilot environment such as a wind farm, a factory, or a physical asset to create a Digital Twin application.

Scope of a pilot implementation

In a large-scale wind-farm environment, we may use one wind farm as a pilot, or in other instances, it might be limited to a single turbine. The initial problem statement will also drive the requirements for the pilot implementation. If we assess the predicted failure on a single turbine, we need a single instance of a wind turbine for the pilot. If we optimize the power generation from a collection of turbines on a wind farm, we need access to a wind farm for the pilot rollout.

Another factor that will determine the scope of the pilot is the perspective that we have for the Digital Twin. In *Chapter 3, Identifying the First Digital Twin*, we described the different perspectives that Digital Twin users have and how their respective use cases will differ. The perspective that we chose for the prototype implementation of our first Digital Twin is that of an **original equipment manufacturer** (**OEM**), which also provides maintenance services.

Getting an agreement on the scope of a pilot is a crucial aspect in terms of delivering a successful outcome. The agreement should be with both internal and external stakeholders, and should cover the following scope dimensions:

- **Geographic**—In which specific geographical area will the pilot be conducted?
- **Organizational**—Which departments or functions of the business will be involved in the pilot?
- **Solution**—The solution scope should match the solution requirement documented in the Lean Digital Twin canvas in *Chapter 4, Getting Started with Our First Digital Twin*.
- **Integration**—Which systems do we need to integrate with?
- **Information technology** (**IT**)—What IT and infrastructure are required for our Digital Twin pilot deployment, such as a public cloud service and other licensed software?
- **Training and documentation**—What training and documentation do we provide for the pilot phase?
- **Change leadership**—What responsibility do we have for change management?

The following diagram provides a straightforward visual approach that clearly demonstrates what is in or out of scope for each dimension:

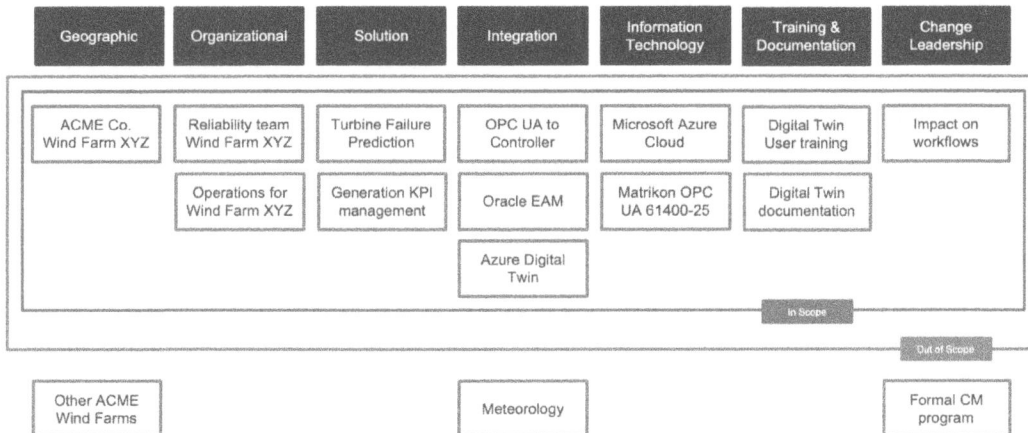

Figure 7.11 – Example pilot rollout scope diagram for wind-farm solution

The **Geographic** scope is limited to **Wind Farm XYZ** in this example for **ACME Co.**, inside the green rectangle. *Figure 7.11* also shows that it excludes the other wind farms that the **ACME Co.** company operates by placing it outside of the red or **Out of Scope** rectangle.

All the other scope dimensions can be easily identified using a similar approach to the **Geographic** scope example. The visual presentation provides clear boundaries for the scope without writing excessive documentation to describe each element. It is easy to present to project sponsors and clearly outlines areas of responsibility and the impact that it will have on organizational resources.

Once the scope of the pilot rollout is agreed upon, it is also essential to establish the success criteria for the pilot phase. Settling on the measures and **key performance indicators** (**KPIs**) upfront ensures that the goalposts are not continuously moving as the pilot progresses. It is also essential that you agree on these success criteria with the project sponsor, stating them in clear and simple terms for all the stakeholders on the project.

Success criteria for a pilot phase

We suggest that you divide the success criteria for the pilot rollout into the three simple categories shown in the following diagram:

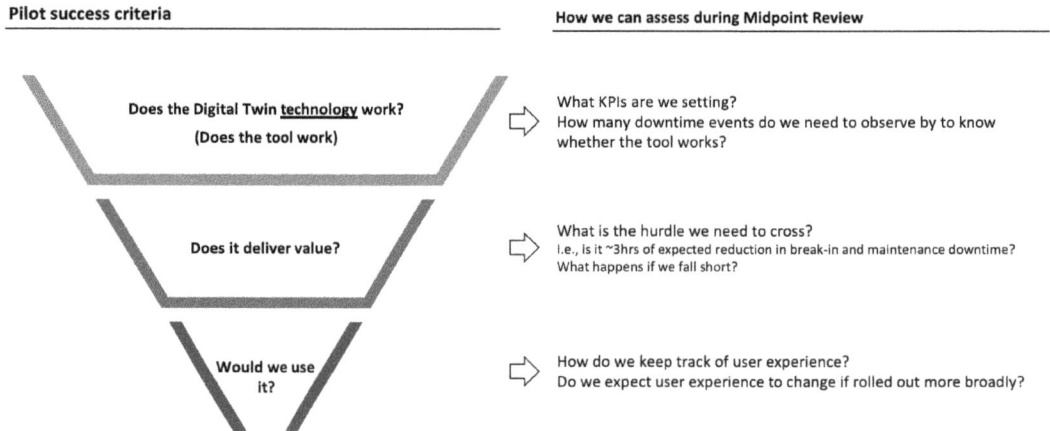

Pilot success criteria

How we can assess during Midpoint Review

Does the Digital Twin <u>technology</u> work?

(Does the tool work)

What KPIs are we setting?
How many downtime events do we need to observe by to know whether the tool works?

Does it deliver value?

What is the hurdle we need to cross?
I.e., is it ~3hrs of expected reduction in break-in and maintenance downtime?
What happens if we fall short?

Would we use it?

How do we keep track of user experience?
Do we expect user experience to change if rolled out more broadly?

Figure 7.12 – Creating pilot success criteria

The first success measure is to determine if the technology and tools are working as expected. In the wind-farm example, we can measure the number of predicted failures, exception events, and alerts that the Digital Twin provided during the evaluation. If we are confident that the technology and application are working, we can move to the next decision gate and success measure.

Measuring the value of the solution ties back to the expected business outcomes that we defined in *Chapter 4*, *Getting Started with Our First Digital Twin*.

This success measure is critical in the pilot phase as it will indicate the expected **return on investment** (**ROI**) when this is deployed at scale on completion of the pilot phase. While the first gate tests the technical success, the question of value is an important consideration for a project sponsor to give the green light for a full rollout of the solution.

The final success measure addressed is change management and the use of the application in the organization. A solution may be technically viable and deliver business value, but users are not motivated or willing to change the way they work. Monitoring the frequency at which users access the system or respond to alerts and actions generated by the Digital Twin provides quantifiable metrics on the use of the application. This success measure should also include a commitment to the ongoing maintenance of the Digital Twin configuration, which includes the Digital Twin prototype and integration points.

Setting these criteria at the start of the pilot rollout makes it easy to decide on the solution's success during the piloting. It also removes the emotional influence of stakeholders as expectations are set at the start and do not change as the pilot progresses.

Timeline and phases of a pilot solution

The timeline and phases for the pilot rollout will vary based on the scope and complexity of your Digital Twin prototype. We propose a three-phase plan for the pilot evaluation of your Digital Twin. **Phase 1** focuses on the solution development cycle, **Phase 2** focuses on the evaluation of the prototype, and **Phase 3** is used to document the results and feedback from the pilot rollout. The following screenshot shows the three proposed phases with typical durations in weeks for each phase. The duration should be adjusted for your project and environment:

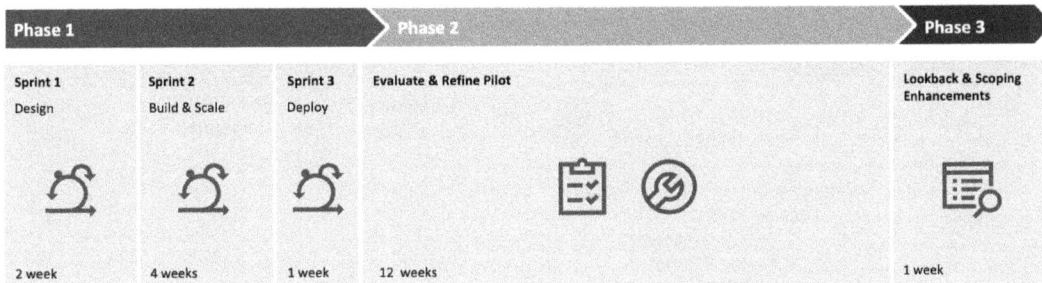

Figure 7.13 – Pilot rollout phases

The following table provides some guidance on the actions in each sprint cycle during **Phase 1**:

Phase 1 Design, Build and Scale				
	Project Management	IT, Integration and Data	Training and CM	Operational Capability

Sprint 1:
 	
Design
	Description
	• Design the logic for one unit/asset
	  o Digital Twin Visualization at asset level (discrete twin)
	  o Data streams logic
	• Design how to scale the logic for multiple units/assets
	  o Digital Twin Visualization at portfolio level (composite twin)
	  o Data streams logic
	• Establish a baseline
	• Deploy software			

	Deliverables			
	• Test plan • Design specification • Sign off	• Integration plan • Data mapping • Target architecture		• UI prototype/s • Data Stream/s • Baseline established

Sprint 2:
 	
Build and Scale
	Description
	• Build the discrete twin
	  o Configure the data streams
	  o Configure the Digital Twin Visualization
	  o Test to the test plan
	• Build the composite twin
	  o Configure the data streams
	  o Configure the Digital Twin Visualization
	  o Test to the test plan			

	Deliverables			
	• Sign off	• Test results	• Material outline	• Data Stream/s • App page/s

Sprint 3:
 	
Deploy
	Description
	• Deploy
	  o IT governance
	  o User training
	  o Post go-live support
	  o Start evaluation			

	Deliverables			
	• Sign off • Start evaluation feedback	• IT governance signoff	• User material	• Live running production system

Figure 7.14 – Sprints in Phase 1: Designing, building, and scaling

We explain the **Agile** approach and **Sprint** cycles in *Chapter 3, Identifying the First Digital Twin*, and it is ideally suited to the prototyping phase of your Digital Twin project.

Figure 7.14 indicates typical actions and needs to be adjusted to your specific project. It addresses specific deliverables for each in-scope dimension during each sprint cycle.

The **IT, Integration, and Data** deliverables include an integration plan and a target architecture in **Sprint 1** of **Phase 1**. The same approach is followed for **Phase 2**, as shown in the following table, to provide a concise scope and description of deliverables presented in a form that is easy to communicate to stakeholders:

Phase 2 Evaluate Pilot 90-day period			
Project Management	**IT, Integration & Data**	**Training & CM**	**Operational Capability**
Description			
<ul><li>Monitor to the success KPI's</li><li>Monitor to the baseline defined</li><li>Evaluate and refine the:<ul><li>data streams;</li><li>integration; and</li><li>monitor the data quality</li></ul></li><li>Evaluate and refine user experience on the Digital Twin Visualization</li><li>Recommendations for optimization's (fine-tuning set points)</li><li>Formal knowledge/skills Transfer</li></ul>			
Deliverables			
<ul><li>KPI's Signed/Acknowledged by Project Owner and Project Coordinator</li><li>Quantify the improvements against the baseline</li></ul>		• User Material	• Recommendations for operations optimization

Figure 7.15 – Phase 2: Evaluating pilot

Next, we look at the **Phase 3** deliverable, as shown in the following diagram, which deals with the optimization and realization phase:

Phase 3 Optimize & Realize
Description
<ul><li>Project lookback</li><li>Scoping the extending of the functionality of this solution for additional capabilities</li><li>Scoping the deployment of this solution to other sites</li></ul>

Figure 7.16 – Phase 3: Optimization and realization

You will increase the likelihood of success of your pilot if you use a combination of the scope diagram, success criteria, and deliverables from each pilot phase to set expectations and manage the pilot's implementation.

The main objective of the pilot phase is to evaluate the solution against the success criteria and identify areas of risk that would impact a full-scale deployment. The pilot phase is a *go/no go* gate for moving to the next phase. It is essential to demonstrate the success (or failure) of the pilot implementation to all stakeholders, including the project sponsors. If the pilot outcomes meet the success criteria, the next step would be to evaluate the pilot implementation for *lessons learned* before embarking on a full-scale deployment.

Presenting pilot results

Project sponsors appreciate a simple and straightforward presentation of the pilot results, and we suggest these results be presented in a single presentation slide, with supporting slides for each metric. The following figure shows a presentation slide based on the initial structure that we described for defining success criteria:

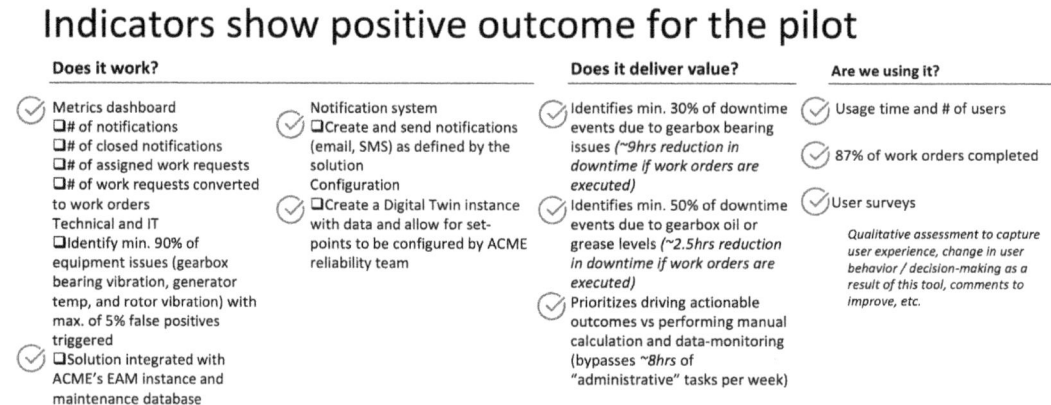

Figure 7.17 – Presenting pilot results

We also suggest that you provide evidence of some of the key operational metrics that support the economic business case to the project sponsor. *Figure 7.18* shows, for example, the performance metrics at the start of the pilot rollout, and *Figure 7.19* shows the impact at the end of the pilot phase.

The following figure shows that several predicted failures were not responded to by the maintenance team, as the business process for the maintenance planners was not yet changed to accommodate the intelligence from the Digital Twin:

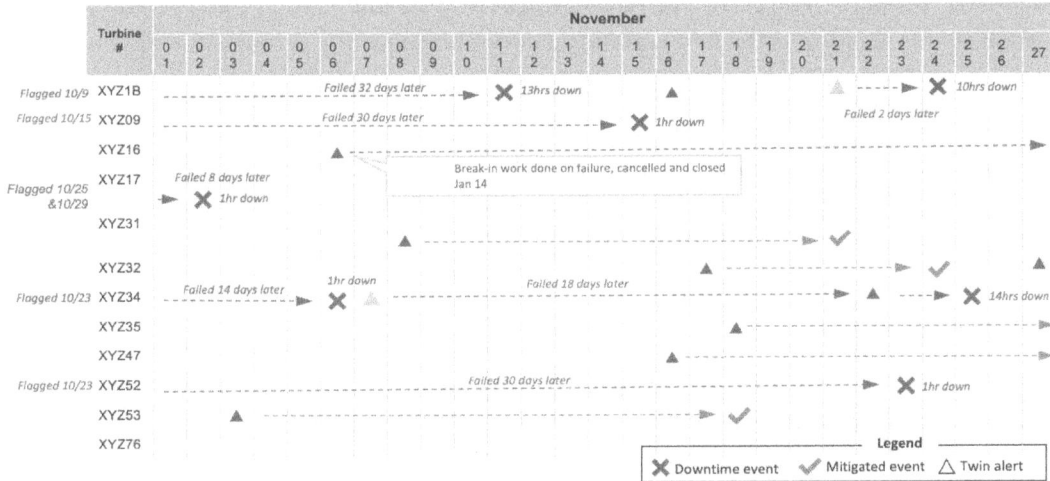

Figure 7.18 – KPI performance at the start of the pilot

The following figure shows the improvement in response to predicted failures, where almost all work is scheduled in advance and eliminated unplanned failures by more than 90%:

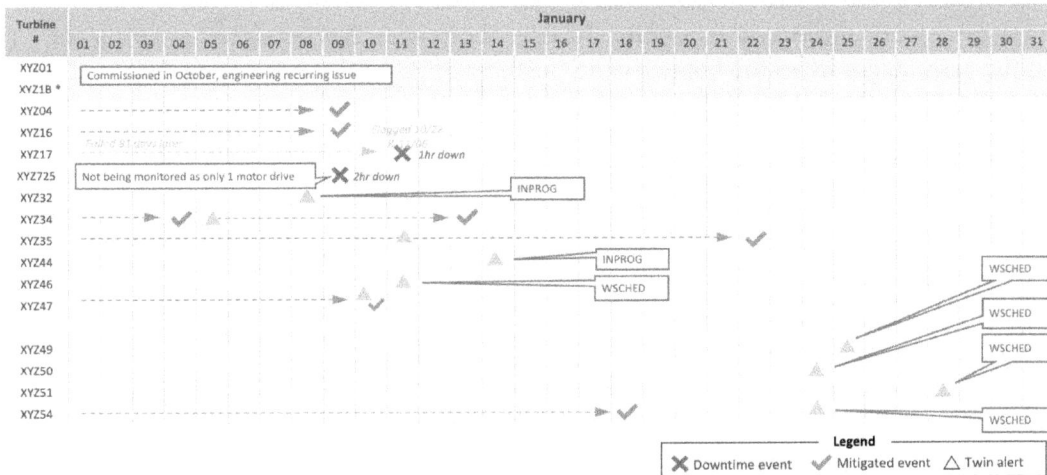

Figure 7.19 – KPI performance at the end of the pilot

In our experience, before-and-after *snapshots* work well to demonstrate the impact to busy executives who need to decide to sponsor your Digital Twin project from pilot to full-scale deployment.

The scope of this book focuses on the development of your first Digital Twin prototype, and piloting this solution is the first significant proof point for the actual value of your Digital Twin solution. For that reason, we provided an expanded explanation of the process and the steps to take during a pilot rollout.

When your pilot implementation proves that the technology works, it delivers value, the business users will use it, and it will secure sponsorship for operationalizing it at scale, then the next phase in *Figure 7.10* is to do a full-scale deployment of your Digital Twin solution.

Full deployment

Now that we've completed both prototype development and a pilot installation of our Digital Twin solution, we are ready to move to full-scale deployment.

We often hear the term *pilot purgatory*, which is associated with pilots that do not move to production. The **IoT World Forum** (**IoTWF**) reported in 2017 that 60% of IoT initiatives stall at the POC and pilot phases (`http://bit.ly/idt-IoTWF`).

This may sound like an alarming statistic, but in reality, it shows that the phased development approach of *Figure 7.10* works as it filters out projects that are likely to be unsuccessful at scale. This means that these projects could not satisfy the criteria of the technology at work, the business value, or the user acceptance. It is better to have projects fail at the early stages when the financial and business impact is limited, rather than end up with expensive failed projects that also damage personal and organizational reputations.

However, the next stage is a full-scale rollout across the new project scope for those projects that pass all the gates. The scope of a full-scale project covers all the scope elements in *Figure 7.11* but will now include the full scope for deploying the Digital Twin solution at scale. Many of the items that were shown as *out of scope* for the pilot will be *in scope* for the full-scale rollout.

This new scope will also define the best approach for deploying your Digital Twin solutions to multiple assets in multiple locations, such as the scenario we have in the wind-farm example.

Next, we deep dive into implementation approaches.

Full-scale implementation approaches

Large-scale distributed software projects typically follow one of two types of scaling deployment approaches. These approaches became popular in deploying complex **enterprise resource planning** (**ERP**) solutions, but provide excellent guidance built on experiences in large-scale software-based solution deployment. Here are these two commonly used approaches:

- Big-bang approach
- Phased approach

Let's now look at the details of each of these approaches.

Big-bang approach

A **big-bang** approach describes a scenario where all the functionality of your Digital Twin solution is deployed across all assets in all locations. This approach means that all the Digital Twin instances go live simultaneously, and it is effective under the following conditions:

- Basic Digital Twin functionality that passed the pilot implementation without any technical challenges
- Limited geographical scope
- A limited number of installations

Complex Digital Twins with extensive integration are not ideal candidates for big-bang implementations. The geographical scope should be limited to close proximity for the different sites—for example, a smaller company with a limited number of wind farms in a county or state may benefit from a single implementation cycle. We would also not recommend a big-bang approach to projects with more than two or three implementation sites for Digital Twins.

A big-bang approach is a higher risk than a phased approach. Still, one of the significant benefits is that an organization can enjoy quicker business value and results from their Digital Twins.

A final point to consider while choosing between a big-bang or phased implementation approach is the impact on the organization. A big-bang approach typically has a more significant effect on resource availability and time that business users need to spend on the Digital Twin system and changing their business processes as a result of implementing Digital Twins.

A big-bang approach may suit smaller-scale, limited-scope projects, but the preferred method is to deploy full-scale Digital Twin projects in a phased rollout to reduce risk and impact on the organization.

Phased approach

A phased implementation approach is precisely as the name indicates. Based on the scope elements, we decide whether to roll out all the functionality on a site-by-site basis or even break it into sub-phases for different use cases.

The complexity of your solution will determine whether you can implement the complete Digital Twin solution in a site-based phased approach. One of the benefits of a phased approach is that you can set milestones based on different scenarios or variables, such as the following:

- Digital-twin use case
- Business unit or plant/factory/site
- Geographic location

The only major drawback of this approach is that it typically takes much longer than a big-bang approach, which means it will take longer to realize the business impact of your Digital Twin project.

One of the most significant benefits of this approach, however, is improved usability and adoption. Employees incrementally build their capability, especially when the phased approach is done not just by site but also by Digital Twin use case.

The following screenshot shows an example of a global mining company that phased its Digital Twin project implementation by mine site and use case. The mining company operates six mine sites for this specific commodity and ranked mining sites based on feasibility and replicability:

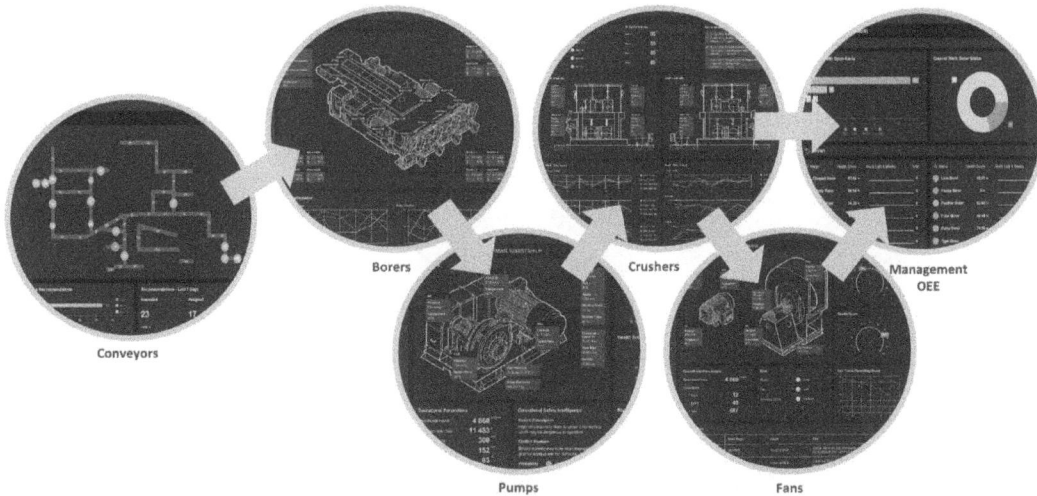

Figure 7.20 – Phased by geography and Digital Twin use case (image courtesy of XMPro Inc)

The pilot project was limited to the underground conveyors, and the lessons learned from this site were used in planning a full-scale rollout of the multiple Digital Twin use cases across the six mining sites.

The site of the initial pilot continued with borers, pumps, crushers, fans, and other Digital Twin use cases, while the other mine site started with the conveyor Digital Twin implementation in a similar phased approach. Not all the mine sites had the same infrastructure, sensors, and systems as the initial pilot site. Their specific phased rollout plan included additional infrastructure components added to the scope that were not required at the initial pilot mining site. This raises an important aspect of a phased approach. The phased rollout plan still needs customization based on feasibility, as the technical environment in large-scale deployments invariably differs.

The following screenshot provides a simple, single-slide presentation of the approach you can use with project sponsors and executives to describe the strategy:

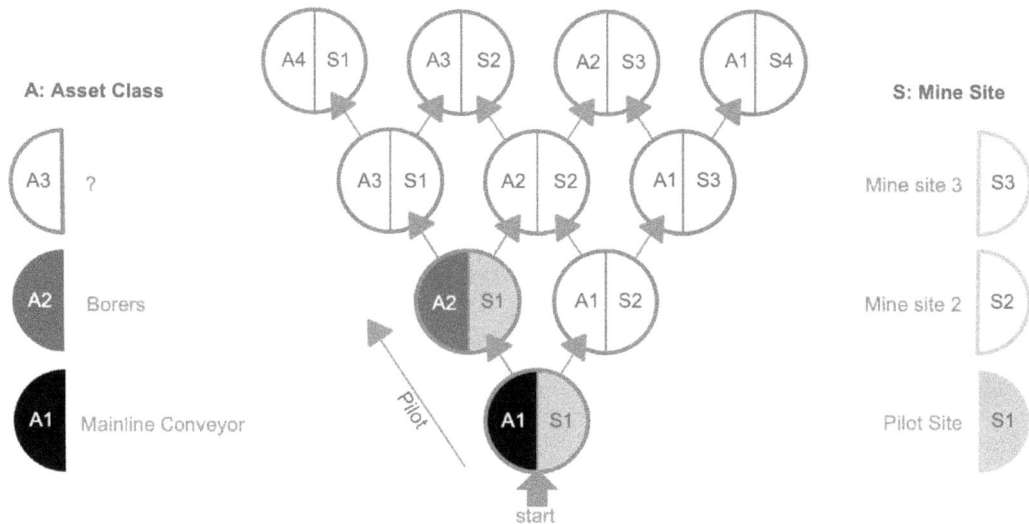

Figure 7.21 – Bowling-alley plan for a phased rollout

The circles represent a specific asset class or use case per site, factory, or geographic dimension. For the mining example, **A1** denotes the conveyor and **S1** denotes the initial pilot site. Upon successfully completing the pilot, the initial site deploys the next Digital Twin use case for borers. As shown with the help of the arrows on the left side of *Figure 7.21*, they move on a trajectory on their own phased rollout of any additional Digital Twin use cases.

Mine site 2, depicted by **S2**, starts with a phased rollout of the conveyors, and the arrows on the right side of *Figure 7.21* show the conveyor digital rollout to all mine sites in a phased approach.

The timeline for the use cases and the mine sites can then easily be phased, as represented in the following screenshot. This is a simple example, but it illustrates the ability to phase by use case and implementation or installation site:

Digital Twin Use Case	Month 1	Month 2	Month 3	Month 4	Month 5	Month 6
Conveyors	Mine 1	Mine 2	Mine 3	Mine 4	Mine 5	Mine 6
Borers		Mine 1	Mine 2	Mine 3	Mine 4	Mine 5
Pumps			Mine 1	Mine 2	Mine 3	Mine 4
Crushers				Mine 1	Mine 2	Mine 3
Fans					Mine 1	Mine 2
OEE						Mine 1

Figure 7.22 – Phased rollout timeline by mine site

This is not the only phased implementation approach that can be used to implement your Digital Twin solutions; however, we found it to be an efficient approach for large-scale complex Digital Twin projects. An alternative approach, for example, would be to roll at all the Digital Twin use cases at a single mine site before moving to the following mine site. Organizational resources, the business case, and user adoption will influence the most suited approach to your Digital Twin project.

The phased approach is lower risk, but it will take a longer time to realize its business value. It typically has a lower impact on the organization, but long timelines can also lead to frustration. Consider the pros and cons of both these approaches and decide what is best for your Digital Twin project implementation.

Let's next focus on the rollout.

Wind-farm Digital Twin rollout

In *Chapter 6*, *Building the Digital Twin Prototype*, we created a prototype of a wind farm with wind turbines on ADT. It is a basic wind turbine asset structure, and the DTDL definition files contain a subset of all the potential properties.

For a full-scale production deployment of a wind-farm Digital Twin, we recommend reviewing the DTDL ontology for Energy Grid (http://bit.ly/idt-energyontology) that is adapted from the **Common Information Model** (**CIM**), a global standard for energy-grid assets management, power system operations modeling, and physical energy commodity markets (http://bit.ly/idt-cim). International standard *IEC 61400-25*, *Communications for monitoring and control of wind power plants* (http://bit.ly/idt-iec61400) provides a standardized data model for information exchange for wind farms and wind turbines.

The standard prescribes a number of logical information nodes for the wind turbine, the controller, and meteorology that can be used in the management of wind turbines and wind farms. *Part 2* of the specification describes the wind turbine and asset-information models, whereas *Part 6* defines a condition monitoring information model for wind farms.

The following diagram shows the logical nodes in the information model as described by *IEC 61400-25*. It lists the components of the wind turbine and the controller unit, alarm information, and meteorology data:

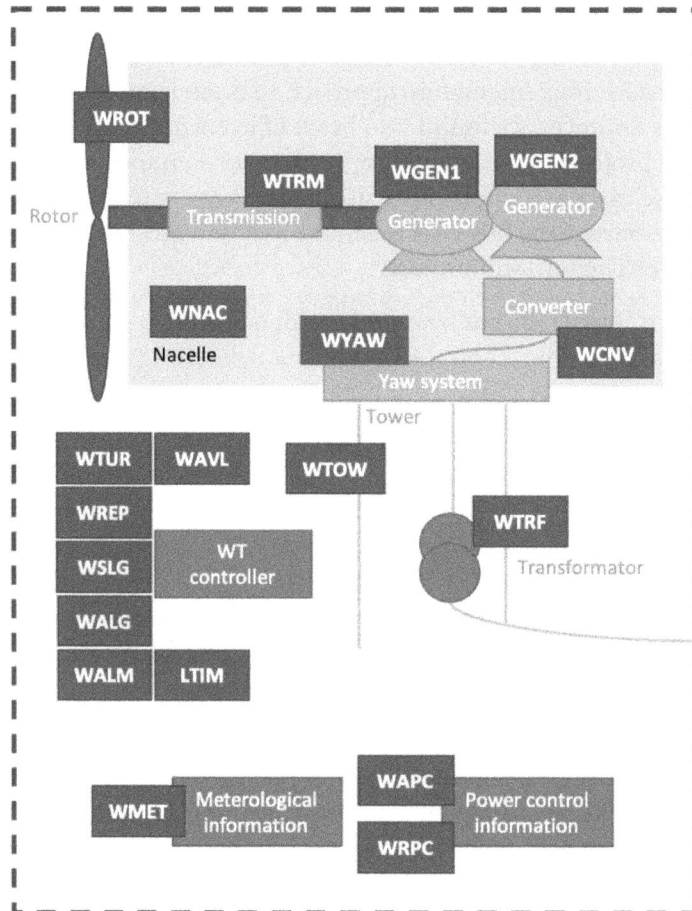

Diagram adapted from IEC 61400-25-2: Communications for monitoring and control of wind power plants – Information models

Figure 7.23 – IEC 614100-25 information model logic nodes
(Image credit: https://bit.ly/idt-iec61400model)

The transmission (**WTRM**) logical node prescribes the data model, as shown in the following table:

WTRM class			
Data Object Name	Common Data	Explanation	M/O
		LN shall inherit all Mandatory Data from Wind Power Plant Common Logical No	M
Data			
Common information			
Status information			
BrkOpSt	STV	Status of shaft brake	O
LuSt	STV	Status of gearbox lubrication system	O
FilSt	STV	Status of filtration system	O
ClSt	STV	Status of transmission cooling system	O
HtSt	STV	Status of heating system	O
OilLevSt	STV	Status of oil level in gearbox sump	O
OfFilSt	STV	Status of offline filter contamination	O
InlFilSt	STV	Status of inline filter contamination	O
Measured and metered values			
ShftBrgTmp	MV	Measured temperature of shaft bearing	O
GbxOilTmp	MV	Measured temperature of gearbox oil	O
ShftBrkTmp	MV	Measured temperature of shaft brake (surface)	O
GbxVbr	MV	Measured gearbox vibration	O
GsLev	MV	Grease level for lubrication of main shaft bearing	O
GbxOilLev	MV	Oil level in gearbox sump	O
GbxOilPres	MV	Gear oil pressure	O
BrkHyPres	MV	Hydraulic pressure for shaft brake	O
OfFil	MV	Offline filter contamination	O
InlFil	MV	Inline filter contamination	O

Figure 7.24 – IEC 614100-25 WTRM logical node information model

Figure 7.24 provides a standardized class name (**WTRM**) and defines three types of data in this example, as follows:

- **Common information**
- **Status information**
- **Measured and metered values**

It further defines mandatory and optional information for each logical node and describes the relationship of the class to the overall data model.

The model and subsequent **data definition language** (DDL) models are more advanced than the example we used in the initial Digital Twin configuration. Our focus for the book is on the technology aspect of the Digital Twin configuration rather than an *IEC 61400-25*-compliant wind turbine Digital Twin. However, for a production system, we would recommend a standards-based approach to ensure interoperability into microgrids and distribution grids.

This section described the entire evolution of the deployment process shown in *Figure 7.10*, starting with the POC ideation, prototype, pilot implementation, and full-scale rollout guidance. The final step in the evolution is not a distinct phase but instead makes sure that we track the value of the Digital Twin solution as it goes from concept to an operational system.

We defined the problem statement and outcomes in *Chapter 4, Getting Started with Our First Digital Twin*. Closing the loop on this initial work is the final task for a project team before handing it to a support organization to maintain and operate going forward.

Value proposition and tracking

In *Chapter 1, Introduction to Digital Twin*, we described the value proposition of a Digital Twin based in terms of the following abilities:

- Reduce complexity to improve understanding. This can lead to a) improved situational awareness and b) improved business outcomes. The improved business outcomes would be reflected in 1) increased revenue, 2) reduced cost, 3) improved customer and employee experience, and 4) improved compliance and reduced risk.

- Transformational value—namely, a) business transformation through digital transformation and b) new or improved products.

- Value at stake, which can be looked at as a) value to industry and b) value to society. The value to industry can be value migration or value addition. The value to society can be economic, societal benefits such as improved skills and/or a safer work environment, and—finally—environmental.

The key elements of all of these value metrics were captured in a lean Digital Twin canvas in *Chapter 4, Getting Started with Our First Digital Twin*, and presented to project teams, executive sponsors, and other stakeholders. It is essential to track these metrics and values during each phase of your Digital Twin project. It is a **continuous monitoring** (CM) process that runs in parallel to all the other activities throughout the development and operations life cycle.

Project sponsors are interested in the financial ROI, but they are increasingly interested in **environmental, social, and governance (ESG)** KPIs due to the increased awareness and legislation on sustainability. Senior executives in organizations are making public statements on sustainability targets, and the continuous tracking and forecasting toward the achievement of those goals are areas of high importance for the executive of an organization.

We recommend building value-tracking metrics into the capabilities and reporting of a Digital Twin—a real-time, self-validating Digital Twin that provides continuous insights into the operations and reduces the continuous effort to track value metrics through manual effort. You have a unique opportunity with a Digital Twin to not only provide value but also quantify the value from a Digital Twin continuously.

Summary

In this chapter, we covered the deployment and scaling of a solution in an operational environment. We addressed four key aspects of turning a Digital Twin prototype into a fully operational Digital Twin solution.

The first key aspect in turning a prototype into a production system is to address the functional testing of the Digital Twin solution. The testing process is to ensure that the Digital Twin solution performs the functions as specified at the requirements at the start of the prototype. In this chapter, we addressed various functional testing processes such as unit testing and black-box testing to illustrate how to test Digital Twins for full-scale deployment.

We described the process of creating a pilot implementation as the second aspect of turning a prototype into a production system. This reduces the risk of a project while proving the capabilities and value in a real-world application.

The third aspect in turning a prototype into a production system is planning and executing a full-scale deployment that builds on the learnings of the pilot phases. We assessed the pros and cons of big-bang and phased approaches and presented a bowling-alley model for a phased approach as our preferred method of scaling out from a pilot.

Finally, we evaluated the success of the solution based on its ability to demonstrate the value it was designed to deliver and we described the process to track the value in a value-at-stake model first introduced in *Chapter 1, Introduction to Digital Twin*.

In the following chapter, we will focus on enhancing the Digital Twin in its ecosystem, describing a system-of-systems Digital Twin approach, and providing some guidance on planning these composite twins.

Questions

1. What are the different functional testing methods that you should consider for your Digital Twin project?

2. Which scope elements will you include in your Digital Twin project?

3. What are the success criteria for your Digital Twin pilot project and how will you present the criteria to the project stakeholders?

4. What approach will you need for a full-scale rollout to take the project beyond the initial pilot?

5. How will you track and present the value of your Digital Twin prototype to create a case to move it beyond a pilot?

Section 3: Enhancing the Digital Twin

In this final part of the book, you will learn how to improve the Digital Twin and plan the twin of twins, as well as considering future enhancements.

This section comprises the following chapter:

- *Chapter 8, Enhancing the Digital Twin*

8
Enhancing the Digital Twin

In *Chapter 7, Deployment and Value Tracking*, we discussed how to perform functional testing and then planned the deployment and rollout of the pilot for the Digital Twin. We looked at the ways to track the **Key Performance Indicators** (**KPIs**) and the overall value of the Digital Twin of the wind turbines. A successful pilot deployment of a Digital Twin often leads to rollout at scale to achieve the targeted business goals.

In this chapter, we will look at ways to enhance the Digital Twin beyond the pilot phase. We will consider the perspective of different organizations to drive economic outcomes. We will cover the following topics in this chapter:

- Defining the Twin of Twins
- Evaluating the First Digital Twin in the Full System
- Identifying related Twins
- Planning Composite Twins
- Enhancements and next steps

Let's start with the digital "twin of twins" concept.

Defining the Twin of Twins

In this context, terms such as composite twins, twin of twins, and system of systems are often used. Let's use the example of the energy ecosystem to understand this concept. In the energy ecosystem, we look at the hierarchy as follows:

- An energy value chain that will consist of a) generation, b) transmission, c) distribution, and d) consumption, as shown in *Figure 8.1*. The grid can have one or many generation sources.

- Energy generation can be broadly divided into a) fossil fuel or non-renewable sources and b) renewable sources.

- With renewable sources, we can look at a) wind, b) solar, and c) hydro.

- Wind farms can be a) onshore (land) or b) offshore (water).

- Each wind farm will often consist of several turbines.

- Each wind turbine has several sub-systems or sub-assemblies and components.

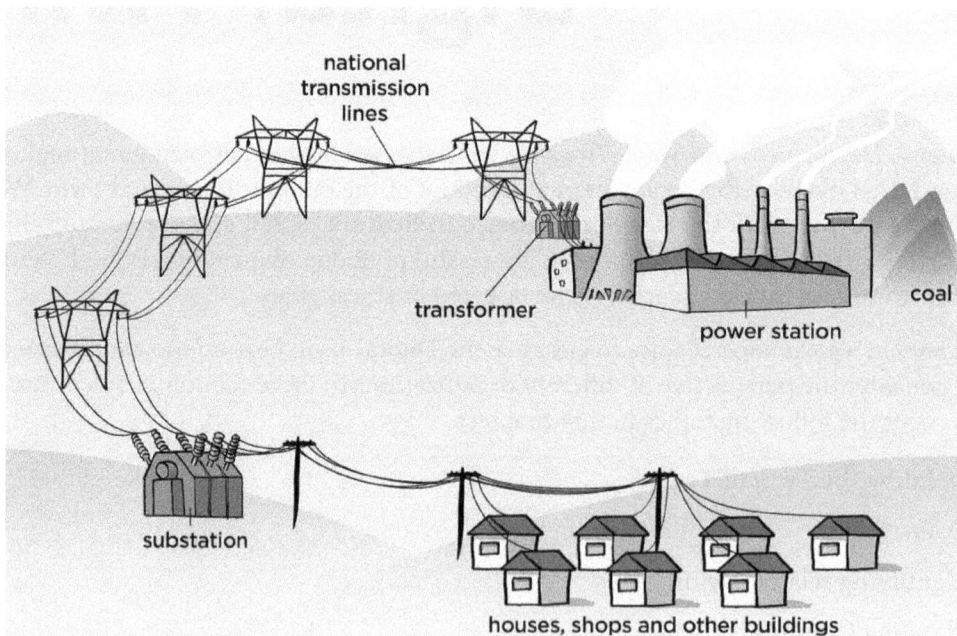

Figure 8.1 – The energy value chain, including generation, transmission, and distribution

> **Note**
> Image source: `https://www.flickr.com/photos/121935927@`
> `N06/13580677703`

A common example of the sub-systems of a wind turbine would be the rotor system, gearbox, blades, nacelle, generator, hydraulics, brakes, and the yaw system. We covered this in *Figure 6.3* in *Chapter 6, Building the Digital Twin Prototype*. The overall reliability or the uptime of the wind turbine will depend on the reliability and uptime of the sub-systems.

For more information, refer to the following:

```
https://www.researchgate.net/publication/271973476_
Reliability_Analysis_of_Sub_Assemblies_for_Wind_Turbine_at_
High_Uncertain_Wind
```

Based on this hierarchy view of the ecosystem, we can visualize the twin of twins shown in *Figure 8.2* at a very high level:

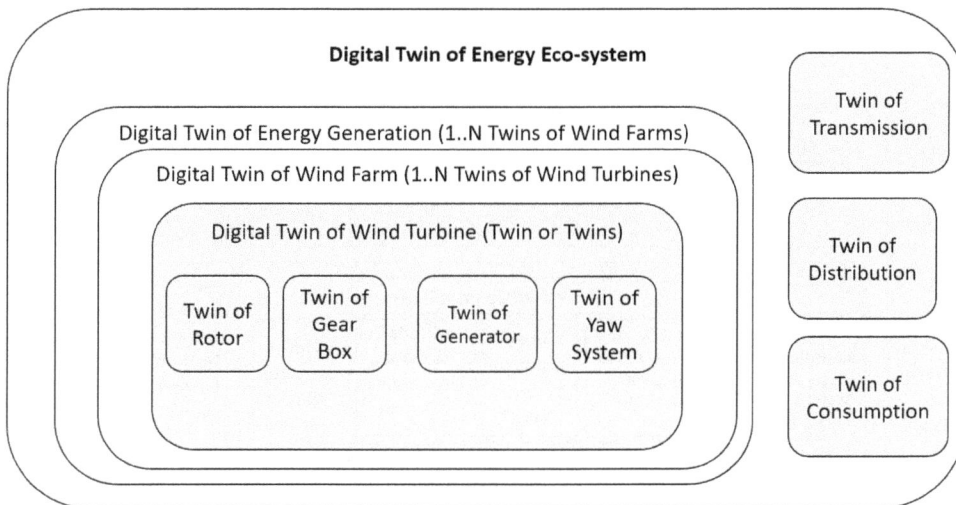

Figure 8.2 – The concept of the Digital Twin of twins for the energy ecosystem

While the prior chapters of this book are limited to the Digital Twin of the Wind Turbine, it is important to understand the concept of the Twin of Twins as shown in *Figure 8.2* to plan for the deployment of the Digital Twin of the Wind Turbine at scale. If we look at the energy ecosystem from the perspective of an energy utility company that uses a wind farm(s) as one of the means of renewable energy, they will look to plan for other forms of generation as well. The other forms of generation, whether a solar farm(s) or gas-turbine power plant(s), may also have an associated Digital Twin of Twins. Hence, it is important to look at this problem statement as a system of systems. In theory, this may seem like a recursive relation, but different other engineering manufacturers of the different equipment could lead to different Digital Twin systems. This leads to the challenge of the interoperability of the Digital Twins in the composite solution.

The role of standards

There are a few efforts to introduce standards, to make interoperability of twins easier. In *Chapter 7, Deployment and Value Tracking, Figure 7.23* shows IEC 61400-25, which describes the standard data model for the interchange of information in the context of wind farms.

Another such body is the SC 41, which is a subcommittee under JTC 1. JTC 1 is the joint **International Organization for Standardization** (**ISO**) and **International Electrotechnical Commission** (**IEC**). SC 41 is working on **Internet of Things** (**IoT**) and Digital Twin-related standards. For more information, refer to the following:

`https://www.iso.org/committee/6483279.html and https://www.iec.ch/blog/moving-ahead-standardization-digital-twin`

Figure 8.3 shows the scope of the work of SC 41 in this context:

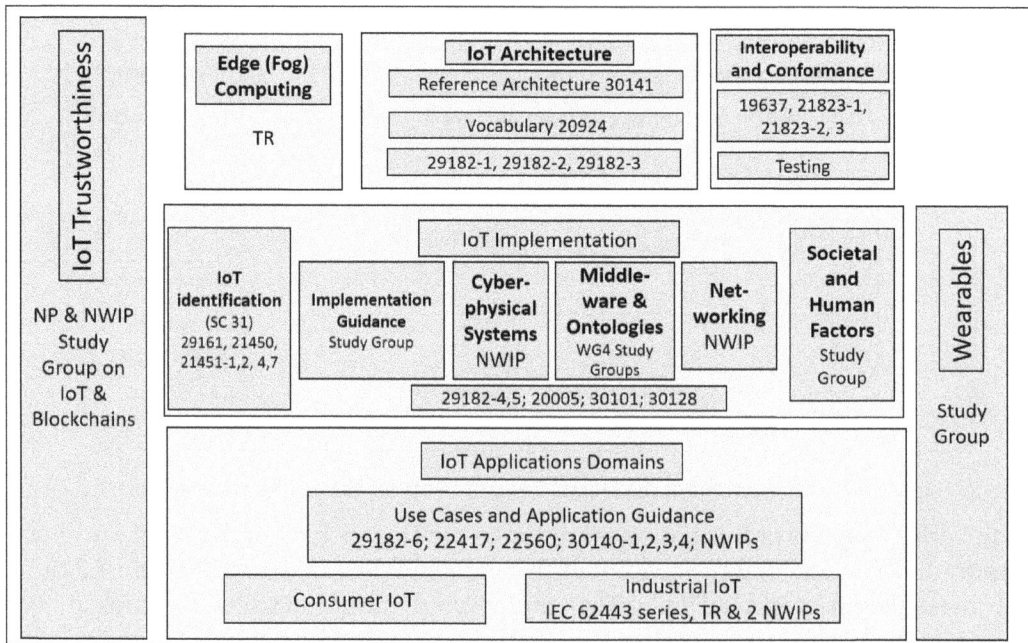

Figure 8.3 – Scope of SC 41 and its activities

> **Note**
>
> Image recreated from source: `https://www.itu.int/en/ITU-T/Workshops-and-Seminars/20180604/Documents/Francois_Coallier_P_V2.pdf]`

In this context of the scope of activities of the SC 41 group, we should consider the term IoT in its broader sense, which would include technologies such as a Digital Twin.

Some of the standards-related work by the SC 41 group includes the following:

- ISO/IEC 21823-2, which describes a framework and requirements for the information exchange of IoT systems. It covers communication between IoT systems and within an IoT system.

- ISO/IEC TR 30164, which describes the general concepts for edge computing for IoT system applications. Our scenario, computing a wind turbine, could be considered edge computing of an IoT system.

- ISO/IEC TR 30166, which covers **Industrial IoT (IIoT)** systems and landscapes. It covers functional as well as non-functional aspects of IIoT. For more information, refer to `https://www.iso.org/news/ref2529.html`.

We can see that the IoT- and Digital Twin-related standards are still evolving. We recommend that stakeholders of the Digital Twin initiative keep an eye on such evolving standards as project PWI JTC1-SC41-5 for the Digital Twin reference architecture. The stakeholders can incorporate them in their planning, to allow for interoperability with other systems. Some of the related documentation can be found here: `https://www.iec.ch/dyn/www/f?p=103:23:0:::::FSP_ORG_ID:20486`.

The **National Institute of Standards and Technology** (**NIST**) is also working on NISTIR 8356 considerations for Digital Twin Technology and emerging standards. For more information, refer to `https://csrc.nist.gov/News/2021/draft-nistir-8356-digital-twin-technology`. This draft document under the "trust considerations" of the Digital Twin talks about a "system of systems" that applies to the twin of twins. When a Digital Twin is composed of twins of different physical objects, the errors and corruption in data originating from the underlying twins can propagate and adversely impact the twin of twins. As a result, this document suggests that the underlying "twins should be wrapped with pre-conditions and post-conditions to determine if the output from one twin will be acceptable as input to another twin."

This section about the emerging standards and guidelines for Digital Twins provides considerations and best practices for twin of twins systems. We recommend that the stakeholders of Digital Twin solutions keep a close eye on such emerging standards and guidelines to make their solutions robust and interoperable.

Let's next look at how to set the vision for the twin of twins.

Setting the vision

In the prior section, we learned about the twin of twins. *Figure 8.4* shows a high-level view of how our first Digital Twin, which is the Digital Twin of the wind turbine, fits in the system of systems. This diagram shows the overall journey of leveraging Digital Twins to drive efficiency and digital revenue streams in the energy sector.

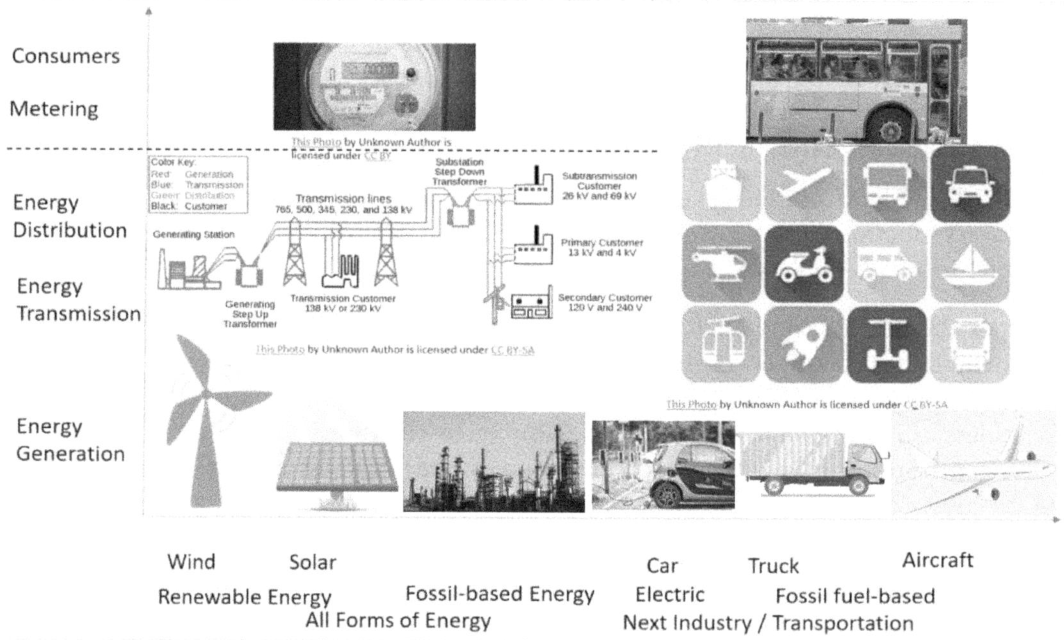

Figure 8.4 – Setting the Digital Twins vision across the industry segments

The Digital Twin of the wind turbine helps to model scenarios such as the following:

- Possible damage to the wind turbine if the wind blew harder than normal, such as a hurricane or tornado

- Impact on energy generation if the wind blew at 25 to 30 miles per hour for a sustained period

- Impact on energy generation if the wind speed was below 5 miles per hour for a long period of time

These scenarios regarding the utility of the Digital Twin help us position the wind turbine and the wind farm in the context of the energy generation grid. In *Figure 8.1*, we showed the whole electricity value chain, which sets the broader context. *Figure 8.4* further depicts how a utility company can plan the future rollout of the Digital Twins of the different modes of energy generation, both renewable and non-renewable sources. Likewise, they can then look at the Digital Twins of the transmission and distribution networks. This is a perfect way to look at the system of systems for Digital Twins.

The **Digital Twins Definition Language** (**DTDL**) ontology for the energy grid, as shown in *Figure 8.8*, would help to build out a Digital Twin application in a standardized manner.

An industrial manufacturing company that operates in multiple industry sectors, such as energy generation, transportation, and aviation, could next look at Digital Twins in the transportation and aviation sector. Examples of such industrial conglomerates include companies such as General Electric (GE), Honeywell, and Siemens.

Now that we have set the larger context of the Digital Twin as a system of systems, let's look at the evaluation of our first Digital Twin of the wind turbine.

Evaluating the first Digital Twin in the full system

In *Chapter 7, Deployment and Value Tracking*, we discussed functional testing of the Digital Twin of the wind turbine. This included testing the Digital Twin infrastructure as well as testing the Digital Twin application. Such testing precedes the pilot rollout of the Digital Twin. In *Figure 7.12*, we showed the success criteria for the pilot of the Digital Twin. Furthermore, *Figure 7.17* to *Figure 7.19* showed how to capture and present the KPIs in this context. Finally, we discussed the two rollout approaches:

- The big bang approach
- The phased approach

The big bang approach works well for mature technologies such as the rollout of **Enterprise Resource Planning** (**ERP**) software, where technology and functionality are very well understood by the stakeholders. The big bang approach for emerging technology adds more risk from technology, adoption, and economic perspectives. We will look at a phased approach here for the purposes of evaluating the first Digital Twin in the full system.

Let's see how a full system may look from a high-level perspective. *Figure 8.5* shows a phased approach rollout of the Digital Twin solution to a wind farm:

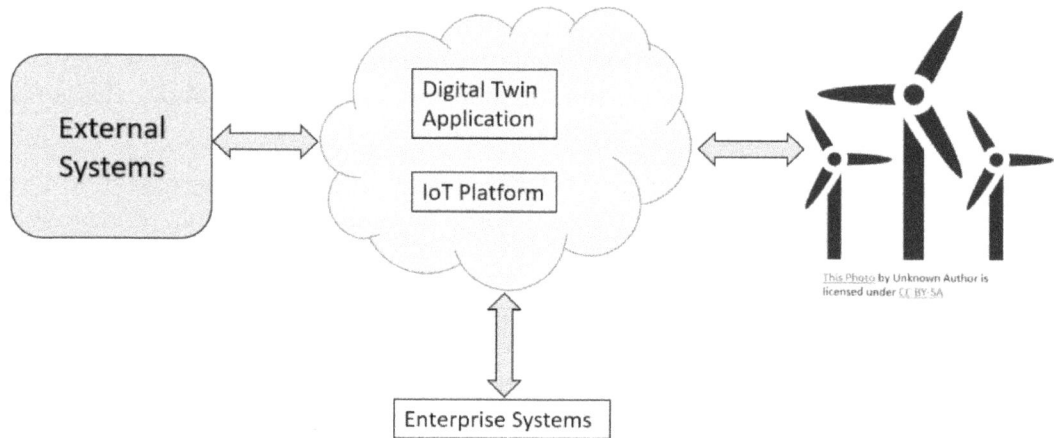

Figure 8.5 – Digital Twin rollout view at a high level

In a phased approach, the Digital Twin is rolled out to one-third of the wind turbines in a single farm. This way, the performance of the Digital Twin and the outcomes can be evaluated against the other wind turbines in the same farm. This provides a good baseline and, generally, the age and the model of the wind turbines in the same wind farm are expected to be similar. They are all subjected to the same environment, such as similar wind speeds and temperatures.

Next, let's look at why we are recommending a phased approach for the rollout of the Digital Twin solution.

Justification for the phased approach

Let's look at our justification for the phased approach using *Figure 8.6*.

For more information, refer to the following:

```
https://blogs.gartner.com/tuong-nguyen/2020/12/07/gartner-
launches-emerging-technologies-radar-2021/
```

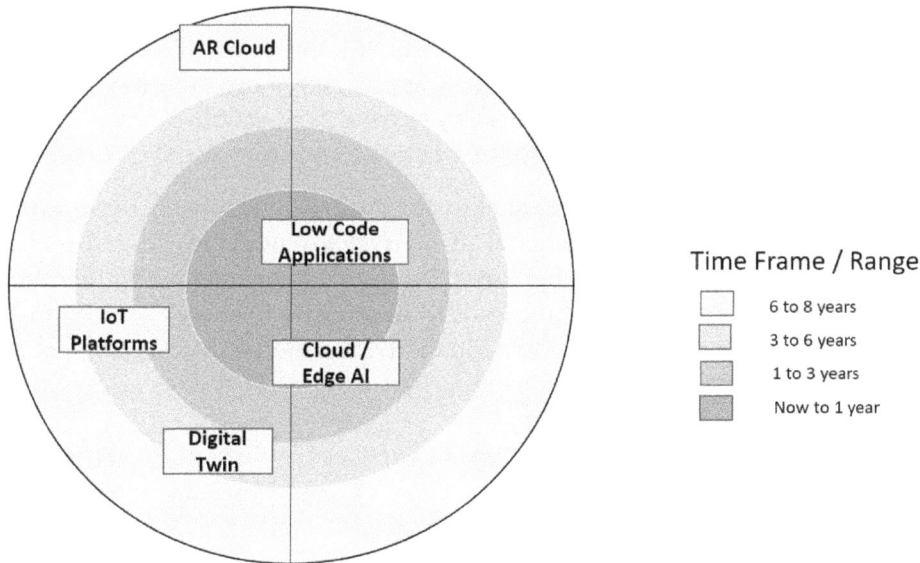

Figure 8.6 – Impact radar for emerging technologies and trends

According to this figure, technologies such as Digital Twin and IoT platforms will fully mature in about 3-6 years. On the other hand, Low-Code Application development is quite mature. This implies that a big bang rollout approach using only low-code application development has a much lower risk and is well understood. On the other hand, a big bang approach using IoT platforms and Digital Twin technology is not very well understood and carries much higher levels of risk. Hence, for an enterprise-wide solution involving the Digital Twin, it is advisable to use a phased approach. In such a plan, the solution can be tweaked along the way as the industry matures.

In the next section, let's quantify the benefits of the Digital Twin solution.

Quantification of the benefits

To quantitatively evaluate the benefits of the phased rollout of the Digital Twin solution for the wind farm, we will assume this wind farm has 150 wind turbines, which is close to the industry average. Let's use the average power generation of 1 megawatt per wind turbine and the average **Operations and Maintenance (O&M)** cost of about $45,000 per year. We will compare the cost for one-third, or 50 turbines, in the **Return on Investment (RoI)** model, as the phased rollout of the Digital Twin is for 50 wind turbines. We show the calculations in *Table 8.1*.

Let's look at the justification of the benefits from the deployment of the Digital Twin solution. A 1-megawatt wind turbine produces about $61,300 worth of electricity at 35% capacity and $87,600 worth of electricity at 50% capacity. For more information, refer to `http://anemoiservices.com/industry-news/how-much-money-does-a-wind-turbine-produce-from-electricity-it-generates/`.

We will target an uplift of about $12,000 of electricity per wind turbine per year, due to the Digital Twin deployment for operational efficiency. For renewable energy, the cost of generation does not have the variable fuel costs. Being able to operate the wind turbine more efficiently and reduce the downtime leads to an increase in energy generation. We expect another $3,000 worth of reduction in predictive maintenance costs per year. This will amount to a $15,000 net benefit per wind turbine on an annual basis.

	Item	Baseline Cost	Twin Cost	Benefit	RoI
1	Current O&M system cost	50 x $45,000 a year	50 x $5,000 a year	$15,000	50 x $10,000 a year
2	Overhead costs due to Digital Twin / cloud computing	0	$50,000 a year		-$50,000
3	Human costs	0	$50K/year		-$50K
				Net >	$400K/year

Table 8.1 – Quantifying the benefits of the Digital Twin phased rollout

We have used variable costs instead of fixed costs for our calculations. While the cost of constructing a 1-megawatt wind turbine may be in the range of $1.5 million, this is a sunk cost from our perspective when we are dealing with an existing wind farm, often referred to as a brownfield project. Since we have proposed the use of cloud computing such as the Azure Digital Twins service as the main enabling service, along with other Azure services, it is easy to look at subscription models of the cost rather than at the capital costs for the purposes of this RoI calculation. Likewise, we have estimated the overheads, such as integration costs, enterprise software, and human costs, on a per wind turbine per year basis. This keeps the model simple and reusable for other phased rollout scenarios, say at 25% of the wind farm or 50% of the wind farm, for Digital Twin coverage.

Let's further look at what kind of real-world metrics can be measured and influenced by the Digital Twin as we derive the business benefits after the rollout. A GE Renewables article discussed these in the context of their Haliade 150-6MW wind turbine, which is one of the most powerful offshore wind turbines. The temperature of the yaw motors of the wind turbine is key to improving its performance. The yaw motor controls the horizontal orientation via the wind turbine's yaw system. To see a detailed view of the cross-section of a wind turbine, including the yaw system, visit this page: `https://www.windpowerengineering.com/wp-content/uploads/2016/04/Haliade_cutaway.png`.

To maximize the generation of electricity, the yaw system keeps the rotor facing into the wind, which is important because the wind direction changes often. This is very important because, in our RoI model, we assume the Digital Twin system deployment will help to increase the energy generation and increase its efficiency from 35% to a higher level, and we can measure the economic impact of the increased energy generation.

The monitoring of the temperature, using the Digital Twin, will allow the development of the application that can decide whether to allow the full power generation and risk a higher operating temperature, which reduces material life, or slightly lessen the power generation. This is done by using the yaw motor to align the turbine based on the direction of the wind. Overall, this would help to increase the power generation without risking the breakdown of the wind turbine. This helps to achieve both higher operating efficiency of the asset as well as reduced cost of the maintenance by operating the wind turbine in the safe zone. These were the two major assumptions in our RoI calculation in *Table 8.1*. For more information, refer to `https://www.ge.com/news/reports/french-connection-digital-twins-paris-will-protect-wind-turbines-battering-north-atlantic-gales`.

In the preceding section, we looked at the business outcomes delivered by the Digital Twin of the wind turbine. We see that as the technology for the Digital Twin for the wind turbine is being proven out, there is investment from the US government such as the **Department of Energy (DOE)** in this direction. A $3.6 million research grant, DIGIFLOAT, was awarded to a consortium by the DOE's **Advanced Research Project Agency-Energy (ARPA-E)** in September 2019. The goal of DIGIFLOAT is to innovate in Digital Twin technology for floating or offshore wind turbines. **Floating Offshore Wind Turbines (FOWT)** are wind turbines in seas and oceans as opposed to land-based wind turbines. For more information, refer to the following:

`https://www.principlepowerinc.com/en/news-press/press-archive/2019/09/26/principle-power-led-consortium-awarded-36-million-for-digifloat-an-innovative-digital-twin-project-for-floating-wind-applications`

In the next section, we look at the identification of related Digital Twins.

Identifying related Digital Twins

In *Figure 8.1*, we looked into the energy ecosystem. The key parts of the electricity system are as follows:

- The generation of electricity – renewable and nonrenewable sources
- The transmission of electricity
- The distribution of electricity
- The consumption of electricity by residential and commercial consumers

This helps us to understand the electricity value chain and to identify future Digital Twins after the initial Digital Twin solution for the wind turbine is rolled out.

Let's look at *Figure 8.7*, the **Digital Twins Definition Language** (DTDL) ontology for the energy grid. Here, the ontology helps to describe the set of concepts and categories in an energy value chain. Furthermore, it helps to visualize the properties and the relations between the major components of the energy grid.

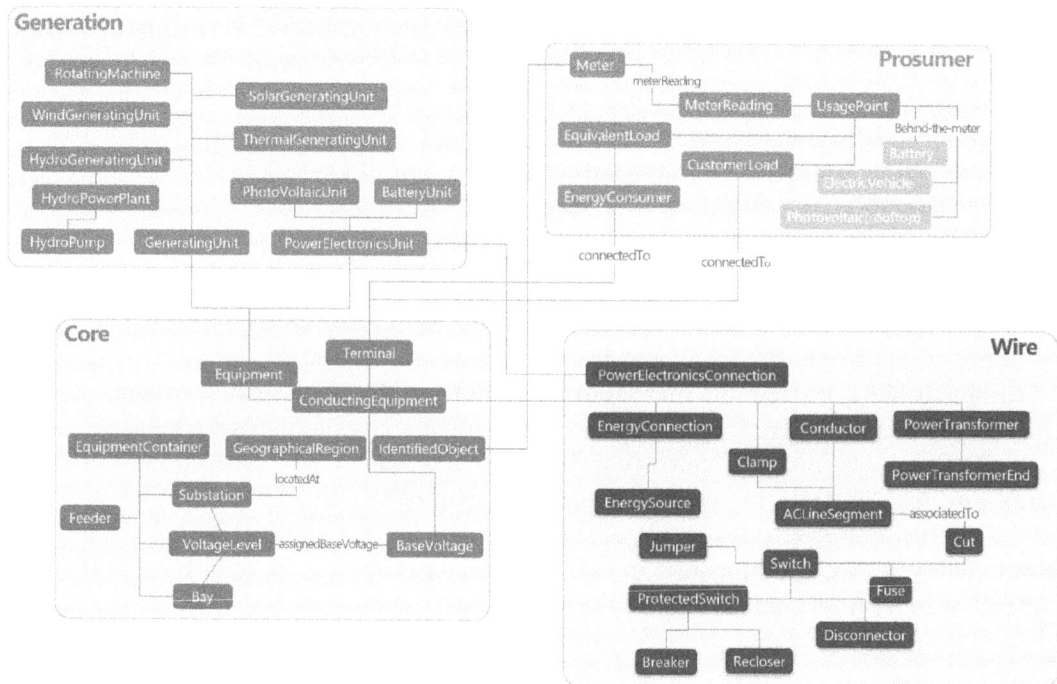

Figure 8.7 – Digital Twin ontology for the energy grid

> **Note**
>
> Image source: `https://github.com/Azure/`
> `opendigitaltwins-energygrid`

Our focus in this book has been on the Digital Twin of the wind turbine, which belongs to the generation part of the energy ecosystem. As a result, the related Digital Twins in the renewable sources of power generation will be as follows:

- Digital Twins of Offshore Wind Farms
- Digital Twin of Solar Plants
- Digital Twin of Hydro Power Plant

Considering the increased focus on renewable sources of energy, we recommend exploring these Digital Twins further. Let's look from the perspective of a utility company. To maximize the energy generation and to meet peak demands, it will have to optimize the generation reliably from all its generation assets. We assume the utility company uses renewable and nonrenewable sources of energy. We will focus on renewable sources of energy here. Let's assume the utility company has wind, solar, and hydro power plants. This is not an unrealistic scenario. One of the largest utility companies in the US, Exelon, has a "balanced portfolio of natural gas, hydro, wind, and solar" power generation. For more information, refer to `https://www.exeloncorp.com/companies/` `exelon-generation`.

In the summer of 2020, northern California faced a power shortage during hot days. One of the reasons was that some of the power plants were operating below capacity. For more information, refer to `https://www.nytimes.com/2020/08/20/business/` `energy-environment/california-blackout-electric-grid.html`.

Deploying Digital Twins for these power plants, such as wind, solar and hydro, can ensure that these assets are maintained properly and are capable of delivering the energy at their peak level on days of higher demand, such as hot summer days, where a large part of northern California has a temperature of over $100°F/38°C$. In some places, it can exceed $110°F/43°C$. The ability to improve the efficiency of the existing power generation assets will be a productive use of the Digital Twin solution.

In the prior section, we identified the Digital Twins related to the first Digital Twin of the wind turbine. Together, these Digital Twins will be transformative to a utility company in improving the productivity of their generation assets, as well as reducing their operation costs by improving the efficiency of predictive maintenance.

Next, let's look at planning for composite twins.

Planning Composite Twins

Let's first understand a simple composite asset before we get into planning composite twins. We are all familiar with commercial aircraft. Companies such as Boeing and Airbus are major manufacturers of commercial aircraft. However, a commercial aircraft such as the Boeing 747-8 (see `https://www.boeing.com/commercial/747/`), which can seat up to 410 people and uses a GEnx-2B engine from General Electric Aviation, consists of as many as 6 million parts, manufactured by about 550 suppliers in as many as 30 countries. For more information, refer to `https://boeing.mediaroom.com/2013-05-29-Boeing-Celebrates-Delivery-of-50th-747-8`.

Figure 8.8 shows a simplified view of a composite asset such as a commercial aircraft. In turn, each major part of the aircraft consists of many sub-assemblies and individual parts. *Figure 8.9* shows the jet engine of the aircraft. A single aircraft such as a Boeing 747-8 would have four jet engines on the wings at any time. Note that aircraft engines can also be taken off the aircraft for inspection and maintenance and replaced with spare engines. To make it more complex, some aircraft allow engines from different manufacturers. An oversimplified analogy would be that you can use tires or batteries from different approved manufacturers for your car.

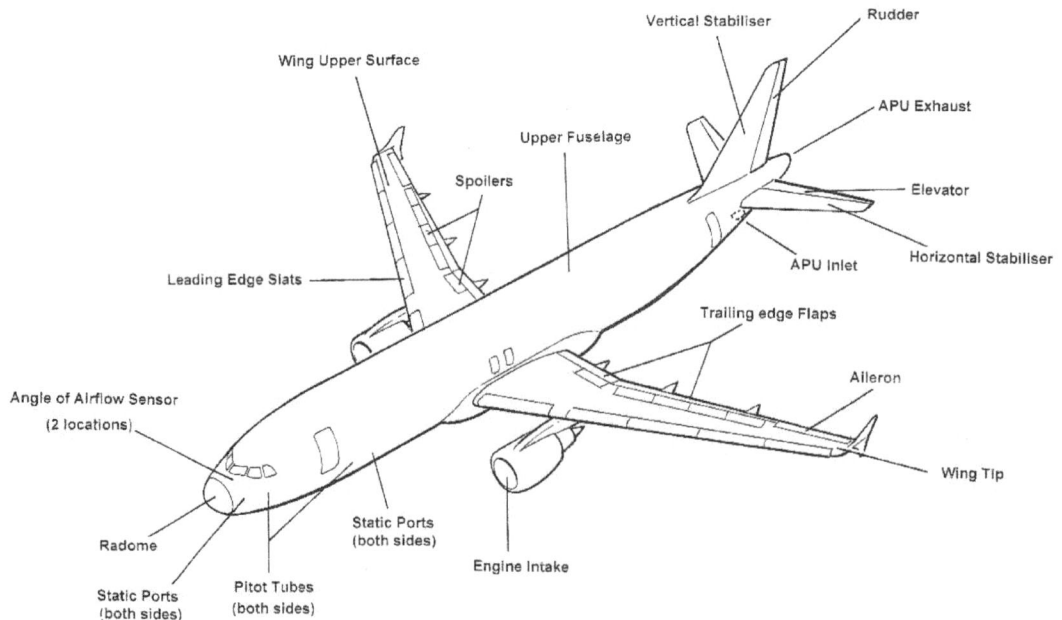

Figure 8.8 – A simplified view of the major components of a commercial aircraft

> **Note**
>
> Image source: `https://it.wikipedia.org/wiki/`
> `File:Aircraft_Parts_eng.jpg`

The jet engine is the most critical and expensive part of the aircraft. A wide-body aircraft such as the Boeing 747-8 uses four jet engines. Some other commercial aircraft, such as the Boeing 777, use two jet engines. An average jet engine can have 25,000 parts from multiple suppliers.

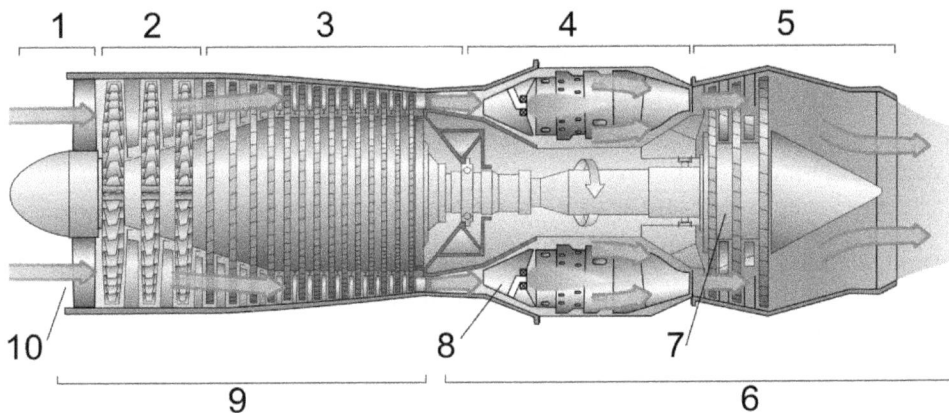

Figure 8.9 – Cross-section view of the engine of a commercial aircraft

> **Note**
>
> Image source: `https://en.wikipedia.org/wiki/Components_`
> `of_jet_engines`

Overall, we notice that real-world assets such as aircraft are very complex in nature and consist of small parts. Likewise, if we look at the other end of the spectrum, such as a fleet of aircraft for an airline, it could consist of not only different aircraft but different models and manufacturers. In addition, the airline may not only own aircraft but other assets, such as de-icing machines, baggage trolleys, **ground power units**, jet bridges, and so on. The whole network from the airline perspective is the *composite* of such a variety of assets.

From an airline perspective, the Digital Twin of its entire airline network would be a composite Digital Twin consisting of the operations of its major hubs, major routes, the fleet of aircraft, and other critical assets.

Now, back to the power generation example, where we started with the Digital Twin of the wind turbine and the wind farm. Next, we look at extending it to the different Digital Twins for renewable sources of power generation. To continue, the composite of the entire power generation for a major utility company would include the Digital Twins of renewable and nonrenewable sources. Next, the utility company would have to look at the Digital Twins of the transmission, distribution, and consumer-level assets such as smart meters.

Next, let's look at Digital Twins for hydropower.

Digital twins for hydropower

The US **Department of Energy** (**DOE**) has an office focused on water power technologies. This DOE office is working on a framework for Digital Twins for hydropower with the goal of accelerating innovation by leveraging a virtual platform. For more information, refer to `https://www.pnnl.gov/projects/digital-twins-hydropower`.

The average life expectancy of a hydropower plant is around 50 years. Digital twins of hydropower simulate the generation, transmission, and distribution systems. The main applications of Digital Twins for hydropower include the following:

- Operations and maintenance – optimizing the maintenance of the hydropower plant with the goal of increasing the uptime, leading to increased power generation.

- Cybersecurity – detecting any intrusions and safeguarding the infrastructure. The Colonial Pipeline ransomware attack on the East Coast of the US in June 2021 created an increased awareness of protecting energy infrastructures. For more information, refer to `https://www.cnn.com/2021/06/07/politics/colonial-pipeline-ransomware-recovered/index.html`.

- Investment and market planning – helping to make the initial investment decisions, expansion decisions, and **RoI** calculations.

According to an article by **General Electric** (**GE**), in 2017, hydropower (see *Figure 8.10*) is a renewable source of large amounts of power on demand as we lack the technology for grid-scale batteries for the storage of energy. Hydropower Digital Twins can help to bridge the gap when wind turbines are impacted by low wind speeds or cloudy weather, and the time of day impacts solar energy. For more information, refer to `https://www.ge.com/news/reports/dam-powerful-ge-connected-hydropower-internet`.

Figure 8.10 – Renewable energy from hydropower

> **Note**
>
> Image source: `https://no.wikipedia.org/wiki/Energi_i_`
> `Afghanistan`

Hydropower Digital Twins can help with similar scenario planning that can impact power generation, such as the amount of rainfall and water levels in dams and reservoirs.

To understand the scale of potential power generation using hydropower, let's look at Quebec, Canada. Due to the abundance of lakes and rivers in this province, hydropower could meet as much as 95% of the electricity needs of the 7 million Quebecois. The installed capacity for hydropower is around 46 gigawatts. For more information, refer to `https://www.cer-rec.gc.ca/en/data-analysis/energy-markets/` `provincial-territorial-energy-profiles/provincial-territorial-` `energy-profiles-quebec.html`. Deb Frodl, a former global executive director of GE Ecomagination, stated that digital hydropower plants are experiencing 1% or higher reliability improvements in their operations due to reduced downtime. This amounts to about 413 gigawatts an hour of incremental hydro generation when scaled globally. To compare it to wind power, it is equivalent to the power generated by a wind farm with about 700 turbines.

Hydropower plants often use a Francis turbine, which is a reaction turbine. As water moves through the turbine, it changes pressure, giving up its energy. For more information, refer to `https://www.sciencedirect.com/topics/engineering/francis-turbines`. A simplified view of such a hydropower turbine is shown in *Figure 8.11*.

The turbine is located between the high-pressure water source and the low-pressure water exit, usually at the base of a dam. This allows us to use water-system dynamics and mechanical torque to turbine shaft equations to create the initial physics-based Digital Twin of hydropower. To learn more about such physics-based computations, see the research paper here: `https://www.researchgate.net/publication/226204151_Torque_model_of_hydro_turbine_with_inner_energy_loss_characteristics`.

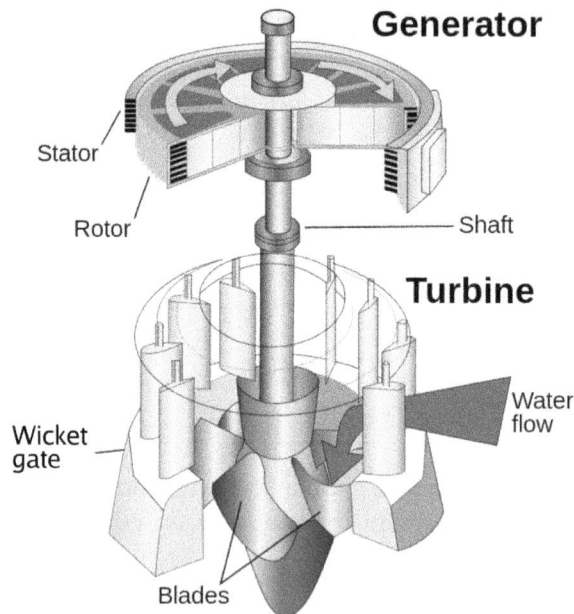

Figure 8.11 – A simplified view of a hydropower turbine

> **Note**
>
> Image source: `https://en.wikipedia.org/wiki/Water_turbine`

In prior sections, we have provided a functional and technical foundation to get started on the Digital Twin of the hydropower. In the next section, we will focus on the Digital Twin of a solar farm.

The Digital Twin of a solar farm

We often see rooftop solar panels on homes, as shown in *Figure 8.12*. The state of California in the US has introduced the California solar mandate, which requires solar panels on all single-family and multi-family residences that are less than four stories high from January 1, 2020. This mandate intends to reduce greenhouse gas emissions by the equivalent of 115,000 gas-powered cars being taken off the road. This mandate was later relaxed and allowed building developers to augment rooftop solar panels with off-site solar power plants.

Figure 8.12 – A residential solar system

In this section, we will mainly focus on commercial solar plants. In 2020, solar energy accounted for 15.4% of the energy needs of the state of California in the US. It produced about 30 **gigawatt-hours (GWh)** of energy through the solar **photovoltaic (PV)** and solar thermal power plants, according to the California Energy Commission. *Figure 8.13* shows a typical solar PV plant. In the next section, we will look at the considerations for building the Digital Twin of a solar plant.

The Gemini Solar Project, with a capacity of 690 megawatts of integrated solar PV and battery storage facility, will be the largest in the US and one of the largest globally. It will be in the US federal government lands near Las Vegas, Nevada. For more information, refer to `https://www.nsenergybusiness.com/projects/gemini-solar-project/`. It will cost about $1 billion and is expected to complete by 2023.

Figure 8.13 – A solar photovoltaic plant

A solar plant, such as the one shown in *Figure 8.13*, connects to the electric grid via the inverter and the transformer, as shown in *Figure 8.14*. The same is true for the wind farm and the hydropower plant, all of which would provide renewable energy for the electric grid, minimizing the need for the use of fossil fuel for power generation.

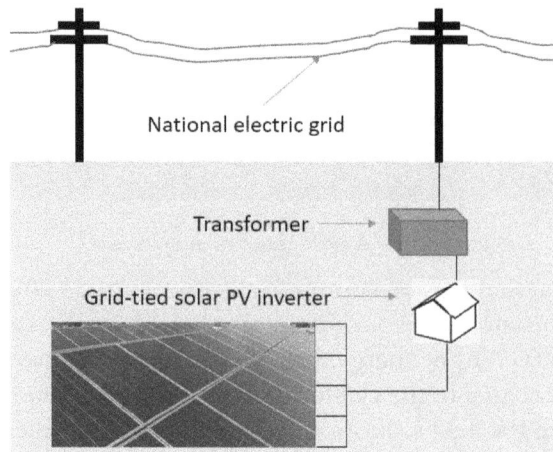

National electric grid

Transformer

Grid-tied solar PV inverter

Figure 8.14 – A solar plant connection to the power grid

One of the authors of this book, Nath, was personally involved in one of the early initiatives for building the Digital Twin of a solar plant as a testbed under the **Industrial Internet Consortium** (**IIC**). For more information, refer to `https://www.iiconsortium.org/press-room/11-08-17.htm`.

To decide the ideal location of a solar plant, solar irradiance information can be used. For more information, refer to `https://www.nrel.gov/gis/assets/images/nsrdb-v3-ghi-2018-01.jpg`.

Irradiance is a measure of the solar radiant energy that arrives at a specific area during a given time interval. It is typically measured in watts/meters squared (W/m^2). The Digital Twin is also considered for feasibility studies of the infrastructure buildout, such as this smart grid Digital Twin project being undertaken by four electrical engineering students. For more information, refer to `https://www.unb.ca/alumni/magazine/2021-spring-summer/solar-energy.html`.

The Digital Twin of the solar plant with a focus on predictive maintenance and operations optimization will include major components (see *Figure 8.15*) such as the following:

- Solar PV panels – commercial-grade solar PV panels are about 78 inches by 39 inches (about 2 m x 1 m) in size with about 72 solar cells. They could weigh about 40 pounds (18 kg) and cost about $250,000.

- Panel strings – a 200 MW solar plant will have about 100,000 panels arranged into 2,000 strings. Ideally, the Digital Twin of each panel and string needs to be maintained as a twin of twins.

- **String Combiner Box** (**SCB**) – these are used to combine several solar panels or strings of panels.

- Inverters – converts the solar panel-generated **Direct Current** (**DC**) to **Alternating Current** (**AC**) before connecting to the grid.

A Digital Twin that considers the major functional blocks of the solar plant can make up to a 4% difference in the operating costs of the solar power plant. We recommend reading the research paper titled *Performance evaluation of 10 MW grid connected solar photovoltaic* to understand the underlying principles of the operating efficiency and the underlying power-conversation factors. This research paper can be found here: `https://www.sciencedirect.com/science/article/pii/S2352484715000311`

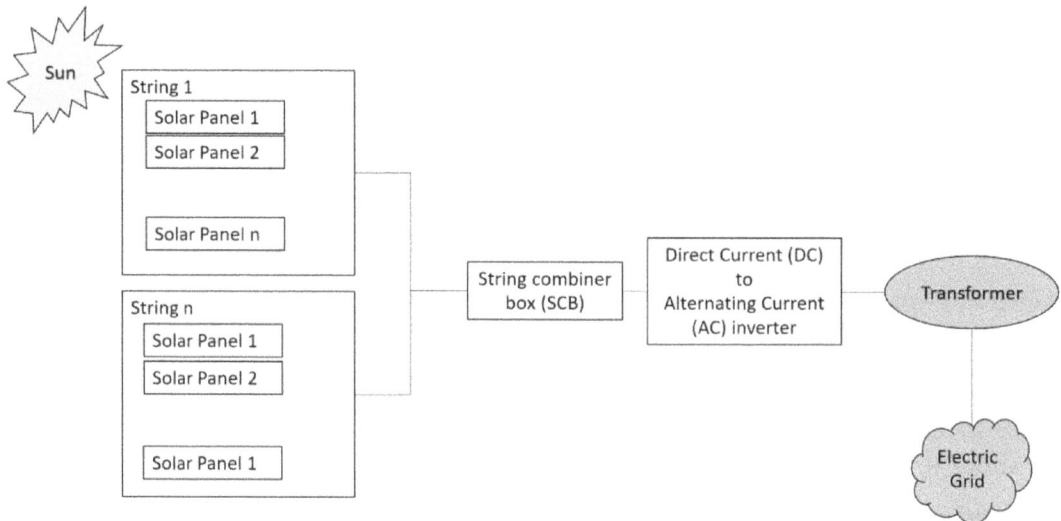

Figure 8.15 – The solar plant block diagram

The Digital Twin of the solar plant can help decide when to replace the solar PV panels to increase the energy output. Likewise, one pilot deployment of the Digital Twin was able to detect up to 83% of inverter failures, a week ahead of the incident. Such increased coverage of failure modes and the increase of lead times are the key overall performance metrics of the Digital Twin solution. The use of Digital Twin solutions for solar plants is driving the industry from the behavior of *install and forget* to more active management of the energy infrastructure. Inefficiencies can be due to several reasons, such as the following:

- The design and installation of the solar PV are flawed.

- There is a mismatch in PV modules connected in series with string modules connected in parallel, leading to lower system performance.

- There is an accumulation of dirt on the solar PV panels over time coupled with the lack of rainfall, especially when the mounting angle is not correct.

- The mismatch is replacement cycles due to different life expectancies, such as 5-10 years for the inverters and 20-25 years for the solar PV panels.

We have highlighted some of the practical issues to monitor and fix with the help of the Digital Twin of the solar power plant. For more information, refer to `https://www.mdpi.com/1996-1073/13/6/1398/htm`.

A solar PV and wind turbine hybrid

The power generation level of a solar plant is dependent on the duration of sunlight, being much shorter on winter days. Likewise, a wind farm may experience lower wind speeds in the summer months than the winter months, based on its location. This provides opportunities to develop hybrid power plants. For more information, refer to `https://www.energy.gov/energysaver/hybrid-wind-and-solar-electric-systems`. *Figure 8.16* shows such a hybrid of solar PV and a wind turbine. Such hybrid power systems are emerging on a small scale today but may appear on a commercial scale in the future. The Digital Twin of a hybrid power plant will require new levels of cross-domain expertise.

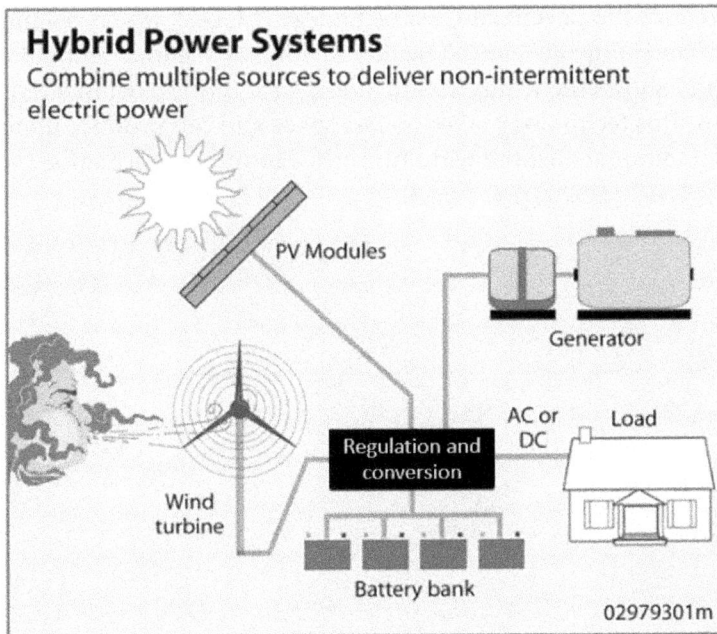

Figure 8.16 – Hybrid power plant

> **Note**
> Image source: `https://www.energy.gov/energysaver/hybrid-wind-and-solar-electric-systems`

In the preceding sections, we have looked at the major sources of renewable energy. We looked at the considerations for the Digital Twin of each of these renewable sources of energy. This information will help plan composite Digital Twins from the viewpoint of the following:

- A large utility company that has generation based on renewable and nonrenewable sources and/or
- An industrial manufacturing company in the energy sector that manufactures energy generation equipment for a variety of these sources

Next, we look at the role of the Digital Twin, due to new innovations related to wind turbine and solar plants.

New innovations in renewable power generation

Let's discuss wind-catching technology in the context of wind energy. Wind catching has great potential to reduce the **Levelized Cost of Energy** (**LCOE**), which is a measure of the lifetime costs of an energy generation facility divided by the total amount of energy produced. *Figure 8.17* shows the wind-catching design for offshore wind energy. It is a floating installation. This technology takes up less space and can produce up to five times more energy than traditional offshore wind turbines. For more information, refer to `https://windcatching.com/`.

Figure 8.17 – Wind-catching design for offshore installation

In wind catching, the energy generation is expected to increase exponentially with the wind speed. Traditional wind turbines tend to limit the energy output when wind speed exceeds about 12 meters a second by altering the pitch of the blades to reduce wear and tear. Hence, a windcatcher can generate a few times more energy from the same area of coverage. The role of the Digital Twin increases when such new technology is rolled out, as we do not have extensive amounts of historical data for predictive maintenance and optimizing energy generation. The physics-based model, based on the product design and data from lab testing of the windcatcher, can help to deploy the Digital Twins of the windcatcher from day one. These Digital Twins will provide key information to help enhance the understanding of the windcatchers as the fleet matures over time. Their expected life is 50 years, which is much longer than traditional wind turbines.

Similarly, in July 2021, Singapore launched a massive floating solar farm. For more information, refer to `https://www.scmp.com/video/asia/3141298/singapore-unveils-one-worlds-biggest-floating-solar-panel-farms`. It has 122,000 solar panels and is about 45 football fields in size. This floating solar plant will power five water treatment plants. *Figure 8.18* shows the concept of the floating solar plant. Due to cooling by water and no shadows from nearby buildings, such a floating solar plant has high efficiency. Again, the Digital Twins of such new generation assets will play an important role in efficient management as we start to fully understand these new assets.

Figure 8.18 – A floating solar plant

In the next section, let's look at the considerations for enhancing Digital Twin solutions further.

Enhancements and next steps

Here, we will take a holistic look at the Digital Twin program from the perspective of a company that is adopting and rolling out such a program. We saw in *Figure 8.5* a high-level rollout of the Digital Twin solution for the wind farm. Next, let's look at an enhanced and more detailed view in *Figure 8.19*. The major blocks from the left to the right are as follows:

- Supply chain networks – these are external networks of the supply chain ecosystem consisting of vendors, distributors, and logistics providers. Considering the disruption in the global supply chain during the COVID-19 pandemic, this area is ripe for supply chain and logistics Digital Twins in the near future.

- Enterprise systems – these consist of the **Information Technology** (**IT**) systems in the enterprise, such as Oracle **Enterprise Resource Planning** (**ERP**), Salesforce.com as **Customer Relationship Management** (**CRM**), or the **Manufacturing Execution System** (**MES**).

- External systems for economic, weather, and market data – these are external sources of reliable data that can be subscribed to and consumed by the other systems to make decisions.

- Business applications – these are often the emerging group of industry-centric applications and digital platforms that will help to drive the next wave of industrial digital transformation. Such applications will often sit on top of the Digital Twin and the IoT platforms and provide business insights. They may or may not reside in the same public cloud or same vendor technology. For instance, IoT Intelligent Applications from Oracle (`https://www.oracle.com/internet-of-things/`) can connect to an Azure Digital Twin-based solution. Other examples include GE's **Asset Performance Management** (**APM**) or more specialized energy trading advisory solutions.

- Digital twin and IoT platforms – these are the building blocks of Digital Twin solutions and provide connectivity to power generation sources, such as wind turbines in a wind farm. Composite Digital Twins are deployed here as more sources of energy generation are introduced.

- **Field Service Management (FSM)** – the industrial asset-intensive industry, such as a utility company or the manufacturer of wind turbines, often manages an extensive field service workforce. FSM applications provide an efficient means of managing the operation and maintenance activities of such a workforce. Digital twins of the FSM workforce is a future area of opportunity.

- Generation sources – this is the collection of the actual generation assets in the power plants and systems that facilitate the connectivity and data gathering, including the edge systems, supervisory control, and data access systems.

- Electricity grid – all commercial-grade generation assets connect to the electricity grid, which manages the transmission and the distribution of electricity.

With this, we have summarized the major systems involved in an enterprise-grade Digital Twin solution rollout:

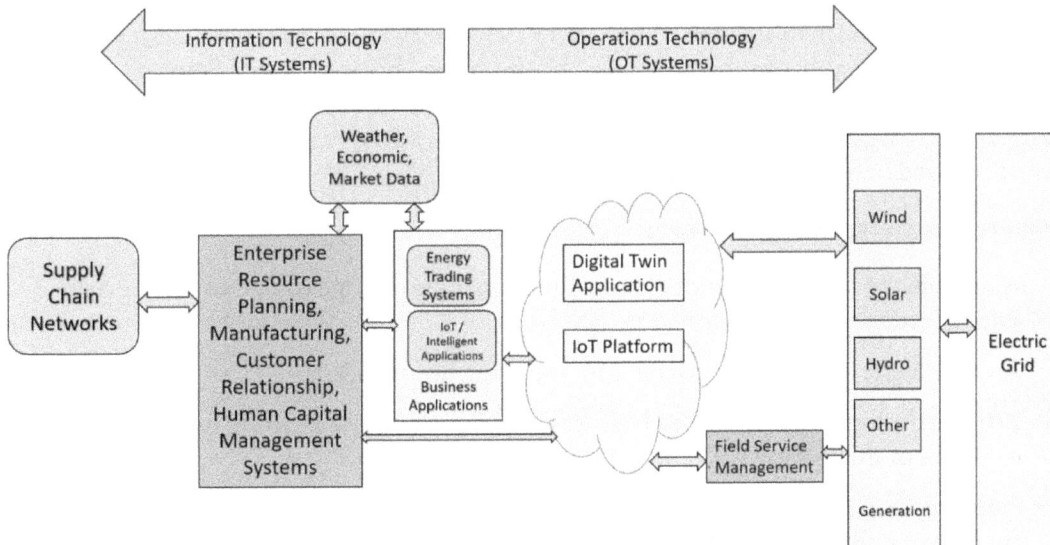

Figure 8.19 – The enterprise landscape for the Digital Twin solution deployment

In this final section, we will look at our recommended organization structure for ensuring the success of such Digital Twin-related programs in a large enterprise.

Center of Excellence for Digital Twins

A **Center of Excellence (CoE)** is often a shared facility with a specialized team dedicated to developing, harvesting, and promoting best practices in a business priority area. General Electric (GE) created a software CoE to focus on the industrial internet in 2012. For more information, refer to `https://hbr.org/2015/01/building-a-software-start-up-inside-ge`. This software CoE later became GE Digital. One of the authors of this book, Nath, was an employee of this GE software CoE and GE Digital from 2013 to 2018. GE Digital has become one of the pioneers in IIoT and Digital Twin technologies. GE Digital supports GE Renewables as one of the lines of business. GE Renewables is one of the largest manufacturers of wind turbines in the world.

CoEs have started to become popular both in the private sector, such as in large global enterprises, and the public sector, such as the Minnesota State Energy CoE. For more information, refer to `https://www.energycareersminnesota.org/`. Another example is Equinor's digital CoE, which includes the Digital Twin in its scope of activities as well. For more information, refer to `https://www.equinor.com/en/magazine/statoil-2030---putting-on-digital-bionic-boots.html`. Some strategies to build a CoE with the goal of driving digital transformation are described here: `https://techbeacon.com/enterprise-it/why-you-need-digital-transformation-center-excellence`.

We summarize these strategies here:

- Assemble the right team with techno-functional knowledge under an appropriate digital leader.

- Provide a clear top-down charter and operating guidelines.

- Provide the right technical and business training alongside a strong focus on a culture of innovation.

- Set governance and put measurements in place, keeping in mind the startup-like freedom for innovation and execution.

We further recommend reading the book *Industrial Digital Transformation, from Packt,* published in 2020. Please check the recommended reading list for this chapter as well. Since Digital Twins are an emerging technology, it is recommended to strongly consider a CoE that can evangelize the Digital Twin program and ensure the delivery of the business benefits from the investment. In the case of a utility company, Digital Twin solutions will improve overall productivity and efficiency, while in the case of an industrial manufacturing company, Digital Twin solutions can drive internal productivity and efficiency as well as new streams of digital revenue by commercially selling this solution to utilities and other companies.

Summary

In this final chapter of this book, we looked at the benefits of deploying a Digital Twin solution from the perspective of an enterprise that would potentially roll out such a program. We looked at how to scale from a Digital Twin of one wind turbine to the wind farm to different sources of renewable sources of energy. We looked at the twin of twins and how to plan and deploy composite Digital Twins. Overall, we looked at how to enhance a Digital Twin solution from its initial pilot deployment phase.

We strongly believe this book provides a strong technical and functional foundation for you to start building their first Digital Twin of an industrial asset and make it production-ready. Such a skill will be a game-changer in industrial digital transformation in the coming years. We thank you for joining us on this journey to build your first digital twin and wish you professional success.

Questions

1. What is a twin of twins?
2. What is the difference between the big bang and the phased rollout of the Digital Twin solution?
3. What are the common sources of renewable energy?
4. What are hybrid power systems?
5. What is the role of a **Center of Excellence (CoE)** in the rollout of digital twin solutions?

Recommended reading

- How to drive digital transformation via technology COEs: `https://enterprisersproject.com/article/2021/2/digital-transformation-via-technology-centers-excellence-COE`

- `https://reveconsulting.com/pages/creating-digital-center-excellence-global-giant/`

- `https://www.coe-iot.com/`

- `https://www.robolab.in/center-of-excellence-in-internet-of-things/`

Interview on Digital Twins with William (Bill) Ruh, CEO of Lendlease Digital

Biography:

A 35-year veteran of the software and internet industries, Mr. William (Bill) Ruh is the Chief Executive Officer for Lendlease Digital. In this role, he is building a new business to help transform the real estate industry. Lendlease Digital is developing the world's first set of autonomous building products to automate design, supply chain, construction, and operations. He also serves on the Board of Directors of Magna International and CADMakers.

Prior to joining Lendlease, Mr. Ruh was the CEO of GE Digital and the Chief Digital Officer for GE. During his tenure, Mr. Ruh led the charge to develop the first cloud-based platform for the industrial world and established the GE Digital business unit. A recognized expert in the emerging Industrial Internet of Things, he helped establish the Industrial Internet Consortium and was a member of the US Dept of Commerce Digital Economy Board of Advisors.

Mr. Ruh is an accomplished author of four books and a frequent speaker on such topics as industrial internet, IoT, industrial AI and ML, and digital industrial strategy:

https://www.lendlease.com/us/company/leadership/william-ruh/

1. **Please share one aspect of you that your formal biography does not cover.**

   I was the lead founder of the Digital Twin Consortium. This has been a true labor of love to create an organization that can help lead the world in the development of a technology I believe holds the key to building a world that is greener, more efficient, and enables better business outcomes. Digital twins are the equivalent of a crystal ball allowing us to see the future or evaluate alternative outcomes. This is a technology that the world needs to deal with the complexity that we face in society, business, and government.

2. **Please share the major focus of your company over the last 1-2 years.**

   The property and construction industries haven't harnessed the power of digital technology. Lendlease is leading the industry advances in cloud, AI/ML, and analytics to automate the design, operations, and experiences in residential, commercial, and retail spaces. The opportunity is large for those that embrace this change – 20%+ reduction in development costs and the ability to create experiences in the workplace and retail settings that make people safer, more efficient, and happier. We are in the early days of the transformation of our industry. Lendlease is leading the way into the future through the development of our Podium Platform.

3. **What is your definition of Digital Twin or one of your unique perspectives on Digital Twin?**

    What is a Digital Twin? I like to think about it as an exact representation in software of a physical object, whether that is a wind turbine, a building, or even a human being. The software can use real-time data to create a model of that object but more importantly allows for a what-if analysis to see all alternative outcomes given a variety of scenarios. Imagine a world where a part never breaks because it's predicted when it will fail and is fixed during standard maintenance. Or a world where you can automate the design of a building down to the nuts and bolts, allowing for optimization of cost, quality, and sustainability. What I think the future holds is that every human will have a Digital Twin that consumes all the data about our lives and is able to guide us to a healthier life or predict significant health issues early enough to enable better outcomes.

4. **How is your company contributing to or embracing the Digital Twin?**

    When I joined Lendlease is early 2019, there was already experimentation with Digital Twin technologies to automate the design of large-scale property development. Over the course of time, we have helped to found the Digital Twin Consortium, created more than a dozen Digital Twins of projects we are developing, and most importantly, have created the Podium Platform, allowing our company to automate the design and operations of buildings. We continue to be at the leading edge of technology working on the Building 4.0 CRC – a research program in Australia aimed at disrupting the development and construction industry. Digital twins are at the center point of our digital activities.

5. **Are Digital Twins ready for production use, pilot use, a bleeding-edge concept, or just hype today?**

    Digital twins have been around for the last 20 years. They have been used primarily in military and space industries. However, in the last decade, they have started to move into high-tech manufacturing industries both in product design but also in maintenance activities. We have reached a point where the technology is moving into the mainstream. The Digital Twin Consortium has hundreds of member companies from all industries who are engaged. All of the major cloud providers are building services related to Digital Twins. We are in the early stages, but Digital Twins are becoming mainstream. The next 20 years are going to be exciting as we push the state of the industry forward.

6. **Any words of advice for those exploring emerging technologies to adopt in their businesses?**

Digital twins hold tremendous promise from automated design to predictive maintenance. My recommendation for any business is a three-pronged approach. First is to ensure the organization is exploring and experimenting with the technology to be able to understand the possibilities. I was fortunate when I joined Lendlease that they were already experimenting and developing talent. The second is to look at the business outcomes that are possible with Digital Twins. At GE we focused on predictive maintenance since unplanned downtime in our industries was a significant problem. Digital twins were a perfect solution to reducing downtime. Finally, focus on using the technology on a few problems. Be careful of boiling the ocean. The technology is very powerful and you need to make sure the excitement of the technology doesn't lead to doing too many things simultaneously. It's a marathon, not a sprint.

Further key links from Lendlease:

*   www.Lendleasepodium.com
*   https://www.prnewswire.com/news-releases/digital-and-sustainable-lendlease-and-google-cloud-partner-to-digitally-transform-the-built-world-301370423.html

Interview on Digital Twins with Anwar Ahmed, CTO - Digital Services at GE Renewable Energy

Biography:

Anwar Ahmed is a seasoned engineering and technology leader leading software product and Digital platform development with extensive experience with Industrial IoT Platforms, Data, Analytics, and Digital Twins focused on the energy domain. He holds a Master's degree in Engineering Physics from Kakatiya University and a second Master's degree in Instrumentation and Control systems from Devi Ahilya University, India.

1. Please share one aspect of you that your formal biography does not cover.

    I have two patents in the related area.

    - Digital Twin Interface for Operating Wind Farms (US9995278B2)
    - Digital system and method for managing a wind farm having plurality of wind turbines coupled to power grid (US10132295B2)

2. Please share the major focus of your company in the last 1-2 years.

    At GE Renewable Energy, our focus is to design wind turbines that are efficient and reliable, and to achieve this we heavily leverage software technology all the way from designing and building powerful turbines to operating them efficiently over its life. The Digital Wind Farm software we built starts at the point of sensors generating data that is collected at the edge and streamed to the cloud for storage and analysis. This allows us to monitor the turbines in real-time and maintain uptime, taking quick actions from an electrically secure perimeter. The historical data is analyzed to detect issues with the turbine and also to predict possible component failures allowing us to move out of unplanned to planned downtimes increasing overall turbine availability. Our focus in the last few years has been to refine our analytics capabilities through machine learning on data we have collected over years of turbine operations and also leveraging the understanding of the physics of our turbine components that we manufacture to drive direct outcomes for our customers.

3. What is your definition of digital twin or one of your unique perspectives on Digital Twin?

    A Digital Twin is a software replica of the physical asset. It's a mathematical model in the cloud of the turbine that continuously learns about its physical pair through machine learning. As more and more data flows over a period of time from the real asset, the model becomes smarter and intelligent allowing us to more easily simulate harsh conditions or situations that could potentially cause component failures. The learnings now can be transferred to the physical asset either as optimized control algorithms or just by manually taking actions like replacing components that are identified by the model that is about to fail. Each asset is unique in its own sense as it may see different physical conditions in its operation so modeling every asset separately is critical.

4. How is your company contributing to or embracing the Digital Twin?

    The concept of Digital Twin is not new, but the term "Digital Twin" is. We have been doing Model-based control for a long time now where a learned model helps drive the control algorithm. Digital Twin is an advancement that takes modeling to a new level where instead of modeling a particular control loop you model the whole asset and continuously keep training this model. We create software models of our new design turbines and simulate wind conditions and various physical conditions our actual turbines see while in operation to see how the model behaves and tune the designs, helping us build better turbines that are more reliable and are built to last its lifetime. We are also using Digital Twins to calculate the remaining component life and perform life-based maintenance instead of fixed schedule maintenance.

5. Are Digital Twins ready for production use, pilot use, a bleeding-edge concept, or just a hype today?

    The availability of the underlying technology is helping make Digital Twin a reality. Powerful CPUs to multi-core GPUs that can perform 15 TeraFLOPS per second have become mainstream. Both Microsoft Azure and AWS offer GPU-based VMs or containers that can run compute intensive mathematical models with ease and also offer all the software and pre-canned algorithms needed to do machine learning and AI. Today IoT hardware is available to even run heavy compute at the edge making it possible to build twins that help turn a new page in how we optimize and run our assets.

I still think it is expensive to build machine learning models of the complete and large physical assets. The key today is to identify a high-value part of the problem and try to solve that specific problem via digital twin such as focusing on reducing unplanned downtime by detecting potential component failures in advance or build a Digital Twin to optimize the power generation of the wind turbine or to increase the overall availability of a wind turbine.

6. Any words of advice for those exploring emerging technologies to adopt in their businesses?

Technology is there and a lot of things are possible! But "Focus", Identify the problem you want to solve that drives a particular outcome for the customers. You don't want to build a solution looking for a problem but rather identify a problem you want to solve and then build your solution.

Any other relevant links:

- Digital twin interface for operating wind farms: `https://patents.google.com/patent/US9995278B2/`

- Digital system and method for managing a wind farm having plurality of wind turbines coupled to power grid: `https://patents.google.com/patent/US10132295B2/`

Packt>

Packt.com

Subscribe to our online digital library for full access to over 7,000 books and videos, as well as industry leading tools to help you plan your personal development and advance your career. For more information, please visit our website.

Why subscribe?

- Spend less time learning and more time coding with practical eBooks and Videos from over 4,000 industry professionals

- Improve your learning with Skill Plans built especially for you

- Get a free eBook or video every month

- Fully searchable for easy access to vital information

- Copy and paste, print, and bookmark content

Did you know that Packt offers eBook versions of every book published, with PDF and ePub files available? You can upgrade to the eBook version at packt.com and as a print book customer, you are entitled to a discount on the eBook copy. Get in touch with us at customercare@packtpub.com for more details.

At www.packt.com, you can also read a collection of free technical articles, sign up for a range of free newsletters, and receive exclusive discounts and offers on Packt books and eBooks.

Other Books You May Enjoy

If you enjoyed this book, you may be interested in these other books by Packt:

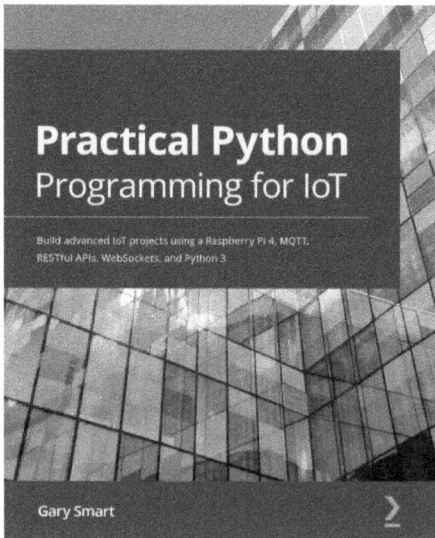

Practical Python Programming for IoT

Gary Smart

ISBN: 978-1-83898-246-1

- Understand electronic interfacing with Raspberry Pi from scratch
- Gain knowledge of building sensor and actuator electronic circuits
- Structure your code in Python using Async IO, pub/sub models, and more
- Automate real-world IoT projects using sensor and actuator integration
- Integrate electronics with ThingSpeak and IFTTT to enable automation
- Build and use RESTful APIs, WebSockets, and MQTT with sensors and actuators
- Set up a Raspberry Pi and Python development environment for IoT projects

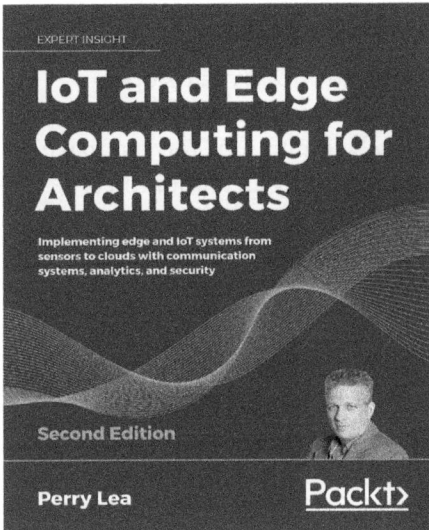

IoT and Edge Computing for Architects

Perry Lea

ISBN: 978-1-83921-480-6

- Understand the role and scope of architecting a successful IoT deployment
- Scan the landscape of IoT technologies, from sensors to the cloud and more
- See the trade-offs in choices of protocols and communications in IoT deployments
- Become familiar with the terminology needed to work in the IoT space
- Broaden your skills in the multiple engineering domains necessary for the IoT architect
- Implement best practices to ensure reliability, scalability, and security in your IoT infrastructure

Packt is searching for authors like you

If you're interested in becoming an author for Packt, please visit `authors.packtpub.com` and apply today. We have worked with thousands of developers and tech professionals, just like you, to help them share their insight with the global tech community. You can make a general application, apply for a specific hot topic that we are recruiting an author for, or submit your own idea.

Share Your Thoughts

Now you've finished *Building Industrial Digital Twins*, we'd love to hear your thoughts! Scan the QR code below to go straight to the Amazon review page for this book and share your feedback or leave a review on the site that you purchased it from.

https://packt.link/r/<1839219076>

Your review is important to us and the tech community and will help us make sure we're delivering excellent quality content.

Index

www.ingramcontent.com/pod-product-compliance
Ingram Content Group UK Ltd.
Pitfield, Milton Keynes, MK11 3LW, UK
UKHW061315231125
9124UKWH00032B/649

9 781839 219078